Dialogue in Intercultural Communities

Dialogue Studies (DS)

Dialogue Studies takes the notion of dialogicity as central; it encompasses every type of language use, workaday, institutional and literary. By covering the whole range of language use, the growing field of dialogue studies comes close to pragmatics and studies in discourse or conversation. The concept of dialogicity, however, provides a clear methodological profile. The series aims to cross disciplinary boundaries and considers a genuinely inter-disciplinary approach necessary for addressing the complex phenomenon of dialogic language use. This peer reviewed series will include monographs, thematic collections of articles, and textbooks in the relevant areas.

Editor

Edda Weigand
Westfälische Wilhelms-Universität Münster

Editorial Advisory Board

Volume 4

Dialogue in Intercultural Communities. From an educational point of view
Edited by Claudio Baraldi

Dialogue in Intercultural Communities

From an educational point of view

Edited by

Claudio Baraldi

Università di Modena e Reggio Emilia

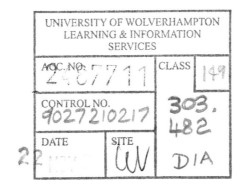
John Benjamins Publishing Company

Amsterdam / Philadelphia

The paper used in this publication meets the minimum requirements of
American National Standard for Information Sciences – Permanence of
Paper for Printed Library Materials, ANSI z39.48-1984.

Library of Congress Cataloging-in-Publication Data

Dialogue in intercultural communities : from an educational point of view / edited by
    Claudio Baraldi.
   p. cm. (Dialogue Studies, ISSN 1875-1792 ; v. 4)
  Includes bibliographical references and index.
    1. Intercultural communication. I. Baraldi, Claudio.
   P94.6.D538   2009
   303.48'2--dc22   2009030327
ISBN 978 90 272 1021 0 (HB; alk. paper)
ISBN 978 90 272 8891 2 (EB)

John Benjamins Publishing Co. · P.O. Box 36224 · 1020 ME Amsterdam · The Netherlands
John Benjamins North America · P.O. Box 27519 · Philadelphia PA 19118-0519 · USA

Table of contents

Introduction

This book presents an analysis of communication processes in educational settings, in international, intercultural contexts. More specifically, it presents a research on CISV (Children's International Summer Villages), a unique worldwide organisation that organizes each year a large number of intercultural villages and camps for children and adolescents, under adults' coordination. The book focuses on CISV's wide and ambitious program of intercultural dialogue among adults and children, by analysing its methodology in conducting educational activities and in managing their organisation. The analysis is based on videotaped interactions of groups of children/adolescents and adults, focused interviews with participants (adults, children and adolescents), and questionnaires.

The book proposes a linguistic and sociological analysis of the interactions, exploring those language cues which hint to the cultural meanings and presuppositions of children's, adolescents' and adults' participation in communication. This investigation concerns the various phases and forms of group activities, particularly the differences among various forms of communication with reference to the main features of speakers' actions which either promote or prevent interlocutors' active participation, understanding and expression, and the main features of decision-making and conflict management in interaction.

The analysis aims to help in planning, conducting and evaluating activities in intercultural groups and settings involving adults, adolescents and children, and to provide useful guidelines for coordinators and facilitators of group interactions who have specific educational functions and are inspired by ideals of effective dialogue and conflict management.

Chapter 1 introduces the theoretical framework that guides the methodological approach and the analysis of the data illustrated in the following parts of the book. Chapter 2 defines the methodological plan of the empirical study regarding CISV villages and camps. Chapter 3 deals with the participants' representations of CISV values and activities, with reference to the social relationships which are developed during villages and camps. Chapters 4–10 are focused on the usage of language for the specific purposes of the organisational and educational activities, highlighting relevant pragmatic structures in the interaction and their cultural presuppositions. Conclusions summarise the ways in which the use of language in interactions provides important cues for analyzing the cultural presuppositions of organisational and educational activities in intercultural settings.

The research which originated this book was made in the context of a national programme entitled 'Mediation in intercultural practices, in managing conflicts and in social promotion', which was mainly funded by the Italian Ministry for the Scientific Research and supported by CISV. I would like to thank the scientific co-ordinator and friend, Guido Maggioni, who is also the director of the Centre for Research and Studies on Families, Children and Adolescents (CIRSFIA), a Centre based at the University of Urbino (Italy) and promoted by four Italian academic departments. Through Guido's coordinating role we have probably achieved the richest and most important Italian corpus of research on children and adolescents in the recent years.

This book could have never been written without the precious contribution of the young researchers who worked on the field and constituted the "strength" of the team. These were the painstaking authors and co-authors of the chapters in this volume, and their contribution goes much beyond the pages written here. I feel utmost privileged in having had the possibility to work with Gabriella, Elisa and Vittorio for so many years and, more recently, with Federico, with his leading enthusiasm and staunch faith in the methods of interaction analysis, Alessandra, Cristina, Elena, Monica and Rosanna, whose perseverance, curiosity, and brilliant observations never let us off. I am deeply indebted to them and I wish to thank them all.

This research would not have even started without the help of CISV people, the members of the International Board (in particular Bastian Küntzel, and Caecilia van Pesky who supported the research from the beginning), the members of the Italian National Association (Jacopo Piccioli and Matteo Zanella), the camp directors, staff, leaders, Junior Counsellors (JCs), and, last but not least, all children and adolescents who participated in the villages and summer camps. A very warm thanks to their families too, who trusted us enough to grant their permission to tape their children for our field research. Although their full names do not appear, they are the real protagonists of these pages.

Finally, I would like to thank my daughter Irene, for giving me parent experience by intensively participating in a CISV village when she was eleven and in other CISV exchanges in the next two years. Now, she is sixteen and I think that her CISV experience has helped her to be mindful of opportunities for active participation and agency in social and intercultural relations, and to nurture genuine interest in equality, empathy and empowerment in the interaction. This book is dedicated to her.

Claudio Baraldi
Modena, June 2009

CHAPTER 1

Empowering dialogue in intercultural settings

Claudio Baraldi

Chapter 1 introduces the conceptual framework used in the book. This frame-work is based on the linguistic and sociological analysis of communication systems and their cultural presuppositions. Cultural presuppositions consist in expectations regarding guiding values, ways of positioning, and results of com-munication processes, specifically of interactions in which the linguistic cues for these expectations can be analyzed. In particular, the analysis considers (1) presuppositions of educational interactions involving children, with a specific focus on intercultural settings, and (2) opportunities for promoting children's agency and active participation in these interactions. Empowering dialogue is observed as a possible presupposition for promoting active participation and effective conflict management in interactions involving children and adults. Empowering dialogue is distinguished from disempowering monologue, which presents different cultural presuppositions.

1.1   Culture, communication, interaction

Culture has been defined and described in many different ways. This book focuses on the description of culture as used in social practices, particularly in its produc-tion and reproduction through communication processes (Carbaugh 2005; Harré & Langenhove 1999; Pearce 1989). We are interested in the production and repro-duction of culture through the use of language in communication.

This interest is backed by conversation analysis (e.g. Goodwin & Heritage 1990; Heritage 1995, 2005, 2008) which provides "a perspective within which lan-guage, culture and social organisation can be analyzed not as separate subfields but as integrated elements of coherent courses of action" (Goodwin & Heritage 1990, p. 301). Weigand (2007, p. 39) identifies a "minimal dialogically autono-mous unit" which consists of action and reaction. Conversation analysis identifies a social organisation of sequences of turn-taking. The minimal unit in this organ-isation is the adjacency pair, based on "the rule that a current action (…) requires the production of a reciprocal action" (Goodwin & Heritage 1990, p. 287), and the turn-taking sequence, based on a mechanism of next positioning, which means that the "current action may project (…) one among a range of possible next actions" (Goodwin & Heritage 1990, p. 288). Turn-taking takes place on a turn-by-turn basis so that after each completed turn, next speaker arrives at the point of possible change (Sacks, Schegloff & Jefferson 1974). In other words, it is possible for all participants to act or take a turn, i.e. to talk to each other.

These approaches imply that social organisation *is* interaction. However, we believe it is necessary to highlight the more general social processes producing and reproducing culture beyond the single interaction and determining important differences among interactions. The understanding of interaction implies "external" criteria or a "background" (Searle 1992) and participants in interaction act according to what they "perceive as other participants' intentions as well as assumptions about the world" (Baker 2006b, p. 325). Participants' intentions are visible in their actions.

The perception of these actions depends on participants' expectations (Weigand 2007), particularly on reflexive expectations (expectations of expectations): one participant expects certain actions (e.g. role performances) to be invoked and the other participant's own assumptions about such patterns of expectations may guide her/his action (Baker 2006b; Luhmann 1984; Searle 1992). These patterns of expectations are the *cultural presuppositions* (Gumperz 1992) of the interaction.

Cultural presuppositions are the fundamental guide for communication processes, the basic premises of their occurrence, and therefore the structures of social organisation. They are the "guidelines" to *select* expectations concerning contents of communication, ways in which participants present themselves and are treated in communication, and results of communication. Cultural presuppositions, i.e. patterns of expectations, can be observed in interactions through *contextualization cues*, which are defined as verbal and non-verbal (lexical, syntactic, structural) signs which contribute to "the signalling of contextual presuppositions" (Gumperz 1982, p. 131), that is they "highlight, foreground or make salient' (Gumperz 1992, p. 232) cultural presuppositions. While production of contextualization cues in the interaction gives meaning to cultural presuppositions, this meaning can hardly be considered as merely a product of single interactions.

Cultural presuppositions are related to more complex social systems. In Western societies in particular, these social systems are differentiated on the basis of specific functions, e.g. legal, economic, political and educational systems (Luhmann 1997). Each of these systems has its own specific cultural presuppositions. In this respect, interaction may be analysed as part of a complex network of communications based on expectations about particular guiding values (e.g. right, money, power, education), particular forms of contribution to the communication process, and particular results of communication. These values, forms of contribution, and forms of expectations regarding results constitute the cultural presuppositions which contextualize the interactions that are relevant within specific functional systems, e.g. judgemental debates, business negotiations, political decisions, teaching, etc. Therefore they structure social organisation. In specific interactions, the cues for cultural presuppositions can be made relevant in different ways, including explicit definitions, explicit meta-comments, and implicit references (Weizman 2008).

Two further concepts may be helpful to explain the complexities of cultural production in communication processes: discourse and narrative. According to Foucault (e.g. 1971), human beings are "acted" by discourses that produce normative expectations of their actions and beliefs. Power is achieved in this discursive production and subjugates individuals, who are trapped in discourse. Discourse analysis conceives power as the only primary cultural presupposition in societies, which generates further distinctions, such as right/wrong, true/false, reason/insanity. In this type of analysis, the differentiation of social systems and relevant cultural presuppositions which differ from power, e.g. truth, love, money, healthcare, education, is undervalued. For this reason, in this book, the concept of discourse, which is recognised as interesting, is used in a more basic way, namely to indicate the various forms of cultural production in communication.

To explain the differentiation of this cultural production, the concept of *narrative* is used. Narratives include all stories that guide actions (Baker 2006a). This concept is inscribed in the more general epistemological stance of social constructionism, asserting that human knowledge is constituted in social relationships (e.g. Gergen 1991; Harré 1984). Narratives constitute rather than represent reality (Baker 2006a), they are social constructions in which the observed reality is interpreted and storied, through different media (oral telling and written documents, but also ballets, motion pictures, photos, etc.). Narratives are not produced only in specific talk or "stretches of language" (Baker 2006a, p. 19), but in series of stories produced within contextualizing social systems. They depend on the organisation of society, namely on communication processes guided by cultural presuppositions. Cultural presuppositions define the space of interpretation of narratives, and narratives are the stories which reproduce and produce cultural presuppositions. Cultural presuppositions are the 'pillars' of culture and inform communicative processes guiding and structuring them; narratives are stories which detail the features of these presuppositions, describing, explaining and legitimising them in communication. In other words, narratives shape the semantic contents of communication processes, which detail their cultural presuppositions, and cultural presuppositions may be observed as narrated in communication processes, in detailed stories which constitute variations of general discourse. Narratives are plural and competing: for this reason, in society the same phenomena may be observed through different sets of categories.

1.2   Positioning in communication

The definition of positions of individual participants is a relevant cultural presupposition of communication. Position has been defined as "a discursive construction of personal stories that make a person's actions intelligible and relatively determinate as social acts" (van Langenhove & Harré 1999, p. 16). Positions are created through "a complex cluster of generic personal attributes" (Harré & van Langenhove 1999, p. 1), which locates participants in communication, conditioning their possibilities of action and the assignment of rights, duties, obligations and entitlements to them. Positions are based on patterns of expectations and are displayed through the use of language in communication, i.e. through utterances. By positioning themselves through their utterances, participants also position their interlocutors, and by positioning their interlocutors, they position themselves. Consequently, positioning is relational, and it is both reflexive (self-positioning) and interactive (other-positioning). Reflexive and interactive positioning may be achieved both in symmetrical and asymmetrical (or hierarchical) interactions. We may observe first order positioning (deriving from participants' direct utterances), second order positioning (questioning the current narrative in communication), and third order positioning (questioning previously produced narratives in new communication systems). Finally, as participants' positions are shaped in structured sequences of actions, the history (or "storyline") of a given sequence is important to understand them and attach meanings to positions.

The concept of position is an attempt at explaining individual contributions to communication differently from what is achieved through the concept of social role (Harré & van Langenhove 1999). In sociology, roles have been defined as patterned expectations about individual behaviours, and have been considered the basic components of the social system (Parsons 1951). In interactions, roles have been observed as "representations" of individuals on the social stage (Goffman 1959, 1974). In general, the concept of role gives relevance to normative expectations to which individual participants must adapt. The concept of position is more flexible: positions include the idea that "there are multiple choices in relation not only to the possible lines that we can produce but to the form of the play itself" (Davies & Harré 1999, p. 42). Participants are not executors or players of roles, but *agents*, i.e. producers and directors or editors (Winslade & Monk 2008) of the interaction. Interactions are co-produced and co-directed (negotiated) by participants. Participants' contributions are reproduced "moment by moment" in conversations, through actions (Davies & Harré 1999). The concept of position highlights participants' agency (Giddens 1984), i.e. presentation of a course of action as one from various possibilities, and therefore the potential production of new narratives through active participation. The concept of position is "sensitive to the subtleties and nuances of moment-by-moment interaction and (…) it locates these subtleties and nuances in the context of wider societal discourse" (Winslade & Monk 2008, p. 98).

The theory of positioning aims to define "what people are" (Winslade & Monk 2008), i.e. their psychology, as socially constructed (Harré & Langenhove 1999). It aims to produce a new cognitive theory based on social constructions (Harré 1984; Gergen 1989), which excludes the 'real' existence of separate personhood/selfhood and attributes relational meanings to the individual self (Gergen 1991). Separate personhood is considered a specific narrative which permeates Western societies. This approach introduces a paradoxical social determinism. On the one hand, "people actively give meaning to things" (Winslade & Monk 2008, p. 104), and cultural norms and traditions are "decisions made by particular people in specific places at specific time" (Winslade & Monk 1999, p. 108). On the other hand, individuals are "bearers of and reproducers of the cultural patterns that are given to them from their cultural world", therefore, their "patterns of thinking are given to them" (Winslade & Monk 2008, p. 103). In conclusion, individuals are clearly agents, "acting to express themselves and to influence others", however they "can be agents only by making use of the discourses that they are familiar with and that dominate their thinking" (Winslade & Monk 2008, p. 111). Individuals actively construct cultures (stories, categories) which in their turn construct the meanings of individuals (their belonging, competence, self-esteem, etc.). The determinism of predefined social roles and cultural groups is replaced by a paradoxical deterministic construction of personhood and agency.

A different theoretical perspective (Luhmann 1984) makes it possible to avoid this paradox without renouncing to the "subtleties and nuances" of social constructions. According to this form of social constructivism, communication systems do not include people's living bodies and thinking systems. The 'world' which is constructed in communication does not include the worlds of individual thinking, although it influences them and is influenced by them, as social systems and thinking systems are "structurally coupled" (Baraldi 1993; Luhmann 1997). Communication systems do not include the specific features of thinking systems, they include the *utterances* of individual participants: only participants' contributions to communication are expected and culturally patterned, and individual positions result from these patterns.

The patterns of expectations concerning individual contributions are differentiated. In the Western narrative, which has largely colonised the global world (§ 1.3.2), we can observe a relevant differentiated positioning of participants, as either *persons* who are able and socially authorised to self-express, or *roles* which perform specific standardised sets of actions and are socially authorised to few variations with respect to generalised patterns of expectations. In our perspective, which differs from the theory of positioning, the distinction between person and role gives meaning to the different positions of participants in communication systems. In other words, person and role are cultural presuppositions of communication systems. The distinction between person and role is directly associated with the distinction between expectations of participants' *personal expression* (or self-expression), i.e. affective expectations, and expectations of participants' *role performance*, i.e. cognitive expectations. The cultural relevance attributed to roles shapes the narrative of individualism, which gives meanings to and details the features of the comparative evaluation among individuals based on cognitive expectations regarding their role performances. The cultural relevance attributed to persons shapes the narrative of personalisation, which gives meanings to and details the features of social processes establishing affective expectations of personal expressions. The distinction between individualism and personalisation makes it possible to understand the different cultural concerns regarding individual positions and contributions in communication systems, both in interactions and in their contextualizing systems.

1.3   Cultural change and intercultural communication

1.3.1   Cultural change

Cultural presuppositions are not fixed contexts of interactions, although they guide interactions. Presuppositions are subject to change, which means that re-contextualization of social systems is always possible (Baker 2006b). Interactions may produce a re-interpretation of cultural presuppositions and may have significant effects on the contextualization of social systems, e.g. on the meaning of guiding values, role performances and personal expressions, and expectations about the results of communication (normative, cognitive, affective expectations). In particular, participants' positions can change through interactions. Weizman (2008) distinguishes two kinds of positioning: interactional roles (which can change) and social roles (which are predetermined). Social roles embody existing cultural presuppositions within contextualizing social systems, and interactional roles embody opportunities to project, and then influence, interlocutors' actions in specific interactions. The difference in participants' power (e.g. between the roles of teacher and student), derives from the contextualizing system. In interactions, what is evident is the influence that participants have on each other (e.g. teachers interacting with students), as a result of their agency. While the general meanings of interactions can be, and often are, culturally predetermined, all participants can always project their interlocutors' actions, influencing the ongoing interaction and the corresponding positioning. Participants' positions depend on both specific interactional structures which allow changes, and structures of the contextualizing social system which can block change.

On the one hand, cultural presuppositions shape interaction, while on the other, interaction may renew cultural presuppositions precisely by re-interpreting them within the local context. Therefore:

1. Interaction is contextualized by a set of cultural presuppositions (guiding values, forms of contribution, and forms of expectations regarding results).
2. Such contextualization derives from social systems which frame interactions and which are significant in society by virtue of their functions (legal, political, educational and so on).
3. Interactions may change these cultural presuppositions; that is, they can re-contextualize contextualizing systems.
4. Contextualization and re-contextualization are made evident through particular linguistic cues in interactions.

In the light of these considerations, the analysis of the relationship between culture and communication requires the integration of two approaches. The first approach concerns the organisation of specific interactive sequences, including (1) adjacency pairs (or dialogic units) and projections of actions and reactions, (2) linguistic (verbal and non verbal) forms signalling the main cultural presuppositions (contextualization cues), and (3) ways of re-contextualizing these cultural presuppositions through specific actions. The second approach concerns the description of the cultural presuppositions which structure communication: guiding values, forms of contribution (persons and roles), forms of expectations regarding results (normative, cognitive, affective expectations).

1.3.2 Intercultural communication and transcultural forms

When different cultural presuppositions contextualize the very same interaction, we may observe *intercultural communication* (e.g. Bennett 1998; Gudykunst

2005; Samovar & Porter 1997; Ting-Toomey 1999). The confrontation of different cultural presuppositions may favour the re-contextualization of the social system which embeds the interaction, but it also implies potential problems in the interaction.

Intercultural communication is related to the process of globalisation, which creates interdependence among societies and cultures that were previously separate. Even though the expansion of economic markets across the world has been the primary aspect emphasised in globalisation, a more general cultural understanding of globalisation has been promoted in social sciences (e.g. Beck 1997; Giddens 1990; Nederveen Pieterse 2004, 2007; Robertson 1992; Tomlison 1999). This perspective suggests that globalisation has an intercultural meaning and is created through intercultural communication. Communication is observed as intercultural whenever different cultural presuppositions prevent the creation of a single, shared culture (Carbaugh 1990), i.e. if and when it presents contradictions (and potential conflicts) on the level of presumably shared symbols. In the literature, intercultural communication is frequently explained through cultural variability that is through the existence of national or ethnic cultures which might be compared and contrasted (e.g. FitzGerald 2003; Hofstede 1980; Triandis 1995). In this perspective, intercultural communication is created through the meeting of different, pre-existing cultural presuppositions, for example different national cultures which are either individualistic or collectivistic, which present different degrees of power distance and so on. This approach gives the highest relevance to the behaviours of individuals as members of cultural groups who bring their cultural presuppositions into communication. Participants are positioned in communication with reference to their cultural identities (Carbaugh 1999; Moghaddam 1999), which are We-identities (Tan & Moghaddam 1999; Ting-Toomey 1999). We may note two main problems with this approach.

Firstly, the globalisation process produces cultural hybridisations (Nederveen Pieterse 2004), whereby purity is cancelled from cultural heritage and can only be reconstructed through new social processes (Winslade & Monk 2008). Consequently, cultural variability is unstable (Verschueren 2008), i.e. cultural presuppositions change and, above all, their differences may be reduced by hybridisation. Secondly, cultural differences are visible only through communication (Gumperz 1982; Gumperz & Roberts 1991). Cultural variability emerges in intercultural encounters; it is constructed via communication processes, not within pre-existing 'groups'. The construction of cultural differences in these communication processes is always unpredictable, although their features can be associated with existing cultural patterns. Intercultural communication is a communication which topicalises different cultural presuppositions that are not accepted by all participants (Baraldi 2006a, 2006b). The construction of the meaning of these cultural differences depends on the specific form of intercultural communication. This means that intercultural communication is always culturally conditioned, and that we can observe different cultural presuppositions of intercultural communication.

Historically, *ethnocentrism* has been the most widespread form of intercultural communication (Pearce 1989). Ethnocentrism is the interpretation and evaluation of others' behaviour using one's own cultural presuppositions, i.e. using a guiding distinction between a positive Us and a negative Them. Ethnocentrism is a form of diversity treatment, based on the attribution of a sense of group belonging and differences; participants' positioning is considered in terms of their being members of a culture, and cultural presuppositions are normatively expected to be stable.

In Western societies, the increasing insensitivity to group belongings and differences has created alternative forms of diversity treatment, such as the pluralism of perspectives, the primacy of role performances (individualism) and personal expressions (personalisation). Today, these cultural presuppositions (pluralism, individualism, personalisation) are features of a functionally differentiated society (Luhmann 1997), which assumes their positive value and the negative character of any other cultural presupposition menacing them (collectivism, hierarchies, denial of individual rights). This approach produces a new form of ethnocentrism, evaluating and refusing any cultural presupposition deemed as a threat to personal freedom, democracy, human rights, individual health and safety, and so on. The paradoxical effect is that by refusing the sense of group belonging, this society adopts an ethnocentric We-identity fixing rigid boundaries of inclusion and exclusion. A society that sees itself as pluralist is not able to accept other societies which are not pluralist; the celebration of diversity denies those who do not consider themselves diverse in the meaning assigned to diversity. This society does not admit cultural diversity as such, but a particular version of cultural diversity; however, it speaks in the name of humanity, observing its cultural presuppositions as a universal definition of rights and needs.

Over the last two decades, however, this approach has failed to create effective intercultural communication in the world. It has failed to ensure effective governance, respect of human rights, generalised education and opportunities for social participation, and frequently it has failed to prevent armed conflicts. Today, the main problem is how to deal with cultural diversities in intercultural communication.

The solution to this problem would require forms of communication coordinating different cultural presuppositions and creating intercultural competence (Spitzberg 1997) and intercultural sensitivity, which is the ability to understand and perform appropriate actions in intercultural situations (Yamada & Singelis 1999). A new effective form of intercultural communication is supposed to produce a "third culture" (Alred, Byram & Fleming 2003; Chen & Starosta 1998; Casmir 1999) based on a "co-created cultural contract" (Onwumechili, Nwosu, Jackson & James-Hughes 2003). This is observed as a transcultural form of communication (Milhouse, Asante & Nwosu 2001) emphasising the conjunction among different cultural presuppositions, producing harmonisation in reciprocity, matching interests and needs, and creating co-constructed meanings. The idea of a transcultural form of communication underlines that the preservation of pure cultural diversity is impossible because intercultural contacts have hybridisation effects on pre-existing cultural presuppositions. A transcultural form of communication produces cross-cultural adaptation (Kim 2001); it opens other possibilities of action and cultural expression. A transcultural form of communication aims at creating a new, harmonised and coherent culture of respect and reciprocity, based on cultural presuppositions such as openness, dialogue, conjunction, and understanding.

This approach presents two paradoxes. Firstly, a transcultural form implies an overcoming of diversity *together with* its respectful conservation in communication, i.e. it implies a simultaneity of conservation of cultural differences and production of a new culture – cultural presuppositions should be preserved and simultaneously changed. Secondly, a transcultural form is based on some selected mono-cultural presuppositions (such as openness, dialogue, conjunction, and understanding) which must necessarily be shared in communication. In the light of these two paradoxes, a crucial issue is the effectiveness of a transcultural form in empirical processes of intercultural communication.

1.4   Empowering dialogue, dialogic mediation and conflict management

1.4.1   Empowering dialogue

A transcultural form of communication needs 'dialogue' between cultures and discouragement of cultural monologues. The concepts of 'dialogue' and 'monologue' have been variously discussed in the literature on the use of language in communication.

Dialogue may be seen as covering the same area of conversation and language use. Specific units in communication, or speech acts (Searle 1969), are seen as "dialogically oriented", that is mutually dependent, as none of them can be communicatively autonomous (Weigand 1994, p. 68). In this perspective, there are two ways of interpreting 'dialogue'. Firstly, dialogue is a sequence of interrelated actions: it is a synonym of conversation and is based on some kind of distribution of turns of talk among the participants. Secondly, in a functional sense dialogue is any communication, as its central feature is the communicative purpose of action, even if interlocutors are inactive or absent (in cases of pure mental reaction). This meaning of dialogue overlaps with the meaning of communication which has been presented in § 1.1: communication is always performed dialogically.

In this book, the concept of dialogue is interpreted in a third, different way. We propose the distinction between 'dialogue' and 'monologue' as specific *forms* of communication, based on different cultural presuppositions. In our perspective, dialogue is a particular form of communication (Pearce & Pearce 2003), which is contrasted with "attitudes such as aggression, hostility, prejudice, sectarianism, and with conflicts of varying degrees, including war" (Wierbicka 2005, p. 677). David Bohm describes it as "the collective way of opening up judgements and assumptions" (1996, p. 53). Therefore, dialogue is a form of communication in which participants' positions are intentionally questioned and negotiated (second order positioning), in order to reach their positive interactive and reflexive positioning. According to Wierbicka (2005), in dialogue the participants' efforts to understand each other and make themselves understood are particularly important. Thus, dialogue "implies that each party makes a step in the direction of the other" (Wierbicka 2005, p. 692).

In this respect, we may speak of *empowering dialogue,* a specific form of communication which creates the opportunity to negotiate contributions and to show positive involvement in the relationships between participants. This idea may be considered normative and idealistic (Ramsbotham, Woodhouse & Miall 2005) as it embodies a positive evaluation and a social ideal. However, in our perspective, empowering dialogue has a technical meaning. Empowering dialogue is based on peculiar cultural presuppositions (patterns of expectations) and implies specific kinds of turn-taking or action-reaction sequences. More specifically, it requires cultural presuppositions which determine:

1. The promotion and fair distribution of active participation in the interaction (*equity*).
2. The display of sensitivity for the interlocutors' interests and/or needs (*empathy*).
3. The treatment of disagreements and alternative perspectives as enrichments in communication (*empowerment*).

Empowering dialogue requires equity, empathy and empowerment as cultural presuppositions of communication; it requires equity and empathy as premises for empowerment. Based on equity, empathy, and empowerment, dialogue enhances expression and acknowledgement of diversity, creating conditions for reciprocity. It is supposed to abolish ethnocentric boundaries and promote cross-cultural adaptation. It may be observed as implementation of a transcultural form of communication, enhancing conjunctions between different cultural presuppositions, harmonisation in reciprocity and matching of interests and needs.

Empowering dialogue is opposed to disempowering monologue. In its more usual version, monologue is intended as a one-sided discussion: a speaker talks and the interlocutors passively listen to her/him, because s/he cannot respond. However, we may also see a monologue as a form of communication which ignores the difference of perspectives in interaction. In a monological perspective "language use is regarded from the perspective of the speaker"; this means that "the meanings of words and utterances are seen as resulting from the *speakers' intentions or strategies* alone, while co-present people are seen as recipients of the units of information prepared by the speaker" (Wadensjö 1998, p. 8).

Monologue may be observed as a way of acting based on expectations of unequal distribution of active participation, lack of sensitivity for the interlocutors' actions, and treatment of disagreements and alternative perspectives as irrelevant or dangerous. In this sense, monologue is a disempowering form of communication.

Disempowering monologue is not absence of understanding or consideration for interlocutors; rather it is a particular form of understanding and consideration for interlocutors. The meaning of disempowering monologue is clarified by some attitudes of speakers: they attach more value to their own action than to their interlocutors' understanding, through their actions they display certainty of their own understanding, they attribute errors to their interlocutors' actions, they display indifference for the consequences of their own actions on their interlocutors and lack of attention to their interlocutors' feelings and thoughts. This meaning of disempowering monologue can be associated with individualism or ethnocentrism, i.e. with a preference for self-perspective or We-identity, with hierarchical positioning of participants in interaction. In a disempowering monologue, a participant claims for an exclusive right to act or at least to control the distribution of opportunities for action, and the interlocutors can react only by taking into account the speaker's power to determine their positioning. In a disempowering monologue, the speaker's interlocutors are treated as irrelevant and hence their perspectives are overlooked, meaning that the speaker lacks sensitivity with regard to her/his interlocutors.

The distinction between empowering dialogue and disempowering monologue is fundamental to understand the management of diversity and conflicts in communication.

1.4.2 Dialogic mediation and conflict management

Empowering dialogue is particularly important in *mediation*. Mediation is considered a way of co-ordinating conflicting parties, modifying their relationship:

"Central to all mediation approaches is that a third party helps disputants resolve conflicts by enabling parties to find their own solutions" (Picard & Melchin 2007, p. 36). The intervention of a third party (the mediator) facilitates communication between the conflicting parties (Bowling & Hoffman 2000; Sahah-Kazemi 2000). Mediators help them to appreciate each other and work together, pleasing both of them (Zeldin 1998). For these reasons, mediation has become very attractive for researchers and practitioners in search of new and effective ways of dealing with what is perceived as an increasing level of conflict in a wide range of social settings.

The interpretation of conflict is particularly important in order to understand the meaning of mediation. While in the literature conflicts are often associated with perception of incompatibilities or opposed and frustrated interests (e.g. Carnevale & Pruitt 1992; DeChurch & Marks 2001; Jeong 2008), they may also be observed as *communicated contradictions* (Luhmann 1984), i.e. communicated refusals concerning both the interlocutor's intentions and the uttered content. Conflicts may be seen as particular effects of (not necessarily intentional) second order positioning, questioning the current participants' positions and stories. Conflicts are based on certain cultural presuppositions and are perpetuated through particular positioning discourses (Baker 2006a; Winslade 2006) in which participants are addressed in terms of their arguments or intentions. These discourses raise uncertainty and doubt, lack of trust in continuing interaction and in obtaining shared meanings or a common ground (Kelman 2005). Hence, persisting conflicts tend to menace existing cultural presuppositions: for example, they can seriously threaten relationships between lovers ('the way you're behaving shows that you don't really love me', 'if you say that, this means that you don't love me'), or political debates ('with this behaviour, you show that you want to destroy my reputation', 'your considerations about the international political situation are completely misleading').

However, conflicts are also starting points for the renewal of cultural presuppositions: starting with communicated contradictions, for example, love relationships or political debates can be repaired through new and more careful actions and words. Consequently, conflicts may enhance changes in the existing social systems (Luhmann 1984; Moscovici 1976), questioning their stable cultural presuppositions and opening up new possibilities for action. Conflicts permit the reproduction of communication in social systems as they lose their rigidity, and make it possible to re-contextualize the social systems in which they arise.

Mediation is a form of conflict management, transforming the uncertainty produced by previous refusals into opportunities for changing social systems. The promotion of change through mediation seems to be primarily associated with the promotion of conflict resolution and final agreements between the parties (Deutsch 2002). However, conflicts can also be prevented or avoided. In these cases, they are not directly visible in the interaction. Prevention means providing the conditions for the absence of contradictions. In the interaction, prevention erases all traces of conflict. Consequently, the analysis of conflict prevention concerns the cultural presuppositions which favour the absence of contradictions in communication. Conflict avoidance means that a contradiction has no consequences; in the interaction, a participant refuses some content or intention and the interlocutor does not react with a new refusal. Conflict avoidance can be observed when a refusal is not followed by a symmetrical reaction. Therefore, conflict avoidance consists in ignoring refusals in communication. While conflict avoidance may be associated with a low level of concern for and involvement in relationships and problem solving (Shell 2001), it may be argued that it is positive in avoiding destructive escalations and defending relationships from stressful and unnecessary disputes (Tjosvold & Sun 2002). Prevention, avoidance and resolution are the main kinds of conflict management and mediation.

Mediation does not manage conflicts by establishing a difference between a right position and a wrong position. Mediation avoids judgements (Bush & Folger 1994; Carnevale & Pruitt 1992; Mulcahy 2001). It is supposed to promote change, both by enabling the participants to find their own solutions together, and by paving the way for new shared meanings. A form of mediation which can create change has been defined as *transformative mediation* (Bush & Folger 1994): it promotes the participants' empowerment in defining issues and autonomously deciding on them, and mutual recognition of their points of view.

Mediators actively intervene as providers of opportunities to talk, encouraging the parties to introduce and deal with particular issues, reinforcing certain roles and identities, making some outcomes more likely than others (Bowling & Hoffman 2000; Brigg 2003; Mulcahy 2001; Winslade, Monk & Cotter 1998), using and treating emotions (Fischer & Shapiro 2005; Katz Jameson, Bodtker & Jones 2006; Maiese 2006; Schulz 2006), and constructing alternative narratives.

Narrative mediation (Winslade 2006; Winslade & Monk 2000, 2008), in particular, underlines the importance of creating alternative narratives with respect to the existing ones, and in particular to existing narratives in which one party is subjugated or emarginated. Narrative mediation is based on the creation of opportunities for the parties to introduce their own stories as personal stories, and gives importance to recovering unstoried experiences. Narrative mediation aims to position participants as active producers and editors of their own stories. In this perspective, empowerment is not the main function of mediation, which is considered in terms of re-authoring stories of relationships. However, it is easy to observe that re-authoring requires recognition and promotion of participants' agency, i.e. empowerment. In our perspective, the distinction between re-authoring and empowerment is only analytical, as empowerment is a necessary requirement for authorship.

Transformative and narrative mediations may be achieved through a collaborative dialogue process (LeBaron & Castarphern 1997; Ting-Toomey & Kurogi 1998). Therefore, its accomplishment requires empowering dialogue, i.e. transformative mediation is a form of *dialogic mediation* (Baraldi & Gavioli 2008). The mediator's actions are supposed to empower both participants' self-expression and effective communications between them (§ 1.7).

The goal of dialogic mediation is not the creation of shared intentionality, common experience or meanings, We-identities, or other shared dimensions, which are frequently considered the necessary outcome of the interaction (e.g. Schegloff 1991; Schegloff, Koshik, Jacoby & Olsher 2002; Searle et al. 1992). Both empowerment and re-authoring, and in general participatory processes and agency (see § 1.6), lead to unpredictable interactional sequences and outcomes, and produce more surprising novelties in communication than sharing.

In intercultural settings, particular attention is given to interlinguistic mediation, which is a type of interaction involving speakers of different languages and an interpreter providing a translation service. Such type of talk is referred to as "interpreter-mediated interaction" (Wadensjö 1998, p. 6). Analyses of recorded and transcribed data show that interpreters are active participants in the interaction: they select the information to translate, ask and provide clarifications, give support to the interlocutors (Angelelli 2004; Baker 2006b; Mason 1999, 2006; Wadensjö 1998). In order to explain the type and amount of work that interpreters do in the interaction, Wadensjö suggests that interpreters play a double positioning in the conversation: they *translate* and they also *coordinate* the talk activity. Such coordinating activity is aimed at making the interaction between the participants of different languages possible and successful and it is concerned with the promotion of their participation, introducing in the conversation a direct support of other participants' personal expressions of feelings or attitudes. This coordinating activity provides for a linguistic-cultural bridging which makes the voice of the interpreter's co-participants effective and their cultural expression possible. It also aims at participants' reciprocal understanding and sharing of information. In addition, the interpreter's support may be very important to make the personal expression of co-participants relevant in the interaction, and to promote participants mutual acceptance and understanding. Specifically, interpreters can mediate cross-cultural encounters (Davidson 2000), and in this sense Wadensjö observes that they "cannot avoid functioning as intercultural mediators" (1998, p. 75). In other words, interpreting assumes the form of dialogic empowering mediation, and the interpreter assumes the position of intercultural coordinator.

Although it is assumed that dialogic mediation may favour both reconciliation and change, doubts have been raised about its effectiveness in promoting symmetrical power relationships and effective changes in important cultural presuppositions. It has been observed that while mediation can effectively entail temporary progress in social relationships, it de-emphasises the importance of the wider social context, of the durability of relationships between the parties, and of their reciprocal stable recognition (Gwartney, Fessenden & Landt 2002). Changes in the social context and its cultural presuppositions are seen "outside the parameter of the mediator's responsibility" (Schoeny & Warfield 2000, p. 254); consequently, mediators "become de facto agents of the status quo invested in maintaining the stability of the current social system and stopping the conflict before it moves beyond the affected institutions' control" (Welsh & Coleman 2002, pp. 345–46). Hence, an important issue remains the effectiveness of dialogic mediation in changing the status quo of social systems and cultural presuppositions, and in empowering the least influent participants.

1.5   Education

1.5.1   Educational systems today

Today, educational systems are particularly interested in empowering dialogue. Educators are interested in the ways in which the cultural presuppositions of education may be implemented in their interactions with children both in assuring the reproduction of education and in managing conflicts with them and between them.

In functionally differentiated societies, the educational system has the function of shaping children's personalities (Luhmann 2002; Luhmann & Schorr 1979). "The idea of education implies that educators (…) have the possibility to effect change in those at whom their education efforts are directed" (Vanderstraeten & Biesta 2006, p. 160). It is "through education, through literally turning 'children' into 'pupils', that they can be introduced into society and come to understand how, as adults, they will find their place within it" (James & James 2004, p. 123).

In this system, the generally recognized educational tasks are (1) guiding children's socialisation, shaping their choices and actions according to shared criteria and values, thus (2) producing reflexive learning (learning to learn) as an instrument of self-regulation. The selection of shared meanings seems to be the best way to accomplish these tasks: the system selects "correct" meanings, binding children to them, in order to allow them to assume social roles. Children are positioned in "forced" (van Langenhove & Harré 1999) roles through communication. Educators intentionally position them in these roles, while they are strategically positioning themselves in a deliberate way. This reflexive and interactive positioning is achieved in a hierarchical interaction, featuring frequent second order positioning in which children's stories are questioned (and evaluated) and third order positioning in which stories are narrated in order to position children effectively in some moral order. The educational function depends on the necessity to create conditions of autonomy and competence in assuming social roles. Education has the function of bringing about changes in children, creating cognitive abilities and adaptation to social norms. This function presumes that children are incomplete persons, not sufficiently responsible and autonomous in their actions with respect to the societal standards: this is the reason why children should be formed.

Education is socially visible when its formative intention is explicit in communication. This requires specific cultural presuppositions:

1. Positioning of participants as roles implying standardised performances.
2. Evaluation of such performances.
3. Cognitive expectations regarding students learning, that is their achievement of knowledge, abilities, competence, and rules.

These three cultural presuppositions guide education as a specific system of communication (Baraldi 2005, 2006a). According to some recent works in childhood studies, education is an attempt to take control of the future through rational knowledge and planning (Prout 2000, p. 306). Consequently, "there are little grounds for thinking that present education systems treat children as competent social actors" (Wyness 1999, p. 354). In educational systems, children are neither creative, nor able to construct meaning and they are positioned by curricular and behavioural rules, incorporating the cultural presuppositions of standardised role performances and cognitive expectations. As the unpredictability of children's construction of meaning is considered a serious risk for the reproduction of cultural presuppositions in social systems, it becomes necessary to shape their meaning construction and guide them towards self-regulation (Hill, Davis, Prout & Tisdall 2004); children are invited to believe that their thinking is part of shared cultural presuppositions, and are invited to adapt to them.

However, the mainstream culture of childhood has recently placed particular emphasis on children's self-realisation (Prout 2000), and on children's agency (James, Jenks & Prout 1998; James & Prout 1997; Prout 2003; Vanderbroeck & Bouverne-De Bie 2006). These new cultural presuppositions lead to the promotion of children's active participation, i.e. children's self-expression (Baraldi 2008) and children's self-determination (Murray & Hallett 2000). Promoting children's active participation means socialising children towards an "understanding of their own competencies" (Matthews 2003, p. 274); that is, to a sense of responsibility and skills in planning, designing, monitoring and managing social contexts.

The success of this new vision of children as social agents has changed educational cultural presuppositions, leading education to use children's self-expression as a resource for reflexive learning (Baraldi 2003). This seems to be possible through empowering dialogue, for example through teachers' active listening and consideration for children's creativity (Gordon 1974; Rogers 1951). Empowering dialogue promotes a change in students' and teachers' positions, and in forms of relationship between children and teachers (Cotmore 2004). In particular, it promotes a new position for the teacher as an "organiser of learning" (Holdsworth 2005, p. 149), who is inventive, leaves pre-planned activities and embarks into the unknown, and is able to understand that children can and must tackle important issues. Empowering dialogue promotes teaching as a "dance with the students" (Holdsworth 2005, p. 150), neutralising the differences between qualified adults and unqualified children.

Over the last fifty years, by adopting techniques of empowering dialogue, education has become increasingly sophisticated and complex. Today, the coupling between education and promotion of personal expression is a key-site for understanding the meanings of innovative interaction between adults and children. Consequently, education is faced with the responsibility for the simultaneous reproduction of different cultural presuppositions, namely (1) individualism which is implied in roles performances, (2) acceptance of normative expectations, and (3) attitudes to personal expression. It is thus particularly important to observe how and under what conditions educational systems promote children's self-expression through empowering dialogue.

1.5.2   Intercultural education

The increasingly multicultural character of society has invested education with an important new task. In multicultural settings, education is intertwined with intercultural communication; this means that interactions have to include the treatment of cultural diversity, expressed by differences in cultural presuppositions (Baraldi 2005, 2006a). In the same communication system, the shaping of children's personalities (including role performances, acceptance of normative presuppositions, and attitudes to personal expression) is combined with the construction of the meanings of cultural diversity. The problem for education is that intercultural communication can create obstacles for shaping personalities, introducing cultural presuppositions which are alien to educational roles, performance evaluation and cognitive expectations. This implies that an educational form of intercultural communication should be produced, shaping personalities *and* cultural diversity. Intercultural education tries to shape cultural diversity, in the framework of shaping personalities.

The main task for intercultural education is to teach children to accept cultural diversity. Intercultural education has the double task of integrating cultural minorities and convincing the cultural majority to accept them, promoting successful communication across cultures. It is based on a transcultural form of communication, which promotes intercultural learning (Dueñas 1994). Intercultural learning is learning from other cultures, which permits the use of new cultural presuppositions, not simply the knowledge of them. Intercultural learning should favour the acquisition of intercultural competence and sensitivity, and leads to the construction of new mixed cultural identities (Onwemechili, Nwosu, Jackson & James-Hughes 2003; Sparrow 2000; Todd-Mancillas 2000): "individuals may keep their own cultural habits and beliefs while 'integrating' aspects of the new culture into their lifestyle" (Yamada & Singelis 1999, p. 707).

This transcultural form of education is considered particularly effective in creating multicultural, global citizenship (Osler & Starkey 2005). Intercultural learning, sensitivity and competence in passing through cultures are considered the main abilities for the new century, and mixed cultural identities are considered the new necessary forms of self.

However, the paradoxical meaning of a transcultural form of education creates practical problems in choosing between the conservation of 'original' cultural presuppositions and the creation of a third culture, which indicates the replacement of these presuppositions. Following these theories, original cultural presuppositions are simultaneously preserved, as they are respected, and changed, as they give room to a new synthesis. Theories of intercultural education invite us to teach reciprocal knowledge, cognitive flexibility, and an understanding based on empathy and intercultural learning. However, the paradoxes of a transcultural approach are encouraged in educational practices. In this respect, the intentional educational proposals clarify the empirical limits of transcultural strategies.

Firstly, intercultural education openly absorbs the cultural presupposition of role performance. Consequently, intercultural learning is contradicted by a clear and unavoidable asymmetry between the roles of teachers and students, based on perceived performance abilities and evaluation necessities. Secondly, intercultural education openly absorbs the cultural presupposition of personalised diversity, represented by concepts such as empathy, active participation, personal confirmation, interpersonal sensitivity. Therefore, the construction of a mixed cultural identity is based on the cultural identity of a personal self. The shaping of mixed cultural identities is contradicted by the explicit necessity to maintain individualism, cognitive expectations and personal attitudes. These educational cultural presuppositions are considered necessary for children's careers.

Intercultural education in a culturally determined educational system requires assimilation to certain cultural presuppositions, which may prevent an effective transcultural education. Without a basic assimilation to the cultural presuppositions of role performance and personal expression, children fail in their careers, losing their opportunities to achieve citizenship rights through education. It seems that mainstream educational strategies do not aim to integrate different cultural presuppositions in a single mixed cultural identity, but different individual identities in a single set of cultural presuppositions. Against this backdrop, transcultural forms seem to be sophisticated forms of ethnocentrism and empowering dialogue seems to be the means used to bring about its achievement.

Is there an alternative interpretation of intercultural education? To answer this question we need to have a closer look at the conditions of participatory processes.

1.6   Promoting participatory processes

The most recent narrative of interaction with children concerns the quality of their participation and self-expression, both in mono-cultural and multicultural settings. In this narrative, children's positions in interactions are intentionally associated with agency and personal expressions, which are considered features of positive positioning. Positive positioning coincides with deliberate self-positioning, through which personal identity is intentionally expressed by stressing personal agency, perspective and/or autobiography (van Langenhove & Harré 1999). Personalisation is recognised as positive and distinguished from individualism (see § 1.2). This new narrative introduces a fundamental ambivalence in society (James, Jenks & Prout 1998; Jans 2004; Jenks 1996): children are considered as either "being" or "becoming", either active or passive, either competent or noncompetent. In interaction, the primacy of children's agency and self-realisation is alternative to or mixed with the primacy of their instrumental usage to realize social aims (Prout 2000).

In many social practices, children control continues to prevail (Hill, Davis, Prout & Tisdall 2004; Maggioni & Baraldi 1999), while in other practices, participation is seen primarily as an instrument for the smooth functioning of a society that is unilaterally designed for adults (Jans 2004; Matthews 2003). In general, the contribution of social systems to children's development seems to be more important than children's active contribution to social systems (Prout 2003) – children are expected to actively participate within an adult-driven framework

(Craig 2003). In this light, however, the goal of changing the societal status quo through children's participation is observed as prominent.

Children's positive participation is primarily observed as involvement in decision-making, which can make them feel influential. To achieve this goal, the promotion of children's self-expression is a primary task which changes the relationships between adults and children: "working in partnership with children requires that adults leave aside the role that society has often prescribed to them of being the teacher with all the answers" (Blanchet-Cohen & Rainbow 2006, p. 122). Adults become "facilitators rather than technicians" and "both children and adults are co-constructors of knowledge and expertise" (Hill, Davis, Prout & Tisdall 2004, p. 84). This means that "children and adults are becoming 'peers' in the way that they both have to learn to give meaning and shape to their active citizenship" (Jans 2004, p. 32).

The importance of the interaction between adults and children in promoting participation is widely recognized. Sinclair (2004) identifies the relevant variables concerning this interaction, i.e. the level of children's active engagement, and the forms of dialogue and engagement. Shier (2001) indicates the most important actions in promoting children's participation, that is active listening, supporting self-expression, taking their views into account, involving them in decision-making processes, sharing with them power and responsibility for decision-making. Matthews (2003) proposes different types of interaction, i.e. dialogue (listening and consulting), development (adults working for the benefit of children), participation (children working within the community), and integration (children working with the community). In particular, Matthews considers dialogue as "the starting point, whereby children are consulted and listened to", ensuring that "their ideas are taken seriously" (2003, p. 268). It is clear that in these perspectives empowering dialogue is fundamental for the promotion of children's agency, participation and self-expression.

It has been observed that the results of children's empowerment are unpredictable: the "adult society must accept that there will be complexities when children express views that do not coincide with those of adults" (Holland & O'Neill 2006, p. 96). Empowerment means seriously taking into account that "when the children are able to determine the issues that they consider to be important, the results cannot be known in advance" (Hill, Davis, Prout & Tisdall 2004, p. 86).

In the light of these assumptions, we may observe that:

1. Empowering dialogue can promote children's active participation and self-expression.
2. Children's active participation and self-expression may provoke conflicts.
3. These conflicts may be managed through dialogic mediation.

4. This kind of conflict management makes it possible to make choices and then to carry out a decision-making process within the interaction.
5. This decision-making process may determine either a reproduction of cultural presuppositions or a re-contextualization of the social system which frames the interaction.

Each of these steps may be more or less articulated and may be more or less successful. In general, they constitute a specific kind of communication system, based on empowering dialogue and dialogic mediation.

The importance of empowering dialogue and dialogic mediation may be observed both in promoting active participation (deliberate self-positioning, primarily as agency) and in managing conflicts arising from this participation. In the first phase, dialogic mediation consists of promoting children's agency, opening various possibilities of actions and self-expression, i.e. expression of their perspectives and emotions. In the second phase, it consists of managing conflicts without denying children's agency and self-expression. Between these two phases, there may be coordination of the interactive *reflection* about the meanings of the ongoing activity and the forms of relationships which such activity is promoting and may promote.

According to Luhmann (1984), reflection is a communication process whereby social systems observe meanings and consequences of their internal processes and structures. Reflection deals with the internal 'reality' of a social system, indicating it as a unit and dealing with this unit in communication, i.e. creating the identity of the system (e.g. education, promotion of positive participation, dialogic mediation, etc.). Reflection may arise in third order positioning of participants in the system, topicalising the narrative about participants' positioning which has been produced in previous communications. Specifically, the dialogic coordination of reflection may elicit the construction of meanings for participation processes, contradictions arising within the interaction, and their possible management.

1.7   Dialogic actions

It is particularly important to understand which actions may enhance dialogic mediation for different purposes (promotion of participation, coordination of reflection, conflict management). Dialogic actions do not determine communication processes; to be successful in communication, they need to be understood and accepted by the interlocutors. Consequently, their success is observable only in the unit action-reaction, and in the organisation of turn-taking.

However, it is possible to observe whether and under what conditions dialogic actions may enhance an empowering form of dialogue, in their positioning participants and projecting participants' reactions. As we have seen, an empowering form of dialogue may be seen as based on conditions of equity and empathy in communication.

Firstly, empowering dialogue requires an equal distribution of opportunities for active participation and self-expression. It implies expression and acknowledgement of different perspectives: each participant observes the others as competent persons, taking into account their perspectives. As knowledge is construed in communication and not owned by privileged groups or competent individuals, empowering dialogue requires balanced communication in order to construe knowledge without denying diversity, in a negotiation process. Secondly, empowering dialogue requires empathy, i.e. showing interest in interlocutors' self-expressions and sensitivity to their needs. Empathy can be observed as addressing participants' interests and/or needs. It means appreciation for emotions and needs, based on the ability to understand them. To sum up, empowerment, positive positioning of participants and re-authoring of stories may be achieved through the acknowledgement of different perspectives and the display of sensitivity for these perspectives.

Features of dialogic actions, which facilitate participants' contributions and promote their interaction, have been described in the literature on mediation (e.g. Ayoko, Härtel & Callan 2002; Baraldi 2006c; Baraldi & Gavioli 2007; Coleman et al. 2008; Gergen, McNamee & Barrett 2001; Littlejohn 2004; Picard & Melchin 2007; Poitras 2005; Royce 2005; Winslade and Monk 2008), on intercultural relationships (e.g. Gudykunst 1994; Kim 2001), and on education (e.g. Baraldi 2003, 2008; Pearce and Pearce 2001). Examples of these features include:

1. Confirming and supporting the interlocutors' self-positioning. Confirmation and support of the interlocutors' contributions can show acceptance and acknowledgement, and create positive connotations of their positions.
2. Narrating personal stories. Narrating personal stories, taking a deliberate self-positioning, enhances a narrative form of mediation which gives room to legitimate expressions of interlocutors' perspectives.
3. Creating stories which include the interlocutor's perspective. The construction of inclusive stories indicates that diverse positions are taken into account, avoiding stereotypes, paying attention to the terminology concerning identities and the expression of meanings about these identities.
4. Checking the interlocutors' perceptions and positions. Perception checking introduces reflexivity, i.e. communication about feelings and thoughts; it shows the will to understand the interlocutors' perceptions of events and positions.

5. Active listening of the interlocutors' self-expression and self-positioning. Active listening (e.g. Gordon 2002) shows sensitivity for the interlocutors' needs and feelings, through signals of involvement in communication, both verbal (encouragement) and non-verbal (glances, postures, smiles, gestures). Active listening reveals personal interests and personal efforts in understanding. In particular, "double listening" (Winslade & Monk 2008) includes listening to interlocutors' sufferance and hope, to their story, and the opportunities for opening up alternative stories. This kind of listening displays "respectful curiosity".

6. Asking for feedback on the effects of actions in terms of the interlocutors' understanding, acceptance and positioning. Asking for feedback enhances the interlocutors' contributions to the communication process and clarifies the possible effects of dialogic actions.

7. Constructing alternative stories (re-authoring) through questions. Asking questions can promote participants authorship and editing of alternative stories, without impositions. Questions can achieve the goal of re-authoring stories towards a positive positioning of interlocutors, favouring interlocutors' self-positioning within new narratives.

8. Formulating the meanings of interlocutors' previous turns. Formulation consists in reacting to the interlocutors' actions with the explicit intention of clarifying their meanings and effects. It consists in "summarising, glossing, or developing the gist of an informant's earlier statement" (Heritage 1985, p. 100). Formulations project a direction for subsequent turns by inviting responses insofar as they "advance the prior report by finding a point in the prior utterance and thus shifting its focus, redeveloping its gist, making something explicit that was previously implicit in the prior utterance, or by making inference about its presuppositions or implications" (Heritage 1985, p. 104). Formulations may make explicit, gloss or develop the interlocutor's self-expressions, i.e. they can be *affective* formulations. In these cases, the gist of the prior utterance is developed focusing on personal expressions, therefore formulations (1) develop and emphasize personal expressions, (2) select what in the prior reports permits to infer the interlocutor's personal self-positioning, and (3) re-present the gist of these reports in order to permit their focusing, topicalisation and elaboration in the subsequent interaction.

9. Appreciating the interlocutors' actions, experiences and positions. Dialogic actions are effective only if they do not produce a negative evaluation of the interlocutors' actions and if they avoid to picture them as problematic people. For this reason, appreciation for the interlocutor's contributions is particularly important. Appreciation concerns the fact of contributing, not necessarily

the contents of contributions. For this reason, appreciation does not imply giving up a personal perspective about contents.

The analysis of these dialogic actions within the interaction leads to an understanding of the possibility and effectiveness of empowering dialogue in empirical situations. Possibility and effectiveness concern promotion of participation, coordination of reflection, and conflict management within social systems which can be seen to play a particular function in society. This analysis can help understand intercultural education as dialogic promotion of participants' personal expressions, avoiding the theoretical traps of paradoxical approaches.

1.8   The passage to empirical observation

The research which will be presented in Chapter 2 aims to analyse the function and cultural presuppositions of (1) educating children to intercultural positive relationships and (2) promoting their positive interpersonal relationships, in intercultural residential settings. The different ways in which this function and these cultural presuppositions are accomplished will be explored in order to understand if and when empowering dialogue is or is not activated and with which effects on intercultural and interpersonal communication. For this purpose, contextualization cues will be analysed in the interaction.

In this chapter, we have posed questions about the effectiveness of a transcultural form of communication, especially in education, to face the problem of cultural diversity and the effectiveness of dialogic mediation to change the status quo of inequalities and power distribution. A linguistic and sociological analysis of these aspects could validly contribute to some clarification of these topics.

Our analysis aims to contribute to this clarification focusing on the possibilities, the successes and failures of the main forms of communication in a particular multicultural social system where children are socialised and intentionally educated to cultural differences and the 'third culture', to cross-cultural adaptation and intercultural learning, and where children's active participation and positive positioning should be systematically promoted.

The research project

Claudio Baraldi, Gabriella Cortesi and Vittorio Iervese

Chapter 2 defines the methodological plan of the empirical study regarding CISV (Children's International Summer Villages) activities. After a presentation of CISV, an international organisation devoted to peace and intercultural education, the chapter focuses on the methodology adopted to observe the cultural presuppositions of interactions within CISV villages and summer camps, in which the participants are children (villages), adolescents (summer camps), adult leaders of children/adolescents delegations, camp directors, and other staff. The field study includes video-recording of interactions, questionnaires and interviews in 12 villages and camps. The analysis is centred on (1) the participant's narratives, i.e. their constructions of the meanings of cultural presuppositions emerged during the activities, and (2) the linguistic cues for the cultural presuppositions of interactions involving these participants during the activities.

2.1   From theoretical framework to empirical research

In Chapter 1, we introduced the conceptual framework which shapes this book. In this chapter we introduce the passage from this framework to empirical observation, which is focused on the cultural presuppositions appearing in and guiding communication processes. Cultural presuppositions may be analysed by looking at the contextualization cues that we can find in the use of language in communication processes. Cultural presuppositions may be observed and enacted only in communication. In our research context, we have observed cultural presuppositions in two ways, which we shall here briefly illustrate.

First, we have considered the CISV narratives: the participants' constructions of meanings of features, characters, events, characterizing CISV's values and activities. As we have seen in Chapter 1, narratives are stories that guide actions, i.e. social constructions in which the observed world is interpreted and storied (Baker 2006a). According to Baker (2006a, p. 10), narratives permit the categorization of actions as valued vs. non-valued, in various specific forms (e.g. normal vs. eccentric, rational vs. irrational, legitimate vs. non-legitimate). Narratives normalise accounts "so that they come to be perceived as self-evident, benign, uncontestable and non-controversial" (Baker 2006a, p. 11). However, it is important to distinguish between categorising narratives and ethnocentric narratives.

Narratives establish categories because they unavoidably fix some kind of interpretations of the world: being social constructions, they always present a "blind spot" (Luhmann 1984) which impedes an objective access to reality and traces the meanings of actions and other events and facts. This means that narratives always use guiding distinctions, i.e. cultural presuppositions which structure their space of interpretation, and depend on the organisation of society. Narratives reproduce and produce cultural presuppositions, detailing their features, describing, explaining and legitimising them in communication. Narratives are plural and competing: this is not only true in intercultural situations, but also in the framework of the same set of cultural presuppositions, when this admits pluralism.

Narratives may reproduce and produce ethnocentrism. Narratives are ethnocentric if and when they use cultural presuppositions and form categories in order to assess the world, in particular contributions to communication, that is if and when they create information as a difference between Us and Them, between a valuable and important way of observing and acting in the world and a non-valuable and unimportant one. It is important to distinguish specific ethnocentric narratives within a more general category of narratives as social constructions, because while categorising is unavoidable, ethnocentrism is applied in certain conditions of social organisation.

Baker (2006a) differentiates among types of narratives: ontological narratives, concerning the self; public narratives, circulating in social and institutional settings; conceptual narratives, guiding scientific research and disciplines; meta-narratives, that is the "great narratives" (Lyotard 1979), which frame all the stories that are produced in societies. The distinction between ontological and public narratives seems difficult to be asserted: narratives of the self are never strictly individual performances, as they are presented and declared in public contexts. Therefore, it is possible to include ontological narratives in the most general category of public narratives and distinguish among different kinds of public narratives, e.g. interpersonal narratives in families (where ontological narratives are particularly important), educational narratives, political narratives, religious narratives, etc. There is a wide variety of public narratives, which are strongly differentiated. Conceptual narratives may be observed as another specific kind of public narratives, concerning the scientific system and its internal differentiation. Moreover, conceptual narratives may be translated into social representations (Moscovici 1982, 1984) which are produced in daily life and in common discourses, e.g. the debates about environmental problems, or economic crises. Finally, the empirical identification of meta-narratives is doubtful: it is difficult to identify which stories are really basic and frame all other stories, although some stories appear to be better rooted in the social organisation. The concept of cultural presuppositions (guiding values, forms of contributions, forms of expectations) seems to be more effective in indicating the basic cultural forms which structure social organisation.

Narratives can be analysed through "textual methods" (Baker 2006a). Analysing narratives means exploring descriptions, explanations and legitimisations of the cultural presuppositions guiding communicative processes. Empirically, this means collecting and analysing the stories which apply the main cultural presuppositions, are documented in written texts (conventions, programmes, plans, assessments, etc.), can be derived from the participants' testimonies, through questionnaires and interviews, can be observed in oral interactions, and can be identified in other visual forms (pictures, ballets, etc.).

In this book, we are interested in studying a particular kind of public narratives – educational narratives – which also include important social representations of conceptual narratives in pedagogy and psychology. The influence of pedagogical and psychological conceptual narratives on educational public narratives is evident in educational systems. This influence is filtered through written texts and conversations among educators, parents, students. By observing educational narratives, we can see displayed features of the main cultural presuppositions of the educational system. These educational narratives are also reproduced in the interaction involving the main participants in the educational systems, namely expert adults and learning children. The relationship between narratives and the interaction is particularly evident in educational systems: narratives are reproduced through interactions and are therefore observable in the interaction, by analysing its semantic characteristics. However, there are two ways of looking at the interaction: we can observe either narratives expressed in the interaction's cultural contents, or the linguistic forms for cultural presuppositions (contextualization cues).

This leads us to the second way in which cultural presuppositions have been observed. As we have seen, cultural presuppositions may be observed as narrated in communication processes, in detailed stories. However, they are not made completely evident through this semantic analysis. Their description and explanation requires a pragmatic analysis, i.e. an analysis of the use of language in the interaction which looks at the verbal and non-verbal forms signalling its structures, intended as the selections which serve as premises for its production as a communication system. The analysis of contextualization cues is a *structural* analysis because it looks for these premises of the interaction, i.e. its cultural presuppositions, and not simply for its cultural productions (discourse and specific narratives). We can observe the production of cultural presuppositions in and through the interaction, only by analysing the linguistic structure of the interaction as a way to understand cultural presuppositions. The analysis of contextualization cues requires videotaping, transcribing, describing and explaining the sequences of turns in the interaction (see Chapter 1).

To sum up, social organisation consists in communicative processes which construct narratives and make contextualization cues available. The analysis of communicative processes is fundamental for understanding the social conditions of cultural presuppositions and their narratives. Social organisation is created through communication processes which are guided by particular cultural presuppositions and include the accounts of their meanings. The analysis concerns social constructions *of* and *in* the interaction; the former implies narratives and the latter implies both cultural presuppositions (i.e. structures) and narratives.

2.2   An overview of CISV narrative and activities

2.2.1 Narrative

CISV (Children's International Summer Villages) is an international organisation which aims to establish exchanges among children and adolescents from all over the world. CISV is based on the narrative that peace is possible if individuals and groups can learn to live together, in friendship. Its primary objective is to prepare children to become active in peace building and in developing friendships, learning appropriate communication skills for these purposes. CISV programs and activities aim to promote children's personal, cultural and intercultural knowledge in order to increase their mindfulness, positive attitudes towards their interlocutors, abilities in living, working and playing with them, without considering different cultural backgrounds as obstacles (CISV 2004). This means promoting peaceful interpersonal and intercultural relations, fostering respect for diversity, reducing prejudices and stereotypes about culture, class, ethnicity, and gender, avoiding conflicts and exclusion, providing opportunities for children and adolescents to coexist. Participants learn that, despite national or cultural differences, they are members of the human community in an increasingly interdependent world. They learn to become conscious global citizens (CISV 2008).

CISV educational narrative is based on experiential knowledge, and is developed through specific activities, based on theories of prejudice and group dynamics. People from different countries and cultures are invited to learn intercultural abilities which should help them establish effective relationships, communicate with minimal loss or distortion, and work together towards common goals. Participants should "learn by doing" and share responsibilities for this kind of learning. Through their active participation, they achieve a better understanding of themselves and their own cultures as well as different cultures, and learn to live in peace with different cultures. CISV aims to offer multiple opportunities to discover informal and educational activities which permit this, at local, national and international level. To achieve these goals, CISV has formulated a set of interactive, cooperative activities and games, which are included in a scheme called *Education Circle* concerning:

1. Global Awareness Education (world citizenship, life support system, interdependence, etc.).
2. Intercultural Education (cultural sensitivity, cultural differences, languages, etc.).
3. Human Relations Education (group dynamics, cooperation, problem solving, crisis management, communication skills, etc.).
4. Personal Development Education (peace at individual and small group level, ability to relate individual values, ethics, trust, etc.).
5. Environmental Education (interrelation between humans and the environment, sense of responsibility for the world, etc.).
6. Development Education (international solidarity, quality of life, social justice, provision of basic needs, etc.).
7. Human Rights Education (fundamental freedoms, justice, individual rights, minorities/groups' rights, etc.).
8. International Education (non-war attitude, international politics, non-violent conflict resolution, etc.).

These activities encourage children to:

1. Know nations in terms of friendship rather than as abstractions on a map or stereotyped patterns.
2. Be aware of the fundamental equality of the human kind and at the same time learn to appreciate differences.
3. Acquire the desire to work to build durable peace in the world.
4. Acquire abilities in communication, even in the absence of a common language.
5. Acquire abilities in administration and organisation.
6. Develop personalities free from psychological barriers and prejudices.

2.2.2 Activities

CISV is organised both at national and international levels. At local level there are local chapters coordinated in national associations which are registered according to national laws. National associations are economically self-sufficient, thanks to the fees paid by the members and some financial aid from external bodies. CISV International is administered by an International Board composed of the representatives of each national association and its headquarters are in Newcastle (UK). This Board provides the guidelines for CISV education, promotes and coordinates it, and checks its quality. An executive committee, the Board of Directors, has the specific function to supervise national associations.

Since 1951, more than 150,000 children have participated in more than 4,000 international activities in 70 countries in the world. English is the official language for communication in all CISV activities, although non-verbal communication is strongly encouraged and translations are provided for those who are not sufficiently skilled in English.

In this book we deal with two important CISV programs: Villages and Summer Camps. The first and most important CISV program of activities is the *Village*, which lasts four weeks (in 2005 there were experimental three-week villages, but this experiment has been abandoned) and offers a wide range of educational activities, games and opportunities for informal encounters. Villages include eleven or twelve national delegations of four 11-year-old children, two males and two females, led by an adult who must be more than 21 years old. In the villages there are also an organisational staff with a camp director and about six Junior Counsellors (JCs) aged 16–17. The *Summer Camp* lasts three weeks and includes six to nine delegations of adolescents (aged 13–15). Each delegation is formed as in villages and the organisation of the activities is also similar to that of villages. However, activities are designed for a different age and this presupposes a greater autonomous participation of adolescents in planning and managing them. Summer camps explicitly aim to promote adolescents' responsibility in planning and discussing important topics.

In addition, CISV promotes other important activities: *Interchange* (exchange between two national delegations of a maximum of ten adolescents aged 12–15), and *Seminar Camp* (involving about thirty adolescents aged 17 and 18 and five international staff members). CISV organises also shorter youth meetings, a three-week program called International People Program (IPP), which enhances important plans (e.g. ecological development, migration, etc.) in cooperation with some institution, and local educational activities.

Villages and summer camps deal with specific themes defined by the staff and are generally based in schools. Participants work together to plan activities and discussions which build on the chosen theme from the preliminary phase carried out by each delegation before the actual villages and summer camps start.

Leaders and staff members of villages and summer camps meet two days before the delegates arrive to get to know one another and prepare the site. They have to create and maintain an intimate atmosphere that makes the experience unique. Every-day village and summer camp life is based on a schedule which splits the day into phases (wake-up times, duties, meal times, bed times, etc.). Four progressively more complex kinds of activities are put forward, aiming to gradually transform superficial mutual understanding into interpersonal trust: name/ice breaking games (introducing participants); running games; contact games; simulation, cooperation and trust games. This progression aims to combine the development of the relationships between children/adolescents with the development or strengthening of communication between them, with consequent disappearance of adults' linguistic mediation. After an experiential activity intended to stimulate observations, emotions and insights in the participants, the CISV routine includes *debriefing*, i.e. an open-ended discussion to reflect on what has been learned.

In villages, activities are organised by leaders and JCs in planning groups, working with the support and supervision of staff members. Each group sets up activities and is responsible for making all necessary arrangements and announcements. Leaders have the important task of translating announcements for members of their delegation. Activity planning is presented at the leaders' meeting, usually one or two days before the date of implementation, in order to allow all adults to understand, review and approve activities. The daily leaders' meeting is also an opportunity for sharing highlights and discussing problems. In summer camps too, there are daily leaders' meetings, but here adolescents plan and perform the activities directly after an initial coordination by adults. The most important aim of summer camps is promotion of adolescents' actions and responsibilities in daily life. Adolescents present their decisions during leaders' meeting. Adults can intervene only if they see major problems. Therefore, the structure of summer camps' daily schedule depends on adolescents' planning. They can decide together the rules, adding them to rules set by the staff and fundamental CISV rules (no smoking or using drugs and alcohol, no sexual relations, no xenophobic or discriminatory behaviour, no physical or psychological abuse or corporal punishment). While in villages adults set timetables and rules that regulate daily life, in summer camps the adults' task is to facilitate discussion among adolescents, and to show them how to handle conflict in a positive manner. Meetings enable leaders, staff and adolescents to discuss and evaluate camps' programmes and life.

Consideration for cultural specificities is different in villages and summer camps. In villages, it essentially takes shape in the *national nights*, during which delegations present exhibitions of songs, dances, games, legends and food tasting from their home countries. This kind of cultural sharing is considered important for promoting awareness of similarities and differences among children. In summer camps, this attention is formalised in the *cultural activities* or *cultural days* planned by each delegation. These activities may be playful (like dances and meals inspired by national customs), educational (such as a presentation of the geographical, historical and political aspects of each country, followed by quizzes or crafts), or promotional, with a reflection on specific topics related to the delegations' specific cultures (e.g. drug policy in Holland, immigration policy in Italy, multiculturalism in Canada, etc.).

In both villages and summer camps, daily rituals aim to create and maintain the sense of community. The most important ritual is *flag time*, in the morning and in the evening, during which the official CISV flag is hoisted or lowered. This ceremony is accompanied by a sort of hymn to the brotherhood sung by all participants. Another ritual is the "kitos", a kind of non-denominational chanted blessing, intoned in chorus after the main meals. In the evening, another ritual is "lullabies time" which sees all the participants together in a special room, during which songs are sung, celebrating CISV. Children and adolescents are responsible for daily cleaning. They have rest time at mid-day, which allows for a quiet break, and about an hour of free-time, distributed throughout the day, to enable interpersonal contacts and friendships. Members of the same delegation are discouraged from staying together during the day. Adults compose mixed groups when allocating the rooms, or during activities such as cleaning and meal times. However, each day, delegations meet during "delegation time", to share experience, problems, and feelings. There is a limited number of scheduled excursions to sites of local interest, and there is usually an "open day", when local people can visit villages and summer camps and be informed on CISV aims and goals. There is also a brief home stay with local families, associated to CISV, which host couples of children or adolescents upon their arrival and, in villages, even during an additional weekend.

These programs are primarily focused on the relevance of adult-children interactions, i.e. on interactions based on educational cultural presuppositions and giving meanings to education. However this is not the only kind of interaction which is important to observe in these programs. Following Matthews (2003), we may also observe the phase of "development", including adults working for the benefit of children and interacting for this purpose, which is particularly important in the system we are observing. This kind of interaction can be observed during *organisational meetings* in villages and summer camps. Furthermore, as Matthews notes, we can observe the phase of "participation", including children working *within* the community in peer-to-peer interactions.

These interactions are particularly important in summer camps, where a stronger meaning of children's autonomy is developed and adolescents are involved in planning the activities and in the *activity time*, where they discuss and assess the activities themselves.

2.3   The research

The research which is presented in this book concerns (1) the participants' narratives of CISV values and activities, (2) the organisational meetings in which planning and decision-making are achieved, (3) the activities with children and adolescents which shape the empirical meaning of CISV educational narratives, and (4) the activities in which adolescents autonomously discuss narratives and cultural presuppositions, with effects of self-socialisation.

The main research questions about all these activities concern:

1. Differences between dyadic interactions and mediation.
2. Relationships between education and promotion of children's participation.
3. Ways in which empowering dialogue can enhance education and children's participation.
4. Relationships between empowering dialogue and intercultural communication.

CISV activities imply expert guidance of dyadic interactions, including interactions between expert adults and groups of children. CISV organisational meetings require some kind of direction, supervision and coordination. However, interactions during activities and organisational meetings are frequently mediated. The difference between expertise and mediation deserves particular attention, specifically in its relationship with empowering dialogue. Empowering dialogue mainly implies interpersonal qualities, such as confirmation and support of personal contributions, formulation of personal attitudes and stories, inclusion of personal perspectives and perceptions, active listening, formulating personal expressions, appreciation of personal contributions. These interpersonal qualities are based on affective expectations and derive from a cultural preference for individual self-expression and active participation.

Important questions include the relevance of empowering dialogue in CISV educational and organisational interactions, its effectiveness in communications which are *potentially* intercultural, and its effects on education in multicultural settings. The effects of empowering dialogue can concern both educational presuppositions (role performances, cognitive and normative expectations) and promotion of children's participation, in terms of support to cultural, mixed or personal identities. Another question concerns the plausibility and the meaning of transcultural forms of communication in these situations: whether these forms may be enhanced by dialogic mediation, in what ways and with which implications.

2.4   The methodology

A strategy of inquiry comprises a bundle of skills, assumptions, and practices that researchers employ as they move from a paradigm of observation to the observed empirical world. Strategies of inquiry put paradigms of interpretation into motion. In Chapter 1, the theoretical framework to which this book refers has been described. The concepts illustrated are used in order to define the methodological plan on which our research is based. From the perspective of this work, methodology is the set of conditions that define the accuracy of research operations (Luhmann 1990). Such accuracy is better understood in terms of internal methodological coherence (self-reference) and in the relationship between theory and external reality (other-reference). This work draws on the theory, the attention paid to the processes constructing the meanings of what is observed as well as who observes, and the requirements of research programs able to direct the observation.

The theory substantially links the action of observation with the construction of knowledge about reality (Foerster 1984; Glasersfeld 1987). This constructivist perspective implies that each system builds its meanings through its operations and observations can be noticed when they are communicated. In this sense, the task of researchers in social sciences is to observe observations. This means that the observations of researchers do not have a greater degree of objectivity than other observations. However, they are focused on the methods of observation of other systems. This attention for the processes of construction of meanings requires a methodology which highlights the choices of researchers rather than the data collected from reality. Researchers need to justify their selections rather than "measure" the information collected. If research is considered construction of meanings, then its methodology has the task of making the choices made by researchers in their systematic observation non-random, coherent and transparent.

Methodology is the result of the theoretical assumptions in their relations with the programs and the object of the observation. Therefore methodology supports the coherence of the act of observing rather than the results of what is observed. Following these premises, the present work tries to reconstruct the forms and contents of CISV villages and summer camps, not only through the perspectives of the participants but also through the direct observation of the interactions which shape the social systems that we name 'villages' and 'summer camps'. Single individuals and their actions are not the object of observation, which is instead the relationships among the participants' actions in the interaction. What is observed is therefore the dynamic and changing sequences of social actions. Individuals modify their actions and reactions according to the actions of their interlocutors in the interaction. On the other hand, the observed interaction is included in a system that tends to determine it according to its own structures (cultural presuppositions). The purpose of this work is therefore to analyze the mutual relationship existing between the systems which frame the interactions and the interactions which are framed within such systems.

CISV presents itself as a system of initiatives aimed mainly at children and adolescents. Its interventions take place in the interaction between adults, on the one hand, and children and adolescents on the other. The analysis concerns the communicative meanings of such interventions, especially the forms of communication that realises them and that they promote. Interventions are seen as communication processes between competent adults and children as recipients, which should ensure the translation of CISV goals into forms of communication that allow their achievement.

According to these assumptions, it is important (a) to know the starting goals and meanings, (b) to observe how communication takes particular forms during the intervention, and (c) to observe the different results that can be produced on the basis of the intervention. While the process is observable in the communication between adults and children/adolescents, the results of the intervention are observable in communications among children and adolescents, that is in the emergence of ideas, doubts, remarks that answer the questions posed as objectives, or, in other words, in the emergence of narratives concerning CISV's cultural presupposition.

The analysis of (a) has been addressed through the distribution of questionnaires and interviews to children, adolescents and adults. The analysis of (b) has been addressed through the video-recording of the most important activities and organisational meetings in villages and summer camps. The analysis of (c) has been conducted by collecting comments from participants at the villages and summer camps through semi-structured group interviews.

These three research areas are closely linked and it is possible to identify the dynamics of CISV villages and summer camps through the relationship between the different meanings developed in these three parts of the research. Similarly, the relationship that binds theory to empirical research is circular; on the one hand, theory can supply meanings for analysing the empirical data collected and on the other hand, these data allow the modification of the theory, opening up new conceptual horizons and raising new questions. The history and characteristics of the research we are presenting attest this close and complex relationship.

The approach characterising this research is the result of various methods and different disciplinary influences. The research team has worked for almost fifteen years on the relationships between adults and children. During this period, concepts and instruments have been refined with respect to different topics and different social systems. The research which has been carried out in recent years has enabled us to test our "work tools" and to adapt them to the complexities that we have approached on each occasion when dealing with various educational systems and services, different forms of education and mediation, prevention of harassment and promotion of participation. In this process, communication studies, dialogue analysis, and conversation analysis have converged in creating a methodology which reflects the theoretical approach described in Chapter 1.

Finally, all research involves necessary choices. Although the search plan is complex and articulated, it has allowed us to observe only some aspects of the investigated reality. As previously mentioned, the task of research is precisely to make selections in a transparent and motivated way from the large amount of redundant information that can be obtained by observing social reality. In our case, the first choice has been based on the definition of intervention. In this sense, we have focused exclusively on 'formal' interactions (those expected in the organisation and development of CISV activities), whereas 'informal' interactions (those realized between activities) have been ignored. This choice is motivated by a need for coherence with the research aims and by a practical need for management of existing resources.

A second set of choices has concerned the selection of the qualitative data to support the analysis of interactions. Since this research has not the purpose of 'measuring' reality, in this book we have chosen to show a selection of data which should be particularly meaningful and easily understandable to the readers. The analysis is based on the observation of interactional sequences and the dynamics through which participants participate in the interaction and co-construct meaning is the core of it. In this respect, quantitative date such as figures related to the percentage of occurrences of actions do not seem central, as the main issue here concerns the ways in which actions are treated, rather than 'how many times' they appear. Some tendencies can although be observed as more pervasive than others in the data, so some observations on interactional sequences that seem to occur many times or even overwhelmingly are provided.

The analyses presented in the next chapters are the result of these two sets of choices, which will be more comprehensible when the analyses are explained in detail.

2.5   The research design

The research was carried out in all CISV villages and summer camps run in Italy in 2006 and 2007. The corpus of data was collected in eight villages (in Bologna, Ferrara, Florence, Forlì, Gorizia, Milan, Modena and Rome) and in four summer camps (in Bergamo, Padua, Reggio Emilia and Trento). These experiences were observed for their complete length.

In the organisational chart of the villages/summer-camps, the researchers covered the role of staff-members, a fact that made the research, and the researchers, integral part of the daily experience of the initiatives. The researchers, as participating observers, were systematically present and involved in the most important parts of the everyday life in villages/camps, selecting from the activities (games, meetings, planning) the most meaningful interactions to be videotaped. Other data were gathered through semi-structured, audio-recorded group interviews and questionnaires concerning the meanings assigned by the children/adolescents and the adults to (a) diversity, dialogue and conflict, and (b) the functioning of intercultural mediation and promotion during the activities.

Questionnaires were administered to all participants both at the beginning (pre-test) and at the end (post-test) of the villages/camps, and their results were compared to those collected through videotaped interactions and audio-recorded interviews.

Overall, we collected 1,353 questionnaires (pre-test and post-test), 95 video-taped group interviews, and 412 hours of videotaped activities. Given this large amount of collected data, we may say that the research was very successful. The few problems which emerged were easily overcome. The main problem concerned the use of English in the questionnaires and interviews, as some children could not speak English very well or at all. This problem was overcome thanks to the leaders' linguistic mediation, which was necessary, although this was an intervening external factor in the relationship between the researcher and the children.

The research involved 482 children (52% females, 48% males) with an average age of 11 in the villages, and 14 and a half in the summer camps, and 216 adults (59% females, 41% males), 54% leaders, 27% staff members, 19% JCs. The majority of leaders were females (67%), while staff members and JCs were fairly uniformly divided between males and females. The average ages were 25 (leaders), 24 (staff members) and 17 (JCs). Adults obtained mainly high school diplomas (39%, 63% staff members), BA or post graduate diplomas (31%), and professional diplomas (14%). All of the JCs obtained a junior high school certificate. Most adults (66%) were students; 12.5% of them were employed, 11% teachers and 6% professionals.

The largest number of delegations came from North-Europe (Denmark, Great Britain, Netherlands, Norway, Sweden – see Table 1), followed by South-Europe (Greece, Italy, Portugal, Spain) and Central-South America (Argentina, Brazil, Costa Rica, Ecuador, Guatemala, Mexico, Peru). Staff members were almost all Italian, as were most JCs.

The data emerging from the questionnaires were elaborated considering the differences in age, gender and cultural origins of the participants and the role played by adults. Videotaped data were integrally transcribed and analysed in their verbal and non verbal aspects. Interviews were used to analyse adults' and children's narratives of villages and summer camps in all their aspects. Video-taped interactions are the main focus of this research as they reflect "real life" in villages and summer camps. Obviously, our ambition was not to videotape everything. We excluded informal life and this was not an easy decision because we were aware of the importance of this kind of social life inside villages and

Table 1. Geographical areas

Geographical areas	% of adults	% of leader	% of young people
South-Europe (Greece, Italy, Portugal, Spain)	41.7	17.9	17.8
North-Europe (Denmark, Finland, Great Britain, Iceland, Netherlands, Norway, Sweden Faroe Islands)	16.2	24.8	23.7
Centre-South America (Argentina, Brazil, Costa Rica, Ecuador, Guatemala, Mexico, Peru)	11.1	15.4	16.0
Centre-Europe (Austria, Belgium, France, Germany, Switzerland)	6.9	10.3	9.1
USA	5.6	6.0	6.4
East-Europe (Bosnia and Herzegovina, Bulgaria, Latvia, Poland, Russian Federation, Slovenia)	5.6	6.8	5.6
West-Asia (Jordan, Israel, Lebanon)	3.7	3.4	3.3
Canada	3.7	6.0	6.6
East-Asia (China, India, Indonesia, Japan, Philippines, Thailand)	3.7	6.0	9.5
Oceania (Australia, New Zealand)	1.9	3.4	1.9
Total	100	100	100

summer camps. However, it would have been impossible to videotape this part of the experience and probably it would also have been unfair to follow the participants in their private life. Moreover it was impossible to videotape all the activities for technical problems (mainly, their overlapping and poor acoustics). We tried to choose the most meaningful activities in terms of relationships and social relevance.

The analysis of the data paid particular attention to the different forms of diversities, such as children/adults, males/females, children from different countries, children who speak English as a lingua franca and children who do not speak it very well or at all. Where these differences are not mentioned, it means that they are not meaningful or that their complexity is too high for this level of analysis.

In order to facilitate the reading of the most complex quantitative data concerning the frequency of important actions in the framework of the interaction, a frequency index was calculated, assigning a value to the main items. Therefore, the frequency of each observed action, in the interaction, goes from 0 (absent) to 10 (always acted).

2.6   The next chapters

In the next chapters, we will illustrate the main results of the research. The huge amount of data that we have collected cannot be reproduced in a single book. Consequently, this book includes the essential and most important aspects of the analysis.

Chapter 3 is dedicated to CISV narratives, collected through surveys and interviews with the participants in the villages and summer camps. The chapter deals with the narrative of CISV values and activities, with reference to the social relationships which are developed inside the villages and the summer camps, and the evaluations of the activities, compared with the participants' expectations.

Chapters 4 and 5 are dedicated to organisational meetings. In Chapter 4, we focus on the presentations and the proposals enacted and debated in the interaction. We have paid particular attention to the treatment of different perspectives, as a key-factor in these meetings is the ways in which active participation is promoted, reduced or blocked. Chapter 5 deals with conflicts and conflict management in organisational meetings, particularly the differences among the forms of conflict avoidance, conflict normative resolution, coordination and dialogic mediation.

Chapters 6, 7, 8, 9, and 10 concern the activities. Chapter 6 concerns promotion of participation in activities involving children and adolescents, in the complex interplay of adults' and children's actions, while Chapter 7 focuses on a particularly important phase of these activities, that is debriefing sessions, in which children are invited to reflect on their development. In these two chapters, we have tried to capture the main features of children's involvement in the activities, describing in which ways adults educate them and promote their participation. Chapter 8 deals with conflict management during the activities. This analysis is useful to understand in which ways the differences of perspectives which emerge from active participation are faced during the activities. Chapter 9 focuses on the interactions among adolescents in summer camps. While in villages the interactions among children are only informal and educational activities always feature some adults working with the children, in summer camps adolescents can work without adults. Although most of the effective interactions include adults, the analysis of interactions among adolescents helps to understand the way in which self-socialisation may be effective in CISV summer camps.

Chapter 10 concerns translation time. Translations are often important for the development of activities. There is a great linguistic gap between children who are either native speakers of English or are very proficient in English as a second language, on the one hand, and children who speak poor or sometimes very poor English on the other hand. The latter have major difficulties in participating in the activities. The limits of communication in a lingua franca are evident above all in the most complex activities, where verbal participation is important and children's contributions are restricted by their linguistic difficulties. In this context, adults' translation is a crucial activity and deserves particular attention.

All the chapters which are dedicated to the interaction (4–10) are mainly focused on the pragmatic use of language for the specific purposes of the activities and on the observation of the contextualization cues. We are not interested in describing and explaining specific games or instructions in villages and summer camps. However, CISV narratives may be easily observed highlighting relevant structures of the interaction and their cultural pillars. The analysis of relevant structures of the interaction can give a meaningful contribution to the knowledge of CISV projects and activities, and makes it possible to describe the ways in which CISV general values and projects are applied in specific interactions.

2.7   The symbols

In this book, in particular for the transcription of interactions, we use some symbols that allow identifying the interactants without revealing their personal identity. We have not identified the single villages and summer camps because the analysis of the data permits us to say that it is not important to distinguish among them: we have not found major differences among villages and summer camps and observations can thus be generalised. The symbols used are as follows:

L = leader
S = staff member
J = JC
D = camp director
M/F = male/female
1, 2, etc. = conventional number of the participant, following the previous symbols
xxx (three letters following the previous symbols) = nationality.

Only in the transcriptions of the interviews:

A = adolescent
C = child

Examples

DMita = camp director, male, Italian
SFusa = staff member, female, American
Mchi = Child, Male, Chinese.
JMnor = JC, male, Norwegian.
F1ita, F2ita = first and second Italian delegates which intervene in the interaction.

In the interviews:

AMdut = adolescent, male, Dutch.

In the analysis of the interactions, we use some transcription conventions which are derived from conversation analysis. The symbols used are as follows:

[text	overlapping turns
(.) (..) (...)	short pauses (less than one second)
(03)	length of pause in seconds
text -	suspended turn
text-	interrupted turn
(text)	unclear turn
(?) (??)	text not understandable
text	high volume or emphasis
°text°	low volume
[....]	information about the context
((comment))	comments of the researcher
>text<	quicker pace
<text>	slower pace
te::xt	prolonged sound
↓	falling tone
↑	rising tone
.,?!	rough signs for intonation in the turn

One problem that is worth mentioning concerns the numbering procedure of the turn lines of the transcription extracts included in this volume. Organizational meetings are distinctly identifiable events, with a clear beginning and end and little or none interruption. So we transcribed these events as long, self-contained interactions starting form turn 1 (the beginning) onwards. The extracts we provided in Chapters 4 and 5 are extracts from these long transcriptions and turn numbering has been maintained in order to give an indication of the position of the extract in the full stretch of talk. Turn numbering in these extracts, then, does not start with 1, unless the extract coincides with the very beginning of the event.

The Activities are, instead, much less clearly identifiable events, as they are frequently interrupted and mixed up with different types of talk. In the extracts from the activities, then, (in Chapters 6, 7, 8, 9 and 10), turn numbering starts from 1, excluding few cases where a clear beginning of the activity is identified and it was thus possible to use the same numbering procedure that we used for extracts from the Organizational meetings.

Following a suggestion by one of the reviewers, those parts of the transcriptions which are relevant for comments are highlighted using bold fonts. In some cases of particular ambiguity, these parts are also quoted in the text, within brackets and in italics.

CHAPTER 3

The CISV narrative

Gabriella Cortesi

Chapter 3 explores children/adolescents' and adults' narratives of their experience of CISV villages and camps. Specifically, the chapter deals with: (1) definitions of cultural and personal differences and their possible forms of management; (2) descriptions of the connections between forms of communication, conflicts, and possible conflict management; (3) descriptions of the forms of differences highlighted in villages and camps, regarding age, gender, nationality, competence in speaking English as a lingua franca; (4) observations of the kinds of actions emerged during interactions; (5) adults' perspectives on children's and adolescents' autonomy and dependence, and descriptions of their corresponding educational intentions; (6) descriptions of the meanings of the whole experience, comparing initial intentions/expectations and final assessments.

3.1   General features of the CISV narrative

As we have seen in Chapter 2, CISV's objective is to promote children's competence to cross cultural borders, which implies the attribution of positive meanings to cultural diversity. Firstly, CISV aims to promote children's social participation and positive and meaningful social relationships with significant adults, peers, and institutions. Through this process social skills should be created, such as co-operative abilities, caring about and respect for interlocutors, social awareness, competence in conflict resolution.

Secondly, CISV aims to ensure the maintenance of cultural specificities, and at the same time their integration into a new cultural form which should transcend them. Therefore, CISV tries to reduce and simultaneously respect cultural diversity, through a transcultural approach.

On the one hand, CISV aims to define and reproduce a We-community which includes the 'We' of all delegations. This community is limited by spatial boundaries, and characterised by symbols, routines and rituals. It is described by the participants as a sort of "parallel world" or "fake world" where it is possible to experience and act differently from the "everyday world": "This is a perfect world: outside all is different" (LMita); "When you live in the real world, you're totally different. This is the perfect world, out is the shit" (LMcan). This "ideal community" tries to close the doors to all external perturbations. On the other hand, CISV positively evaluates cultural diversities, and their manifestations, understanding, respect and acceptance.

These two aims require the construction of shared normative expectations, which are based on affective expectations (empathy, respect, appreciation of others) on the one hand, and on cognitive expectations (intercultural learning) on the other. Participants are treated both as autonomous individuals and members of the community. Empowering dialogue seems to be the way for managing and harmonising the problems created by diversity, while respecting, listening and appreciating interlocutors.

In this chapter we shall observe how this narrative of CISV cultural presuppositions is interpreted by the participants in villages and summer camps.

Firstly, this narrative is reflected in the participants' expectations at the beginning of the activities (see Tables 2 and 3).

Adults expect mainly that children/adolescents find it important to live with people from other countries and cultures (84%) and learning new and important things (76%). Further, according mainly to leaders in summer camps, adolescents should play an active role in taking decisions. This expectation is shared

Table 2. *Villages:* Important factors in children's experience

Important factors in children's experience	% Leaders		% Staff		% JCs		% Children	
	pre-test	post-test	pre-test	post-test	pre-test	post-test	pre-test	post-test
Meeting friends of their/my age	5.0	16.0	2.7	11.1	2.5	4.9	11.4	12.5
Living in a new place, different from their/my home/s	3.8	2.5	–	3.7	–	4.9	2.2	1.7
Living with people from other cultures and countries	75.0	51.3	89.2	59.3	90.0	51.2	29.0	29.3
Having fun together	12.5	10.0	8.1	18.5	7.5	26.8	19.9	16.5
Making friends with a number of children	3.8	20.0	–	7.4	–	12.2	32.5	33.0
Learning English	–	–	–	–	–	–	2.2	2.4

Table 3. *Summer-camps:* Important factors in adolescents' experience

Important factors in adolescents' experience	% Leaders		% Staff		% Adolescents	
	pre-test	post-test	pre-test	post-test	pre-test	post-test
Meeting friends of their/my age	–	8.6	–	11.8	15.4	15.9
Living in a new place, different from their/my home/s	–	2.9	9.5	11.8	1.6	2.9
Living with people from other cultures and countries	88.9	37.1	90.5	58.8	34.1	23.9
Having fun together	8.3	22.9	–	17.6	19.5	14.5
Making friends with a number of children	2.8	28.6	–	–	22.0	34.8
Learning English	–	–	–	–	1.6	2.9

by the majority of leaders in the villages, yet 40.5% of these leaders primarily expect children to follow their suggestions. Moreover, children's/adolescents' expression of spontaneity is expected by a small minority of the adults (21%), with the exception of staff members in the summer-camps (60%). Finally, children's fun and new friendships are expected in very few cases (11% and 4%) and almost exclusively by the leaders. The majority of children/adolescents expect above all to learn something from the experience (64%), and secondly to have the possibility of free self-expression (25%). They rarely expect to reinforce their values (10%).

All these expected results of CISV experience (construction of the meaning of diversity and friendship, learning and active participation, adults' contribution) are connected in a narrative in which we can observe a selective appropriation (Baker 2006a) of concepts and ideas belonging to a more general culture of adult-children interactions and adequate intercultural relationships. This narrative features the property of relationality (Baker 2006a), which means that its different parts should not be considered in isolation. However, it is useful to deal with its single parts separately in order to analyse its meanings.

3.2   The narrative of diversity and friendship

In the participants' narrative, cultural and personal diversities are closely interrelated. Firstly, the narrative of diversities includes three different ways of observing the relationship between culture and personality, fixing particular causal emplotments and different "story types" (Baker 2006a):

1.   Culture moulds and overwhelms individual personalities.
2.   Individuality is a specific expression of culture.
3.   Personal difference is stronger than cultural difference.

Secondly, in general, adults agree with the idea that cultural specificity should be shown in communication, although this can lead to misunderstandings, lack of respect and prejudices. Stories concerning the expression of cultural diversity are emplotted and typed in different ways:

1.   Expression of cultural diversity through interpersonal relationships.
2.   Consideration for cultural diversity through cooperation and interaction.
3.   Expression of cultural diversity through acceptance of different cultural forms.

The adults' approach to cultural diversity is paradoxical: on the one hand, they stress the importance of its acknowledgement and expression; on the other hand, they set it aside as quickly as possible, to guarantee a successful communication. In fact, minority cultures are given up or repressed in order to achieve an integrated village/summer-camp: "The more you abandon your own culture, and the better things work" (SMita); "In CISV we even try to hide cultural differences: we are all friends, we are part of CISV" (JMfin).

In the attempt to construct an 'ideal' intercultural community, and to protect it from the risk of conflicts, discussions about cultural diversity (e.g. regarding religious beliefs) are dodged or closed quickly:

SMita: We handled too many cultural differences with kid gloves. Let's conform.
SF1ita: You should also respect others. As in the case of the activity on religion, which was turned down because it might offend people.
SF2ita: Some leaders and the staff ((didn't accept cultural diversity)). To us it seemed like it would be a debate, but then maybe you risk inflaming people or touch on values that for some people are important. Therefore it is best (..) that they come out when they decide to express themselves, to let others know. You need to be a bit careful.

Cultural/national nights and cultural activities are the official time when cultural diversity can be shown. Here, however, the expression of cultural diversity is reduced to a description of national features, therefore contradicting the statements on diversity.

Adults stress their disappointment with the fact that the 'We-village/summer-camp' is constructed on activities which reflect specific forms of Western culture, which are proposed as the only valid ones to the participants. At the same time, however, they consider children's acceptance of certain aspects of Western verbal and non verbal communication, which are initially considered embarrassing or inappropriate. This consideration may be problematic from the perspective of cultural diversity. For example, Chinese and Japanese delegations declare that they find the persistent laughter of other participants incomprehensible, the non-ritual way the other delegates refer to adults improper, the Western proxemics with friends excessively intimate and therefore disrespectful ("In China if a boy hugs a girl, it means they are boyfriend and girlfriend").

With the exception of language, differences among delegations appear more personal, character-related than cultural, to both adults and children. Children state that they listen to the same music, they know the same VIPs, they dress the same way: they do not notice any difference concerning their friendships which are related to cultural habits and belongings. Adults explain that cultural diversity is not connected with delegations' geographical and national origins because those taking part in CISV come from very similar social and family contexts.

The only important exception concerns East-Asian delegations (especially Chinese, Japanese and Thai): cultural diversity is observed and pointed out by these delegations, and attributed to them by other delegations in connection with their habits (e.g. the way of eating). East-Asian children and adolescents observe many difficulties in establishing relationships outside their own delegation, also because they speak bad English, and they notice considerable differences in ways of communicating. In fact, most participants in these delegations withdraw from communication in villages and summer camps. The contrast between different instances of cultural-We is important for both adults and children:

> Cultural difference does exist, but in a village it is often stigmatised on one or two groups. And this really bothers me: people say 'CISV is great, we all stick together', but then the Westerners all stick together, and the Japanese or the Thais, who are the only ones with a large cultural difference, have many problems. And CISV does not have tools to overcome them. Because all the activities are inspired by Western culture. If there were more different cultures in a camp (SFita)
>
> It's true that until we have a camp in which there are 50% Westerners and 50% Easterners [...] There is an immediate factor of exclusion, orientated on that specific person (DMita).
>
> The Chinese delegation try to be always together. They don't want to be also with the others [...] They don't try. Well (..) In the night, in the room, we always chat. One day we put all together the beds. We told her ((a Chinese girl)): "Do you want to come?" She said "No, I'm tired", but ten minutes before she was talking with Y. ((another Chinese girl)) [...] I think they are afraid that people don't see them like they want. So they do not try to make friends [...] Sometimes ((they are)) afraid, but sometimes good, because they are in their delegation and. They can't talk as

they want, but they are in delegation» *((They make fun of Chinese children's way of speaking))* (LFmex)
They don't know really English, but I try to talk (..) I try, they don't. They are not here to be with other delegations (LMdan)

East-Asian children and adolescents meet considerable problems in adapting to CISV programmes, resulting from their lack of competence and training in participation in social life in villages and summer camps. These difficulties are never formally addressed in communication, and adults underestimate them highlighting that the Easterners who take part in CISV initiatives are 'Westernised', coming from families from higher social backgrounds, who have lifestyles similar to those of Western families.

According to all participants, however, new friendships in villages and summer camps are easy, as they are affected by the peculiar conditions created in these CISV initiatives: children and adolescents are aware that they have something in common, that is the choice to accept certain conditions of social life.

Nevertheless, children's and adolescents' judgement on personal diversity does not really change after the CISV experience. Two thirds of them (66%) observe ambivalent personal diversities (sometimes positive and sometimes negative), while one third regard them as always positive. Only 6% of adolescents change their opinion on personal diversity, shifting from ambivalence to positive opinion, while only one child defines it as always negative.

At the beginning of the experience, children and adolescents support three different narratives about diversity in general (see Table 4):

1. It should be tolerated even when it is not accepted (42.5%).
2. It should be protected (28%).
3. It should be substituted by a set of common values (27%).

Tolerance is slightly higher among children (5% more than adolescents). At the end of the experience, the idea of tolerance is reinforced among adolescents (56%: +17%), while it is stable among children, who slightly increase their idea of protection. The interviews reveal that the meanings of tolerance, respect and acceptance often overlap, both in children's and adolescents' and in adults' perspective.

In CISV you learn to have a relationship with the others. You learn to *((she asks the leader))* Come si dice sopportare? *((How do you say "sopportare?"))* You learn to sustain other cultures, other people, other points of view (AMita).
Respect means that you accept other cultures and other religions. Respect for people (…) Our leader don't respect person (AMnor).
Respect is that you don't laugh of other people for what they say, what they do or whatever (AM1Dut)

Table 4. Thinking differences

Thinking differences	Pre-test				Post-test				Difference pre/post	
	Total	Child.	Adol.	Diff.	Total	Child.	Adol.	Diff.	Child.	Adol.
Not responded	2.3	1.5	4.3	–	5.1	4.5	6.5	–	–	–
Differences in other people should be protected	27.8	27.0	29.9	2.8	29.2	32.5	21.5	−11.0	5.5	−8.3
Differences in other people should be tolerated even if we hardly accept it	42.5	43.9	38.8	−5.1	44.0	38.6	56.2	17.5	−5.3	17.3
People should overcome problems of differences in other people, in order to establish a set of common values	27.0	26.1	29.1	3.0	25.2	27.1	20.8	−6.3	1.0	−8.3
Differences in other people should be challenged, as they are threatening	2.8		2.2	−0.7	1.6	1.7	1.5	−0.2	−1.3	−0.7
Total	100	100	100	–	100	100	100	–	100	–

> To have respect for something doesn't mean that you accept something. I accept (..) it's like you say 'Ok, It's all right, you can do it', but if you respect that's like 'Yes, I can try to do that too', because you think is something good (AFnor)
> But if you don't accept somebody, you can still respect them. If you don't respect them, you accept them neither (AM2dut).
> We have to be tolerant, in a certain level during thirty days. Tolerance is understanding people that cross the boundaries that they don't know. And also to respect the people who don't understand how we are (LMbra).
> During delegation time, my kids didn't want to mix with the Thai kids ((they were without their own leader, who had a day off)). They were afraid of them (…) not afraid, suspicious. I told them to talk about the cultural differences, I told them 'They are different from you, that it's why you may feel like that'. […] They made me some little examples of what they found strange. We talked about that, and I told them to be tolerant. Now they are not best friends, but it's better (LFphi).

It seems that tolerance is the main meaning of personal and cultural relationships, and that its relevance is affected by the CISV experience only for adolescents.

3.3   The narrative of learning, autonomy and active participation

CISV programmes aim to promote children's and adolescents' autonomy and participation, in particular their competence in self-expression and decision making, which can affect their lives and have public resonance. However, adults find it difficult to observe children's and adolescents' autonomy because the narrative implies a particular kind of temporality, children's development, and a particular kind of causal emplotment between education and autonomy.

Children are defined "dependent" because of their inexperience, in need as they are of an adult who leads and "regulates" their behaviours. Children and adolescents are often considered unable to express their reasoning in absence of an adult who assists and guides them. Children are considered autonomous only if they behave responsibly, that is according to meaningful adults in relationship with them (parents, teachers, CISV volunteers). Therefore, adults do not believe that children and adolescents participating in the villages/camps are autonomous. They appear to have fun, but not to meet their duties and conform to fundamental rules, such as respecting the commitments set for the day, and looking after their own hygiene and appearance. Moreover, children are not considered autonomous because of their insufficient knowledge of English, which makes them dependent on adults' linguistic mediation. In their turn, in this perspective, adolescents fail in managing summer camps. Only few adults define autonomy as the ability to choose and be responsible for the consequences of the choice made.

> Making or having good judgement. Autonomy is when kids can already decide if their actions would be best for them and for their peers and are keen to observe progress in the children's degree of autonomy during the programmes, highlighting that this result is not expected by adults (LFphi).

The observation of children's and adolescents' dependence goes hand in hand with the emphasis on educational forms of communication, based on two methodologies: learning by doing and educating through living together. Both methodologies include rules aiming to guide children's and adolescents' actions, according to "internationally accepted values: respect, discipline" (LFphi). These rules lead the children to accept compromises between different lifestyles and behaviours in the villages/camps. This educational process is reproduced in the daily routine and creates a "safe" context where children are able to self-educate. In villages in particular, through this educational process, some adults aim at teaching children how to manage relationships. In summer-camps, on the other hand, only some adults believe that through education adolescents can develop critical sense, responsibility, autonomy and the ability to cooperate.

It is interesting to note that children and adolescents do not think it necessary to express their own autonomy, with the exception of some Italian adolescents.

> Up to now these activities have not thrilled me. I like activities in which we are a bit more autonomous, you don't always have to follow everyone, you can also make decisions, activities that even last all day [...] You are under the control of the leaders, but not too much. For us children it is practically a dream to be more autonomous. [...] Even when you start getting your own house keys (AFita).

Among adults, the idea of children's social participation is ambiguous. It is defined as the "second touch of education" (LFecu). In this narrative, promoting participation means allowing children to express their own contribution whilst they are educated to play a role in society, preserving universally accepted values.

> First we need basic education, then we can talk about bringing out the abilities of every single child. [...] If he/she has not learnt courtesy and respect (SFita).
> We educate them to be more socially engaged, to be aware of what's going on, make positive changes (LFusa).

According to both adults and children/adolescents, children's self-expression is effective during delegation times and free time, while it is restricted during educational activities. Moreover, according to adults in the villages, children's self-expression is limited by the rules which guide their action, and children's active participation in decision-making is not supported, because it is not included in the aims of the villages.

> The rules forced them to express themselves just in some particular moment, instead of being just themselves all the time. This is the difference between a kid and an adult. An adult knows when he can act in some way or in another way. A kid is just himself, and finds out (LMeng).
> But then there is whole a series of stratagems designed not to let them express themselves at certain times. Because sometimes it's necessary. Education is about helping them understand when something can be done and when it can't (SMita).

In general, children accept these conditions, which are perceived as necessary and similar to those observed in other contexts in which they are involved (school, sport group). Only the Italian children complain and contest the limitation of their self-expression and autonomy. Adolescents blame the linguistic difficulties which limit their expression in the planning group, and affect the course of their experience. They expect the leader to facilitate their discussions, without interfering or censuring the themes and procedures they adopt. However, especially in the first phase of the experience, they also expect the leaders to take an active part in the discussions and give them clear guidelines, explaining how to achieve the aims of the camp, manage group communication, and take decisions collectively.

Consequently, leaders frequently appear to them either excessively intrusive or absent. Adolescents declare that during planning meetings they often spend their time talking with co-delegates, or they lose interest in the group discussion as they do not understand what is happening. In addition, those who speak bad English feel intimidated in expressing their ideas in front of those speaking it fluently.

> There are some more than others who assert themselves within the planning group. I think I am one of those who assert themselves, who manages to slightly manipulate people, and this is not always such a positive thing, because perhaps I am pushing out the more timid ones. It depends on your personality: if you are someone who asserts themselves it's not difficult to manage a group. So I even make decisions more as an individual. Instead one should try to listen to the whole group, which is heterogeneous (AFita).

AF1bra: We have a lot of chances to make choices, but it's very hard to make decisions as a group. It's complicate because if you make a decision and this decision affect only you it's more easy than affect all group.

AF2Bra: If in the group there is a part that thinks one thing and another part that thinks another thing; it's difficult to find a solution.

AF1bra: It's difficult. We have to think as a group.

Adolescents often observe that discussions are reiterated and submerged by chatting or games in small groups. In camp meetings these problems seem to be emphasized. Conflicting positions in the debates are indiscriminately received with supporting applause by the participants, highlighting the scant attention to contents. Collective decisions are rarely taken, and nearly always through ballot, a method that adolescents consider inadequate, given that the losing minority does not change its minds and does not adapt to the will of the majority. According to adolescents, these factors lead to failures in managing decisions.

It is interesting to note that staff members appear to be aware of this perspective, mostly sharing it, whilst leaders notice the lack of interest in activities which involve a certain degree of attention. Consequently, in the camps staff members highlight that leaders do not manage these dynamics, thus only partly fostering adolescents' personal expression.

SF1ita: What was missing was the condition of allowing them the freedom to express themselves, allowing them the freedom to find their own place within a group. I know we helped them with the translations, but the fact that this did not always stimulate their interest, and that it was so clear that the key was not the language problem, made me think. The fact that only a few people spoke, even if it is those predisposed to being leaders, and that the leaders were extra-assertive in discussions, blocked the situation, did not allow it to develop. The weaker people clashed with the very strong people. Even when they would have liked to enter the equation, they were blocked by a question of character and not language.

SF2ita: But who were the strong ones?

SF1ita: The English-speakers, in the way in which they set about things and formed a group. And the leaders. The fact that the leader speaks in front of a child during the discussion activities, is not right. There was not a single discussion activity where a leader didn't speak, not to facilitate the discussion, but to express an opinion. This, in my opinion, cut off anyone who would have liked to oppose this vision. Unless someone is strong enough to challenge the figure of a leader.

SMita: In the village you have many more activities and you have a group of leaders made up of people who know what to do. In the summer-camp which is self-managed, where you have people who do not have very clear ideas about what they can do, who have expectations either way (…) given the miscellaneousness, given that nothing is specified, there will always be someone who says 'You followed too much', and another who says 'You followed me too little', because they expected something more or less.

SF2ita: But in this way there was no reflection. Here when things went well or badly, there was no responsibility.

LFita: It's also a matter of maturity. My kids were involved in running games, in the discussion they fall asleep. Even if I try to translate (…) Sometimes I feel to translate for myself.

Despite recognising and understanding the inconvenience caused by linguistic problems, staff members and leaders notice that adolescents lack the self-confidence to take the opportunity to express their own opinion, to affect discussions: "To say one's opinion, takes great courage" (LFdut).

3.4   The narrative of conflict and conflict management

The difficulties in considering cultural diversity do not seem to affect the narrative of CISV relationships. Children observe that it is easy to interact with their peers: 81% declare that it is possible to accept everybody in villages and summer camps. Children add that they do not meet difficulties in establishing relationships with their peers. Particularly in villages, adults confirm the existence of new friendships among children from the beginning, despite the fact that most of them do not speak or even understand English. Children are able to communicate through drawings and gesture: "I've learnt to use my hands, like Italians ((laughter))" (CFcan). Children and adolescents feel like they become friends.

However, the large majority of them (63%) report difficulties in accepting *some* peers, and 46% experience difficulties during the activities. In villages, 33% of children find it difficult to talk to the members of other delegations and 45% find it difficult to accept them. Moreover, for adolescents more than for children (24% vs. 17%) it is not always possible to accept everybody. Surprisingly, difficulties in accepting peers are more common than outside CISV, for example with classmates (–9%; 36%).

The temporality of the narrative is evident: interpersonal relationships improve over time: children and adolescents feel progressively closer, more friendly, having become more fluent in English and having shared everyday life. At the end of the experience, however, adolescents, unlike children, notice that friendships are not generalised, but they are selective. A twofold picture emerges: 38% feel at ease with the other delegates, while 30% have difficulties in accepting them. One of the causes of this situation is that groups are formed on the basis of language affinity (English-speaking, Latin-speaking), and are exclusive, causing frustrations and conflict. Further, these groups include subgroups based on more intimate communication. Only towards the end of the experience do interpersonal relationships intensify and are cross-sectional friendships more easily created.

Native speakers of English are recurrently judged as arrogant, dominant and excluding by those who do not speak this language well, especially in the first phase of villages and summer camps. The fact that they refuse to speak English slowly to help the interlocutors' understanding is seen as lack of respect.

> I think that they ((the English-speaking people)) need to respect us. They had to speak slowly. We have to help each other to understand each other, like we do ((she points at Italian and Bosnian boys and girls)) (AFbos).
> Also because the Canadians and English, after you've asked them to repeat themselves twice because you don't understand, say: 'Nothing, it doesn't matter', instead of trying to explain it in simpler words and by speaking slower (AFita).

According to adolescents, non-English speakers feel incapable to self-express, and have considerable troubles making friends outside their delegation. Consequently, they consider their possible participation in the activities limited, if compared to English-speaking participants who enjoy the language advantage in decision-making and an allegedly better background. While English-speakers notice these difficulties, they end up blaming their non English-speaking mates for their lack of responsibility in camp work.

Children declare fewer conflicts with their peers (20% with other delegates, 16% with co-delegates), than in other contexts (34.5% with schoolmates, 30% with friends), while adolescents declare more conflicts during summer camps and similar experiences inside and outside the camps (33.5% with other delegates or schoolmates; 25.5% with co-delegates or friends).

The main reason for conflicts among delegates is misunderstanding (30%), arising in particular from a different sense of humour and an insufficient knowledge of language.

AM1ita: When we stayed with the host-family, we thought that ((*two Chinese boys*)) were calling us names, so we also started calling them names.
AM2ita: They used to watch us, say something and then start to laugh. So we started calling them names.
AM1ita: We thought they were mocking us.

> Sometimes somebody jokes with us, we didn't know that it is only a joke, so we get angry (AFchi).

Some disputes are recurrent inside the delegations: they are considered a feature of friendship, defined futile, and linked either to different opinions and personal characteristics or to tiredness. More generally, the causal emplotment of the conflict narrative is based on the attribution of conflicts to the interlocutors: the origin of conflicts is observed in unfair actions of the interlocutors (25%), in the interlocutors' blames and critiques (21%) and in their lack of care for relationships (20%). Important conflicts more frequently involve the members of different delegations (24%) rather than those of the same delegation (18%); however, this selectivity does not seem very relevant.

Conflicts are essentially resolved by talking (65%), similarly to what happens outside CISV (63%). More frequently than adolescents, children declare they use their intelligence and wit (20%), assert their perspective (16%), or, infrequently, call for a third party to help (12%). Third party mediation is infrequent even outside CISV (8%). Although children believe it is good to resolve conflicts by talking, in certain situations they consider useful to assert their point of view, for example when the interlocutors do not do the right thing (54%), blame and criticise (50%), are careless (46%, especially according to children), and do not understand (40%).

Leaders observe these dynamics, blaming the lack of respect among adolescents, and only rarely their failure at promoting effective communication among them. In general, when conflicts involve children of different delegations, conflict resolution is the leaders' job. Leaders discuss the problem, present it during the leaders' meeting, then deal with it with their delegates in order to resolve the conflict. This form of conflict management prevents direct confrontations between the two parties, and favours a quick conflict resolution, through the adults' intervention, preventing the undermining of the activities.

If the leaders' intervention fails, the CISV routine prescribes the intervention of a staff-member (preferably the camp director) as a hierarchically higher third party that, again, usually avoids confrontation between the conflicting parties, talking with each of them separately.

Children are aware of this procedure. Nevertheless, they prefer the JCs as first interlocutors. According to children, leaders usually ask their delegates to apologize with the other party, and to promise to stop immediately and not repeat the dispute. This intervention, however, does not lead to shared solutions:

AFita: We continue to quarrel, because we think they are nasty girls, perhaps they are not. We try to be friends with them, but (…) you can only try.

AM1ita: The biggest problem was in not listening to the other person. Slowly slowly also with the help of our leader, we managed to confront each other and understand each other.

AM2ita: I found that I rarely managed to follow what the other person was proposing, and I was always judging. Instead this is exactly wrong. [...] As bad as the idea may seem, it should never be judged. Now, with the help of our leader who acts a little like a mediator, we managed to solve the issue a little. We always try to respect the ideas of the person proposing them.

AF1ita: Anyway we overcame most of the problems we had by talking.

AF2ita: Because the division happened more between boys and girls, the leader 'broke up' the two parties and said that there was no point talking behind people's backs. She tried to build connections, the willingness to talk. It went well overall. It was the leader who sat down and listened to the two parties and said: 'There is some good here, let's work this out'.

Surprisingly, adults find difficulties in managing conflicts between children and adolescents and rarely declare that they mediate between the conflicting parties:

> ((I told my children)) 'You have to pay attention because there are cultural differences, you have to know how to express yourself in a very good way, you have to be very calm. Try to speak slowly. Please came to me, ask me, I can help you'. At the end the problem was solved. Me, the two kids and the other leader we talk together, we translate for them. They apologize (LFita).

In summer camps, few adolescents report conflicts with adults (14%). However, they declare that conflict avoidance is prevalent because "it's not worth discussing it with leaders. If you have very different ideas (...) the discussion became so hard, and maybe in the future you have some problems. It's better to let them talk" (AMbra). 10% of the children find it difficult to accept the staff-members' actions, and only 6% clash with adults. In general, conflicts with adults in villages/summer camps are narrated as less frequent than those with other meaningful adults (24%

of the adolescents and 14% of the children declare conflicts with their parents; 33% and 20.5% with their teachers).

Conflicts between adults are mainly a consequence of misunderstandings connected to different personal perspectives. These conflicts concern essentially different expectations about roles, efforts in engaging in the activities, and informal hierarchies arising among the leaders, based on differences in experience and assertiveness. Even among adults, conflicts are often avoided or immediately closed, as they are considered to threaten coexistence and the activities: "Sometimes you don't say anything, because you know that's gonna be a mess" (LFfra). The more experienced leaders declare that they try to maintain the focus on the topic, avoiding negative personal judgements in order to continue working together.

Conflicts between staff members and leaders arise from the former's distrust of the competence of the latter and, according to the leaders, from the imposition of hierarchically higher roles, and therefore from the fact that staff members do not listen to different perspectives.

3.5   The narrative of adults' contributions to empowering dialogue

Participants narrate their awareness of some forms of action that are supposed to promote self-expression and intercultural mediation, and therefore empowering dialogue, such as expression and display of personal meanings and personal involvement, checking interlocutors' perceptions, active listening to interlocutors' perspectives, giving positive feedback on interlocutors' actions, and appreciating interlocutors' actions and proposals. Participants declare that they often trust their interlocutors' expressions and respect the opinions which they do not share, but also that they rarely act and seldom observe actions which promote dialogue. In particular, they notice unequal opportunities in expressing opinions and difficulties in listening to their interlocutors.

In particular, adults declare that they stimulate children and adolescents to express their emotions, and to look for a shared solution in cases of disagreement. They declare that they pay attention to the consequences of their words and actions, and highlight the positive aspects of the different opinions expressed by children and adolescents, although this form of action is difficult to preserve during CISV programmes. This difficulty is demonstrated by the fact that leaders assert their point of view before listening to children and adolescents, they talk sharply in order to convince them, instead of staying calm, they do not ask for confirmation or clarification of what children and adolescents say, and they judge them on the basis of what they do or say (Table 5).

Table 5. Leaders' behaviours in the interactions (frequency indexes)

Leaders' behaviours in the interactions (frequency indexes)	Pre-test with young people	Post-test with young people	Diff. pre-post	Post-test with adults
Ask others what they feel rather than saying what they feel.	3.3	6.6	−3.3	4.5
In case of disagreement, try to find a shared solution/ try to understand whether it is convenient to win over or accept what others say.	3.8	6.7	−2.9	5.6
Trust/do not trust others' expressions of thoughts and feelings.	8.3	8.1	0.2	7.6
Respect/do not respect others' different opinions.	8.2	7.6	0.6	7.5
Be worried/do not worry about the consequences of one's actions or talk.	7.7	7.0	0.7	5.9
Point out the positive aspects of others' opinion/point out others' drawbacks.	7.7	6.5	1.2	5.5
Judge/do not judge others on the basis of what they did or said.	5.0	3.7	1.4	2.5
Understand others' different opinions/ influence people who have different opinions.	8.1	6.6	1.5	6.8
Speak calmly to favour others' listening/ speak sharply to convince others.	7.0	5.1	1.9	5.4
Ask/do not ask for confirmation or clarification.	6.4	4.0	2.4	4.1
Same/different chances to express one's opinion.	6.3	3.4	2.9	2.7
Listen to others' points of view/ above all express one's opinion.	5.1	2.1	3.0	2.7

Leaders consider the care of their delegates' emotions as the most important task undertaken during the CISV experience (61%): "I'm just a mum, that's my job. Talk with them, take care of them" (LF2ita).

They also declare that they try to encourage children's creativity and leading roles (46%), especially in the summer camps (78%). Finally, they try to increase children's competence in communicating and ensure that they have fun (35%). Staff members, as well as leaders, declare that they try to support children's expression (74%), and to encourage their creativity and their leading role (76%). JCs aim especially at allowing children to self-express (60%) and to have fun (50%), by promoting their communication skills (33%) and encouraging them to make new friends (33%).

However, leaders find difficulties in carrying out their role: they find it awkward to manage relationships with children/adolescents. They note especially that they do not know how to manage the authority connected to their role, for instance which limits and rules they should give to children, and if and when they should ask for their respect. Their educational narrative is rarely translated into practice due to their inexperience and desire to have fun, although there is an unexpected amount of work to do. These difficulties are confirmed by staff members, who declare that they constantly remind leaders of their function, urging them to be an 'educational model' for the children, to show that they are active and responsible in their daily commitments, as well as respectful and collaborative vis-à-vis all participants. Staff members see these expectations frustrated and demonstrate their disappointment to leaders, thus triggering tensions.

The greatest difficulties in "actively listening" emerge in the interactions between leaders and participants of other delegations, especially if adolescents: in summer camps 60% of the leaders declare that self-expression is not balanced, and in villages about 31% of the leaders declare that opinions are expressed before listening to the interlocutors. These difficulties have a surprising consequence: leaders' attempts to check children's perceptions are quite frequent with other delegates (frequency index 5.4), while they are almost absent with their own delegates (2.7).

> In my delegation we stop talking for a while. We talked about it during a delegation time. I needed to mediate, and I remind them the importance of respect other people (LFcor).
> In my delegation we fed up of each other. But it's normal (LFdut).
> They don't understand that they are four against one person: they are four persons with different needs, different stuff, different questions for you. And that is why most of the time I can't keep control (LF2ita).

These difficulties in the interaction are confirmed among the adults. Respondents rarely observe equal opportunities of expression and their own efforts to listen to the interlocutors. These difficulties are above all in the interaction between leaders and staff members, according to 44% of leaders and 33% of staff-members, and with JCs (40%): "Sometimes you don't say anything, because you know that's gonna be a mess" (LFbra). Therefore, they concern hierarchical relationships. However, judgements of the interlocutors' words or actions are observed very frequently by one third of the leaders with other leaders, by 40% of the JCs and by 42% of the staff members with everybody. Therefore, difficulties are also observed in the interaction between adults who play the same role. Only occasionally do adults check the interlocutors' perceptions. JCs declare that they tend to self-express rather than waiting for the interlocutor's self-expression, and rarely pay attention to the consequences of their actions.

Finally, adults, especially leaders and JCs, show difficulties in defining dialogue and its possible use in conflict management, when speaking in general terms of listening, respect and tolerance.

> Respect what the other says, listen and tolerate (LFmex).
> Passing the free-time not playing soccer, but staying seated and asking: 'What do you usually do when you are at home? How many hours do you spend at school? Which are your parents' jobs? What time do you usually have dinner? What do you usually eat?' This is the dialogue that children can have. An exchange of information, of ideas. This is very important; we all should have to make it (SMita).

In general, adult males declare non-dialogic actions more frequently than adult females.

Children and adolescents confirm that leaders put the expression of their feelings and opinions first (see Table 6).

Children observe some opportunities of self-expression with their leader (5.2), and very few with other leaders (2.7). Adolescents observe more opportunities of self-expression with their leaders (7.2) and with other leaders (4.1). Children define leaders' different opinions positively (6.7), much more than adolescents (3.7).

In the interactions with their leaders, children/adolescents declare that they act dialogically more frequently than outside CISV programmes with other meaningful adults such as parents and teachers. Children and adolescents are careful in understanding and respecting adults' points of view, although they judge them. In the interactions with leaders, adolescents rarely negotiate a solution in case of different perspectives (2.7), whereas children make more efforts (4.6). Adolescents notice that, during the experience, they have got to know their leaders in-depth, but not the other adults in the camp; 23% of the children find difficulties in talking with leaders of other delegations, 38% of adolescents even with staff-members.

Nevertheless, children's and adolescents' expectations towards their own leaders are fulfilled. Firstly, they observe that the leader supports them when they feel dejected (52%), an action which is considered very important (32%), and helps them to express their feelings and thoughts, mostly during delegation-time (38%). Secondly, they observe that the leaders provide them with opportunities to have fun (37%) and with important information (37.5%), while they rarely observe them as guides and examples to follow or as helpful managers of their conflicts.

Table 6. Children's/Adolescents' behaviours in the interactions (frequency indexes)

Children's/Adolescents' behaviours in the interactions (frequency indexes)	With their own parents	With their own teachers	With their own leader	With other leaders
Same/different chances to express one's opinion.	2.6	−0.2	5.9	3.2
Listen to others' points of view/ above all express one's opinion.	0.5	2.6	0.6	1.7
Speak calmly to favour others' listening/ speak sharply to convince others.	4.5	5.8	5.4	6.0
Understand others' different opinions/ influence people who have different opinions.	4.6	5.0	6.4	6.5
/do not respect others' different opinions.	6.2	5.9	7.3	7.3
Point out the positive aspects of others' opinion/point out others' drawbacks.	4.9	4.2	5.9	5.7
Judge/do not judge others on the basis of what they did or said.	3.5	1.2	3.4	3.0
Ask/do not ask for confirmation or clarification.	3.7	4.0	2.5	3.2
Ask others what they feel rather than saying what they feel.	2.4	2.4	3.1	4.2
Trust/do not trust others' expressions of thoughts and feelings.	7.4	5.0	7.3	6.7
Be worried/do not worry about the consequences of your actions or talk.	4.5	5.0	4.5	5.0
In case of disagreement, try to find a shared solution/try to understand whether it is convenient to win over or accept what others say.	3.7	3.5	4.1	4.0

3.6   The narrative of the experience

According to adults, the overall meaning of activities changes during the experience. In particular, as for the temporal aspect of the narrative, at the end children and adolescents find it important to live together with people from different cultures, but less than expected (52%). Adults observe having fun together

(20%), making new friends (13%) and meeting people of the same age (10%) as the aspects that children find really important. The gap between expectations and results is remarkable above all among leaders in summer camps (the importance of the coexistence of different cultures drops from 89.5% to 37%), but also among JCs (from 90% to 51%) and staff members (from 90% to 59%). Additionally, according to adults, children tend follow their guidelines (59%) rather than taking an active role in decision making (41%). This is observed also for adolescents, with disappointment of leaders' expectations (42%). Part of the leaders of villages who expected a more active children's participation highlight the same disappointment (27%). Consequently, children's fun seems to be the most significant aspect of the experience, if compared to initial expectations. Children and adolescents confirm most of this narrative.

Firstly, children and adolescents declare that their actions have been similar to those with other peers, outside villages/camps. However, they also declare that they act more dialogically with other delegates than they usually do with their classmates. In particular, they more frequently speak calmly to help other delegates to listen, and to try to understand their feelings and opinions highlighting their positive aspects, thus encouraging a certain degree of mutual trust. Moreover, they declare that they act with their co-delegates similarly to how they act with their friends (see Tables 7 and 8): they trust their interlocutors' expressions, and they are prepared to understand, appreciate and respect their different opinions, if expressed fairly.

Secondly, however, these positive relationships among delegates do not coincide with a general positive consideration for the interaction. Children and adolescents observe primarily monologues in their interactions. Only on few occasions, however, do they avoid judgements, and pay attention to the consequences of their actions. Moreover, they hardly ever provide feedback.

AMita: Our main problem was not being able to listen to our own delegates. With the help of our leader, we have slowly succeeded in confronting each other, in understanding each other.

AFita: I have found that I hardly succeeded in following what the others were proposing, and I always judged them. But, that is wrong. As negative as can seem the others' ideas, you don't have to judge them. Now, with the help of our leader mediation, we have partially solved this problem. We always try to respect the other's ideas.

Neither adolescents (3.8) nor children (3.6) observe equal opportunities in expressing opinions. In cases of disagreement, adolescents declare that they tried to find shared solutions (2.7 within delegations, 3.0 between different delegations), much less frequently than children (5.6 and 5.2). Although one of the main aims of summer camps is precisely to promote negotiation skills, adolescents try to understand whether it is convenient either to win over or accept what the interlocutors say, and they very often judge interlocutors' expressions (2.9), stressing mistakes in their assertions (3.8).

On the other hand, the expectations that children and adolescents would learn new and important things are generally confirmed, although 11% of the

Table 7. Children's/Adolescents' behaviours in the interactions (frequency indexes)

Children's/Adolescents' behaviours in the interactions (frequency indexes)	With classmates	With other delegates	With friends	With co-delegates
Same/different chances to express one's opinion.	2.3	3.6	4.5	6.0
Listen to others' points of view/ above all express one's opinion.	1.3	1.0	1.0	0.0
Speak calmly to favour others' listening/ speak sharply to convince others.	3.6	5.1	4.0	3.8
Understand others' different opinions/ influence people who have different opinions.	4.7	5.8	4.8	5.5
Respect/do not respect others' different opinions.	5.9	6.9	6.7	6.2
Point out the positive aspects of others' opinion/point out others' drawbacks.	4.7	5.6	5.2	5.2
Judge/do not judge others on the basis of what they did or said.	1.5	2.5	3.0	3.1
Ask/do not ask for confirmation or clarification.	3.6	3.4	3.5	1.6
Ask others what they feel rather than saying what they feel.	3.6	4.7	4.3	3.3
Trust/do not trust others' expressions of thoughts and feelings.	5.4	6.2	7.3	7.2
Be worried/do not worry about the consequences of your actions or talk.	3.4	4.0	3.8	3.5
In case of disagreement, try to find a shared solution/try to understand whether it is convenient to win over or accept what others say.	3.8	4.5	4.5	4.7

Table 8. Children's/Adolescents' behaviours in the interactions
(<u>Average</u> frequency indexes)

Children's/Adolescents' behaviours in the interactions (<u>Average</u> frequency indexes)	Pre- with peers	Post- with peers	Diff. pre- post	Pre- with adults	Post- with adults	Diff. pre- post
Same/different chances to express one's opinion.	3.4	4.8	−1.4	1.2	4.5	−3.3
Listen to others' points of view/ above all express one's opinion.	1.1	0.5	0.6	1.6	1.1	0.4
Speak calmly to favour others' listening/speak sharply to convince others.	3.8	4.5	−0.7	5.2	5.7	−0.5
Understand others' different opinions/influence people who have different opinions.	4.8	5.7	−0.9	4.8	6.4	−1.7
Respect/do not respect others' different opinions.	6.3	6.5	−0.2	6.0	7.3	−1.2
Point out the positive aspects of others' opinion/point out others' drawbacks.	5.0	5.4	−0.4	4.6	5.8	−1.3
Judge/do not judge others on the basis of what they did or said.	2.3	2.8	−0.5	2.3	3.2	−0.8
Ask/do not ask for confirmation or clarification.	3.5	2.5	1.0	3.9	2.8	1.0
Ask others what they feel rather than saying what they feel.	4.0	4.0	−0.1	2.4	3.7	−1.3
Trust/do not trust others' expressions of thoughts and feelings.	6.4	6.7	−0.3	6.2	7.0	−0.8
Be worried/do not worry about the consequences of your actions or talk.	3.6	3.8	−0.2	4.7	4.7	0.0
In case of disagreement, try to find a shared solution/try to understand whether it is convenient to win over or accept what others say.	4.2	4.6	−0.4	3.6	4.1	−0.4

leaders, especially in summer camps, and 20% of the JCs mainly see self-expression as the final result. According to adults, children and adolescents especially learn to manage new emotions which arise from living with many people: "For the first time they have felt certain emotions or understood that they can be felt" (SFita). Also children's and adolescents' expectations of learning are confirmed, although in villages the observation of learning is slightly higher than in summer camps (65%, +7.5%), especially among males (+10%). Nearly all children and adolescents who knew little or no English declare that they have learnt the basics of the language (especially children), or acquired greater fluency in communication (especially adolescents). Children also declare that they have learnt to make friends quickly, while adolescents have learnt to overcome shyness and to respect and tolerate their interlocutors. Moreover, children and adolescents emphasize the importance of having forged new friendships (34%), having met peers (14%), having had fun (16%), but also having lived with people from different cultures (38%). At the end of the experience, the importance of close friendship increases, especially in summer camps (+13%).

Participants see their expectations partially confirmed even with regard to the possibility of being able to actively take part in decisions. Over two thirds of adolescents (69%) and about a third of children (30%) declare that they participated in the decisions taken in the delegations during the preparation of the national nights and, in some cases, of the open days. Children, however, declare they have mainly followed the guidelines of leaders (70%). Moreover, the opportunities for active participation appear to be lower than previously expected in both summer camps and villages (about −7%).

According to children and adolescents, the CISV experience will influence their future relationships because they have learnt to open themselves, to see other people's similarities in spite of their differences, and to avoid immediate judgements. CISV villages/camps seem to achieve the objective of promoting a unique experience for children, one that they will always remember. Nearly all children appreciate the experience totally, especially because they had fun with their new friends. For this reason, according to children, the most important part of the experience is the informal one, especially free-time and the national/cultural nights, during which the interactions are particularly intense. However, the predominance of this aim seems to overshadow the other aspects of the experience. Consequently, according to adults, children have 'stored' information and stimuli, but have 'decoded' only a minimum part of their real meaning: "They are not aware of what they are learning" (SMita). Only in the future will they fully understand the special meanings of the activities that they have carried out.

Surprisingly, adults are not able to say whether they have gained any new knowledge from this experience with regards to their communication competence with children and adolescents. The inexperience of leaders and staff-members may considerably influence the overall meaning of the experience. As we have seen, adults find difficulties in working together, and promoting dialogic communication. Some leaders report lack of participation and involvement in co-ordination (villages) or facilitation (summer camps) tasks. Some of them complain about their difficulties in 'building their own group'. These dynamics make the experience of leaders more difficult and less enjoyable than expected.

Adults underestimate the potential of the CISV experience, in particular children's competence in constructing articulate meanings from their experience, and children's autonomy. Their intervention is frequently interpreted as a form of control of children's actions rather than a promotion of their active participation. Promotion of children's agency and self-expression is alternated or mixed with invitations to align to adult-driven patterns. Through the interaction with adults, above all in villages, children's self-expression and agency are used as resources for educating them to self-regulation. Participants notice the difficulties in creating an educational intervention in a context where the expression of children and adolescents should be systematically focused on.

Children enjoy the activities of villages: however, they find simple activities allowing participants to get acquainted boring, and complex activities rather unclear, especially for the linguistic difficulties in understanding the instructions. Children would like to repeat the experience, although some of them appear hesitant, fearing they might be homesick again as happened during the experience. Adolescents declare difficulties in taking part in the planning groups and in contributing to the most complex activities. These difficulties are overcome with the proposal of playing standard games for entertainment, which are unanimously approved. Adolescents' agency seems to be insufficiently promoted in the interaction with adults. Consequently, adolescents feel a partial sense of failure in the educational programme. Both adolescents and adults define the experience in summer camps "enjoyable", but not within the "CISV spirit".

The major critiques, however, concern the organisational aspects of the activities. Nearly all children criticize the poor hygienic conditions of bathrooms and showers, as well as bed times set by adults. Adolescents criticize the large amount of time spent inside the buildings.

Children also provide some suggestions to improve the experience. They propose parallel activities among which they can choose, depending on their interests. Adolescents focus on the difficulties in speaking English, expressing the need to pay greater attention to linguistic mediation, and suggesting the use of written translations of the most important instructions.

3.7   The influence of cultural variability on CISV narratives

An important question about villages and summer camps concerns the impact of cultural diversity on the narrative of the experiences and its results. On the whole, this impact seems to be relatively marginal, yet there are some cues which indicate the importance of cultural variability.

Firstly, there are some difficulties that seem to be related to culture. Children/adolescents of East-Asian delegations (especially Chinese, Japanese and Thai) experience frequent difficulties in accepting the interlocutors (54%).

AFchi1: We come from different schools, we don't know each other and we can't understand each other.
AFchi2: Sometime we are happy, sometimes no.
AMchi: Sometimes we are unhappy because we don't have the same ideas.

At the end of the experience, these children/adolescents reinforce their evaluation of the ambivalence of diversity (+13%) and their need for a set of common values to overcome problems arising from different perspectives. Similar results concern the delegations coming from East-European countries (Bosnia-Herzegovina, Bulgaria, Slovenia, Latvia, Poland, Russian Federation). The initial idea of protecting diversity leaves room to the need to create common values (+18%), and diversity between people is considered neither positive nor negative (63%), although it is necessary to tolerate it (50%). Both leaders and children/adolescents from East-European delegations frequently declare the importance of non-dialogic actions, and often observe inequalities in the opportunity for expression: "Everything was on a trivial level, like 'Don't care, don't do that, stop it'" (LMpol).

Many delegates from Central and Southern Europe (53%), declare that they feel uncomfortable in talking with other delegates, and express their need to tolerate cultural diversity. Children coming from the most northerly nations (Canada, Iceland) observe many conflicts with other delegates. Almost all Central-South Americans (82%) consider it useful to assert their perspective in case of conflict.

Secondly, the main changes after the experience affect the narrative of West-Asian delegates (Israeli, Lebanese, Jordanians). They see the value of diversity much more frequently in a positive way (+28%, from 19% to 47%). At the same time, they reinforce their idea of tolerance (+32%, from 8% to 40%) and protection (+16%, from 31% to 47%), abandoning the initial idea of managing diversity through the creation of common values, although they often experience conflicts with other delegates for lack of understanding (60%). Some English-speaking delegations change their opinions on the value of diversity, especially delegations from USA who increase their acceptance of peers from other delegations (22%).

More generally, the value of diversity changes positively inside American and Australian delegations.

Finally, most of the children/adolescents from West-Asia (68%), North-America (68%), and Oceania (75%) report that they have followed the guidelines of their leaders more than they expected (+23% for West-Asia; +37.5% for Oceania, +32.5% for North-America). The West-Asians also claim that they have been given less chance of free self-expression than expected (−25%, from 44% to 19%). Adults confirm these tendencies.

ChFchi: Sometimes we have some problems, and we talk in our delegation. Our leader decides who is right who is wrong.
Researcher: And you don't like this way?
ChFchi: We don't like it. We wish ourselves say who is right or wrong (…) ((she can't translate what she is thinking))
Researcher: Oh! You prefer to solve alone the problem.
ChFchi: Yes, yes.
Researcher: And did you talk with her about this question?
ChFchi: No. In China we don't have to talk with our teacher, telling her what is right or wrong (…) That is a secret.

In general, these narratives do not seem to confirm that cultural variability is a main issue in CISV experience. However, they indicate a need to check some particular situations concerning the relationships involving different delegations, above all the use of a lingua franca and the different relational styles in different parts of the world.

3.8   Conclusions

To sum up, the meanings of the village and summer camp experience may be seen as determined by the combination of four interrelated aspects of a general narrative: (1) participation in activities and decision making, (2) self-expression, (3) intercultural learning, and (4) having fun. However, the transcultural and participatory ideals which characterize CISV abstract meta-narrative are affected by some significant difficulties which emerge in the previously described narratives.

1. In constructing a We-community, which aims to transcend the existing cultural diversities, the diversities are theorised as being important, but they are rarely faced in communication. In particular, in the community, personal diversities are stressed much more than cultural diversities. Consequently, the success of the CISV experience is linked to the fact that cultural diversities are

set aside, if not abandoned, as quickly as possible. Creating and maintaining the community involves asserting its new culture, and avoiding intercultural conflicts. The potential clash that could emerge from the comparison between cultures is avoided, in order to protect the new community from the risk of destabilisation and to highlight the differences from an external reality that is characterised by contradictions and relational difficulties. Moreover, the routines of the community are built on particular aspects of Western culture, proposed as the only valid ones to all participants.

2. Consequently, the most frequently observed result is that children learn to observe different people as similar. Paradoxically, adults link these results to intercultural learning, that is to the fact that children learn that there are people from different countries with different customs.

3. These factors imply a reinforcement of children's and adolescents' perspective on the ambivalent value of personal diversity and on the need to tolerate it even without accepting it. The meaning of tolerance is identified as equivalent to that of respect and acceptance. This perspective is corroborated by the fact that alongside the creation of friendships, there are difficulties in relationships between peers of different delegations, especially when they do not speak the same language. Adults find it difficult to manage these situations and act as mediators, especially because of their inexperience in playing these roles.

4. Adults' contributions are generally guided by the observation of children's and adolescents' lack of responsibility and autonomy. They are considered in need of guides for their actions. For this reason, adults believe it necessary to emphasise normative and cognitive expectations, albeit supported by the affective care for children. The forms of actions just described can enhance empowering dialogue and guide children's and adolescents' competence in managing their emotions in the interaction. The same forms of expectations are frequently observed in interactions among adults, which are either formally asymmetric (e.g., leaders vs. staff-members) or informally asymmetric (e.g. experienced leaders vs. inexperienced leaders). The least experienced adults or those playing a lower role are regarded as not responsible by those who have a higher status or are more experienced.

5. In the interaction, the participants observe disempowering monologues more frequently than empowering dialogues. They declare their trust in the interlocutors' expressions and their respect for different opinions, but at the same time they give more value to their action than to their interlocutors' understanding; they show the certainty of their understanding and attribute mistakes to their interlocutors' actions; they judge the interlocutors' actions, and they lack explicit attention for their interlocutors' perceptions. The adults'

narrative includes their attention to the interactions with children/adolescents, and consequently their inclination to listen to them. However, this narrative includes also the adults' assertion of their own perspectives in order to pursue their educational purposes.

In the CISV narrative which is constructed in villages and summer camps, the community has the highest value for its peculiarity, i.e. its being a 'perfect world' based on friendship and respect for others, while the external reality is observed as featuring opposite values. The success of this narrative is clear among children and adolescents, but it is based much more on fun and selected friendships than on the learning of new communitarian ideals. Consequently, the narrative of the perfect world emerging from the field experience does not seem to fit perfectly with CISV cultural presuppositions. This situation requires a careful analysis of what happens in naturally occurring interactions during villages and summer camps.

Organisational meetings 1

Promoting participation

Claudio Baraldi and Cristina Caiti

Chapter 4 analyses the organisational meetings held daily in CISV villages and summer camps in order to plan educational activities. The chapter explores the ways in which adults discuss and decide on the kinds of activities and their organisation, underlining the ways in which active participation is either promoted or reduced in interactions. It explores if and in which ways empowering dialogue is enhanced during these meetings and which obstacles can prevent its achievement, focusing on (1) the linguistic and cultural differences between projection of empowering dialogue and projection of normative expectations, (2) the linguistic and cultural differences between processes of coordination and mediation in decision-making and forms of assessment.

4.1   Organisational meetings

This chapter concerns the presentations of planned activities and problems arising during organisational meetings (OMs) in CISV villages and summer camps. These meetings aim to take the most important decisions about daily life in villages and camps, specifically concerning activity planning. In particular, we will observe the process of dealing with proposals in these meetings, including participants' expectations and contributions. The point of departure of this analysis is the two-part sequence in the interaction, i.e. proposals (first part) and promotion or assessment (second part).

In villages, participants are leaders, staff members and Junior Counsellors (JCs), while in summer camps participants are leaders, staff members and adolescents. These participants are supposed to be trained before the village/camp, and therefore to know and share the basic CISV cultural presuppositions (see Chapter 2). However, we have seen in Chapter 3 that their level of experience is highly differentiated. Communication processes are influenced by these premises.

They should be characterised by openness and listening, respectful actions and expectations of friendship, cooperation in problem solving and decision making. The analysis conducted reveals whether and when this occurs in the empirical interactions involving different people with different experiences.

4.2   Projecting empowering dialogue

During the OM, presentation of planned activities and problems is the main opportunity to promote participation. In the starting turn, speakers (leaders, JCs, and also adolescents in summer camps) present proposals or problems concerning both organisational and educational issues. In these presentations different ways of promoting participation and positioning interlocutors can be observed: all of them include questions as first part of main sequences. All presentations are combined with requests for understanding, discussion and support.

4.2.1 Inviting clarification questions

After their proposals, speakers ask for feedback in order to check understanding and invite requests for clarification. Recurrent linguistic cues are used to project this kind of feedback, such as 'Do you know it?', 'Everyone knows or have I to explain?'.

In S1, JFarg introduces her proposal concerning the activity, checking if the participants know the game (turn 407). After LFger's feedback (turn 408), she starts explaining the activity (turns 409, 411, 413), while answering LFcan's indirect questions (turns 410, 412). In this invitation, there is a change of footing (Goffman 1981), i.e. a change in the projection of the speaker's position in the interaction: in particular, this is a change from a collective positioning ('we') to a self-positioning 'I' (turns 407, 409). This change underlines JFarg's personal responsibility for her interlocutors' participation.

(S1)
407. JFarg: the first activity **we were thinking** about doing -, eh: the first part of the
        first activity (??) doing the mafia game, you know? (Where you have to
        kill) (??) **or I have to explain?**
408. LFger: **yeah, explain**
409. JFarg: well, basically it's like they all sit -, **we should divide** them (??) in three
        different groups or something like that and they all sit in a circle and then
        we pick a policeman, a killer, a doctor and **I think** also (02) (??)
410. LFcan: **and the rest** –

411. JFarg: and the rest are like –
412. LFcan: **the civilians**
413. JFarg: yeah, the civilians and then they all go to sleep and then there's like a narrator (??) and he wakes them up and he describes (??) they're all died and then basically (..) it's also about -, well, persuasion and discussion, you have to, like, say why or not you're (??) or basically, the killer points at someone who wants to kill then the doctor wakes up and points at someone he wants to save and then the policeman wakes up and points at someone who he thinks <u>is</u> the mafia and (??) to say yes or no or whatever and then the town wakes up and somebody' s dead and they have to start defending themselves like why they didn't do it, or why they think another person did it and basically (??) the game we did –

In cases like this, an explanation of what is being referred to is preceded by a check on interlocutors' previous knowledge of it and coupled with answers to their questions. It is not very frequent for all participants to know the activity and, in any case, checking their knowledge is necessary to avoid misunderstandings. However, this invitation for requests of clarifications has a *relational* rather than an informational aim: through this invitation, the speaker can promote the interlocutors' active participation, thus facilitating their sharing of the planning.

In some cases, after the introduction and explanation of their proposals, speakers invite their interlocutors to ask for more information or to make comments, projecting different perspectives. In these cases, the linguistic cues are less directive, e.g. 'Questions?' 'Any doubt?' 'What do you think?'. Alternatively, after completing the explanation, a short pause may constitute the *transition relevance point* (Sacks, Schegloff & Jefferson 1974) to the interlocutors' questions.

In S2, after explaining the planned activity in details, SFisr asks for questions (turn 1). This invitation projects SFusa's question, followed by LFnor's answer. This kind of opening activates a process of interaction among the participants because it introduces details which are "food for communication".

(S2)

1. SFisr: All the kids will be divided in two groups (.) the majority are rabbits, then there are foxes, some less are hunters, (??) and there is one (??). Exactly we have food life chain, food chain, but the rabbits are the bottom of the food chain and so it goes up (.) the rabbit go with eleven (?), they go around the area, they have to find envelopes with small pieces of paper which are food (.) every time they find an envelope they can take only two pieces of food from that envelope (.) and then they keep running around (??) the foxes are (?) and the foxes can catch rabbits (.) if they catch a rabbit they take two pieces of food from the rabbit (...) after few minutes the

hunters go and if they catch a fox they take two pieces of food (.) if they catch a: rabbit they take <u>four</u> pieces of food (…) then the diseases go out (.) let's say they catch a hunter they get two pieces, fox four pieces, rabbit six pieces (.) and then the death goes and releases and then if he catches someone that someone is (.) dead (??) (03) so they go on and lots of times goes the circle of food (??) (03) so they realize that if they work together they can get more food and they get caught less (?) and so the cooperation (time) there (…) **questions?**

2. SFusa: **What happens if they get caught and they don't have any food?**

3. LFnor: **They die**

In cases like this, speakers' invitations can open up more differentiated developments and positioning, as they are less directive and restrictive. Interlocutors are invited to formulate more detailed and complex questions, thus becoming more actively involved in the interaction than through questions as 'have I to explain?'. The former kind of questions directly promotes the interlocutors' active participation and self-positioning, while the latter indirectly promotes the continuation of the first speaker's explanations, via her/his questions and the interlocutors' other positioning of the first speaker.

4.2.2 Asking for support

After the introduction of doubts about the planning, the speaker may ask interlocutors for support. Its main cues are linguistic forms such as 'No idea?', 'We were actually asking for support'.

In S3, JMdan explains some activities (turn 13), receiving appreciation in turn 14, then in turn 15 he presents a problem about an activity and asks for support. This request for support is enhanced though the use of 'but' which may be interpreted as a cue for self-disclaiming, i.e. disclaiming the position of the speaker (JMdan). This self-disclaimer promotes the interlocutors' personal contributions, through a mitigation of the speaker's positive position, in this case opening to the request for support ('*so maybe have any ideas?*'). The self-disclaiming 'but' is a cue for promoting the interlocutors' participation, reducing the speaker's authoritativeness. Furthermore, JMdan's change of footing from 'we' to 'I' allows his self-positioning as responsible person in planning activities. LMusa aligns to this request trying to find an alternative proposal, which seems to be successful (turn 17). In turn 18, JMdan projects a new support for his proposal (turn 19) through a repair concerning the amount of time requested for the activity, which responds to LMusa's assumption on 'that time you left'.

(S3)

13. JMdan: erm regarding to you:, some name games regarding tonight, **we're gonna start** with the lion hunt, performed by yours truly, and (04) yeah, and then mini banana, and then erm: **we're** also ((reading from a sheet)) going to: to do some games, and **I wish** (run) one of those

14. *((Many leaders appreciate the proposal))*

15. JMdan: and then **I will run** the, **we have** twenty minutes (as) last time, **we just wrote** energizers **but (they're) just too (plain) just do energizers for twenty minutes, so maybe, so maybe have erm: any ideas?** do maybe really good name games (the time that lasts the activity), last erm

16. LMusa: (??) different erm translations, as time maybe (??) **that time you left** ↓

17. Some leaders: yeah

18. **JMdan:** well the- **these things are not taking a lot of time**

19. LMusa: well explain all (??), taking time and tell the kids even in Danish so we have delegations' and translations time, (taking a round)

Asking for support, the speakers invite the interlocutors' to deliberate both self-positioning and collective solidarity.

These different openings – asking for clarification questions, especially those directly promoting the interlocutors' reactions, and asking for support – can promote active participation and interlocutors' deliberate self-positioning.

4.3   Projecting normative expectations

Opening turns may also project normative expectations, and this can create problems in the interaction, blocking active participation and forcing the interlocutors' positioning. This happens when opening turns are assertive critiques or suggest interlocutors' negative performances.

In S4, turn 69, SMita complains about leaders' performances, invites them to use a more correct behaviour, and suggest some actions to solve the problem. At the beginning of this turn, Smita's 'but' is an other-disclaimer, combined with a confirmation token ('*ya*'). The combination 'yes but' is a cue for a mitigated other-disclaiming, as it combines positive self-positioning (confirmation in the first clause) with negative other-positioning announced by 'but' (Van Dijk 2000). In this case, 'but' introduces a hierarchical disclaiming of the interlocutors' positioning. Furthermore, Smita's repeated change of footing between 'I' and 'we' denotes his hierarchical self-positioning ('*I think, know, say what we need to do*'). This turn projects LFbra's reaction (turn 70) through another mitigated other-disclaiming 'but' which defends her subordinated position: in this way, she defensively reacts to SMita's turn, although this was not addressed either to her or to any specific leader. It is evident that SMita's normative position promotes a conflict (see Chapter 5) with LFbra (turns 70, 71): LFbra refuses LMita's explanation about her presumed mistake, while in turn 73 SMita maintains his perspective about the problem.

(S4)

69. SMita: ya. Today **we can see** that the planning group planned everything **but** because **I think** this was a bit complicated with things to do etcetera and **we only briefly went** through the concept of the activity yesterday, **the leaders didn't know what was going on, okay? Or didn't know how to help out** and **I know** because it's hot and people are a bit tired then because you don't know then **I saw leaders wandering around not doing anything**. I mean, **I'm saying,** I'm not in group green or group yellow so therefore I'm not doing anything. Um, **which is untenable but that shouldn't be the case,** so **we have** two options, I mean we have two things that need to happen at the same time. On the one hand the leaders should be active because, they've gotten out of the activity, umm in trying and get involved in the activity so if you do other things, that is not an excuse to say 'oh well they didn't tell me so should try what's the activity about' **so try and learn** what it's about and how can I get the kids to do what they are supposed to be doing. On the other hand **the planning group maybe should find a way to get the leaders informed,** maybe right before the game or while describing the game (.) maybe making sure they go into details even if the kids do not understand it because the leaders will understand it. So you can have a very detailed description of the games so the leaders will understand it and then the translation comes later with what they see and what they think for the kids.

70. LFbra: **yeah but the reason why myself and Michel weren't participating today was we had a misunderstanding,** we were both in group Green and then Martega said 'you have to go over there, no yellow group is here, okay, no green is there' 'okay' and then we were back and forth and back and forth, that's why it was hard.

71. LMita: **I asked you what group you are and you said green and I said okay leader's here and it's green so I'll go over there that was the green spot and I thought you got the game leaders it's not your problem actually,** maybe I didn't explain that and so I told everybody go on the other side, but everybody who is moving has already *((putting his hands in his hair))*

72. LFbra: **and I stayed on the side as I was supposed and then you said no, Green there and I went there**

73. SMita: **it means it's problem**

In S5, LFeng's first long turn opens with a clear expression of greater expertise (*'It's obvious like, from last night, like there are few people who are experienced in the games'*) followed by a number of requests, in forms which are both positive (*'It's very unfair on the few people that have got their name down'*, *'you should just go and start working on it'*, *'keep in touch with your planning group'*, *'help them'*, *'you have to rely on each other'*) and negative (*'don't leave everything to that one person'*, *'Like someone shouldn't have to come and get you to prepare it'*, *'do it'*, *'like don't walk off'*, *'Don't make one person chase you'*). These expressions signal normative expectations. Turn 1 is followed by a very short alignment (turn 2) and a long silence of twenty seconds. LFeng's turn projects neither active participation in the planning, nor reflection about it; rather it projects embarrassed alignment and silence. Its clear hierarchical form blocks participation. In turn 4, DMita introduces a new topic, breaking the silence and highlighting the embarrassment caused by LFeng's long normative contribution, and giving up opening any reflection about it.

(S5)

1. LFeng: eh! (??) about planning groups and stuff, like (..) **it's obvious like, from last night like there are- there are few people who are experienced in the games**, and they are like on planning groups like, every other day, and (.) I just think (02) when it comes (??) planning groups (02) **don't leave everything to that one person**, like (..) the getting of the materials, the cleaning up, the setting of stuff, and like (.) if you know like- This is no reflection on my planning groups (today) like is not- I'm saying it as a general (..) thing, I don't think I'm having, like- but I just think (02) If you know you're in a planning group and you know how to prepare something, **like someone shouldn't have to come and get you to prepare it**, **you should just go and start working on it** (..) like, coz we're all adults that doesn't need to have to- doesn't have to be somebody going: "Come on, let's go to this, this, this, this, this" like (02) if activities need cleaning up (..) then clean up after it, something- **it's very unfair on the few people that have got their name down** on every single day (.) to be doing (.) everything: get the materials, do the activity, and then cleaning up everything afterwards like - that's- planning groups are really (pulled) together, and if you plan to do something, like some more planning in siesta time, or (.) you plan to do something in free time, then (..) **do it, like don't walk off** and like- have- (..) have other people doing it for you kind a thing like, really **keep in touch with your planning group** all day to maybe meet the (??) before the activity, and five minutes after the activity you clean up and you know where (??) all day, because it's obviously the (big sight) to know where (your) people are (.) So I just think it's really

important to remember that (02) if someone's leading the activity, (..) they're not doing on their own, so **help them** with the materials and then also **help them** to clean up, and to set things out, and to be on time to where (.) things are happening and to be available, and if you're meant to do something like, do it. **Don't make one person chase you** around the whole building because it's just (..) it makes it very stressful (02) and **you have to rely on each other** for these games.

2. LFmex: (all right)
3. (20)
4. DMita: we have time?- (02) We have time for the kids' (room)?

In S6, LMnor makes a direct request, with the indirect illocutionary force of a complaint about the confusion caused during lunch by a song that children usually sing while waiting for food (turn 1). She asks to prevent the children from making noise. After some clarifications are provided, this proposal projects the alignment of LMswe and LFdan (turn 6–9), promoting a sort of "Nordic alliance". However, in turn 10, LFarg introduces her doubts about this solution and in turn 14 she motivates her preference for the children's fun. Therefore, the normative expectations introduced by LMnor are only partially successful and thwarted by the affective expectation of children's fun.

(S6)
1. LMnor: **I'm asking you to tell** in your delegations to stop to make noises during lunchtime
2. SMita: be:[cause -
3. LMnor: [I saw my children, they can hardly eat –
4. LFjor: [you mean that song
5. LMnor: [they start beating on the tables so your dishe:s ((imitating the movement of the plates on the table)) like a earthquake, you know
6. LMswe: **I think I understand the girl who starts the whole think**
7. LFdan: do you know her?
8. LMswe: **I think I got the voice**
9. LFdan: **so her leader can pick her and asking to stop -**
10. LFarg: **wait (.) I'm not sure this is a good idea**
11. LMusa: [I:
12. LFarg: [because the kids ((*noticing LMusa is upset for her interruption*)) ah, so:rry
13. LMusa: no, no go away
14. LFarg: **they seem to having so much fun**

Sequences 4–6 show that the introduction of normative expectations in the first turn of the interaction may create conflicts, both in hierarchical (S4, S5) and reciprocal (S6) interactions. Hierarchical interactions are opened by a first turn which projects a hierarchical structure, based either on the organisational role (S4) or on expertise (S5). Normative expectations project either defensive reactions or silent alignments. In reciprocal interactions, these expectations may project uncertainties in participation, due to a mixture of alignment and opposition. In both cases, active participation becomes improbable in OMs, and, most importantly, coordination in decision making fails.

4.4   Coordination and mediation in decision-making

4.4.1 Coordination

Attempts at collective decision-making require *coordination*, i.e. a dialogic construction of decisions involving various participants in interactive positive positioning. Coordination in decision-making is fundamental to achieve a shared planning of the activities and take effective decisions. Coordination means acceptance and support of participants' personalised contributions on the basis of deliberate self-positioning and reciprocity, i.e. without asymmetries. Coordination therefore is based on affective expectations, i.e. expectations of self-expressions. Coordination is constructed in sequences of actions and is not the result of individual initiatives.

In S7, turn 8, LFleb explains a planned activity. In turns 9, SFita asks for clarifications, and in turn 11 she confirms and then gently (smiling) formulates (see Chapter 1) the meaning of LFleb's proposal. As suggested by Hutchby (2007), this formulation is introduced by a prefatory 'so'. The formulation projects LFecu's further suggestion to the proposal in turn 12. In turn 13 SFita aligns with this suggestion, showing appreciation for it. In turn 14, after the suggestions received, LFleb refines her proposal and completes it.

(S7)

8. LFleb: ok, this is one while the other one is splitting in two groups, they have to choose fifteen movies related to the theme, like not (.) in some ways they think related to the theme, they put in two boxes and then they switch the boxes. The group one take from the box a movie and then start to act it to his group

9. SFita: switching boxes mean that they have the movie of the other group?

10. LFleb: ya

11. SFita: ok. **So you have the box of the other group and: they have to guess the movie. And the group that win at the end (..) just (..) they drop the other** *((smiling))*

12. LFecu: can I suggest for the movie they switch in group divide for planning
             group (in order to think to compare the groups) It could be more funny?
13. SFita: **I also think that I like this one** because it's most related to the theme so
             they start to think about it, the switch is funny and so it could be coupled
             with a good discussion in an attempt to talk about the theme.
14. LFleb: it's just asked to each group to erm: when they play the movies erm: **just
             (..) they just act first and then they explained, maybe just why they
             choose that movie.**

The final proposal is the result of coordination among three contributors, showing involvement through both questions and formulation of perspectives, respecting and appreciating the interlocutors' initiatives. In this process, the formulation (turn 11) enhances further support (turn 12 by LFecu) and anticipates further supporting comments (turn 13 by SFita) which help LFleb to adjust her proposal (turn 14). The supporting and affective way in which the formulation is enacted is crucial to avoid its being considered as a correction or a cognitive suggestion and instead promote its acceptance as support. Affective formulations can be seen as fundamental dialogic actions in the coordination of decision-making processes (Baraldi & Gavioli 2007).

In S8, LFnor is coordinating the meeting. DMita has proposed a game and in turn 65 LFnor encourages him to continue its description and to enhance the understanding of the group. DMita does not seem to understand her intentions (turns 66 and 69) and JFita and LMisr (turns 67, 68, 70, 71) help LFnor to clarify them through an other-initiated repair, thus achieving solidarity in conversation. In this phase, the participants coordinate in clarifying the requested task to DMita (turns 67, 68, 70, 73). DMita fulfils this task in two very long turns (74 not presented, 78). In turn 76, DMita's self-disclaiming 'but' mitigates possible negative expectations about his position, enhancing his positive role. His first clause in turn 76 is a self-repair, projected by the hilarious reaction of the leaders to his explanation and introducing a negative position. This self-repair is however followed by a positive positioning, introduced by 'but', which allows him to conclude his proposal. After the conclusion of DMita's long and detailed explanation, LFnor leaves the floor to other participants (turns 79, 81, 88), promoting active participation and supporting it (turn 83).

(S8)
65. LFnor: **we wanna continue?! Yea?!**
66. DMita: **what?!**
67. JFita: **the game.**
68. LFnor: **describe what we are gonna do.**
69. DMita: **do what?!**

70. JFita: **explaining the game.**
71. LMisr: **and the water game over there.**
72. DMita: **do you want me (to go through the tasks)?**
73. LFnor: no (..) oh, yea, then what we are gonna do after.
74. DMita: *((Long explanation))*
75. *((Laughing))*
76. DMita: **very stupid thing and (..) but I mean, this is the simplest thing.** If you say "Hello" instead of "Good morning" you should say -
77. JFita: chicchiricchiiiii!
78. DMita: chicchiricchi (..) o qua qua, and instead of (..) if it's in the morning and so on. We can decide which words should be substituted by the Chicken language. That's the first. Second is dresses colours. They can decide the way to dress in that moment, so that means for example you say white you have to be all white. Or white trousers or skirt and blue t-shirt or (?). I thought of things that are not influencing our daily rules and daily schedule. This week they have an activity with coloured (?) so on. They could decide the way of awaking or the cup game shortly or something about jc shop and I'll finish, I'm not finished with the things. So the scheme is: we prepare in advance the four commissions, which should be more or less one of each delegation. Now we have to think of translation problems and...well, the big work is (there o their), we have to do good (?) grouping and...So they meet in the parliament and we will do an explanation also altogether. They will be divided in commissions, the commissions will work for a certain amount of time and they have to come to a decision and they will go back to the parliament and they will introduce, they will present the law and they will discuss briefly with the possibility for anybody to suggest amendments or not if it's complicated and they will vote them, simple majority as our parliament and then we will see how the laws will work the day after.
79. LFnor: **Maria, you wanna say something?**
80. JFita: no.
81. LFnor: **Hellen?**
82. LFnz: I'm just thinking at if you want to split into four commissions, we could actually do it by delegation (..) three delegations?! And that would help with the translation (.) maybe.
83. LFnor: **yea, and so leaders can be in the commissions.**
84. LFnz: yea so (?) with the translation.
85. LFusa: New Zealand, Canada and the US can maybe be together.
86. LFnz: just put my kids rather than pick the kids.
87. LFusa: yea.
88. LFnor: **any other (?) activities?**

89. LFnz: I think also if parliament doesn't, if parliament sort of finishes after two
            (?) we can have a big village Human Knot. Does everybody know what
            Human Knot is? Everybody goes and grab hands and you gonna try and
            (?) just a bit of fun after all of the talking.

LFnor is not as active as SFita in S9, however her actions are equally effective in
promoting participation. The comparison of S8 and S9 allows us to state that in
OMs, coordination can have two different forms: proposal/support (formulation)
and distribution of turns. Both forms are effective in promoting active participation, although the former seems more effective in elaborating the proposals.

In summer camps, adolescents present their planned activities in OMs. During these presentations, leaders and staff members frequently act to support and
promote adolescents' actions. In S9, Mcos and LMbos enact a joint presentation
of the planned activity. In turn 1, Mcos starts explaining the activity. SMita asks
for a clarification and LMbos immediately supports Mcos's action (turn 3). In
turn 5, Mcos asks for feedback signalling understanding and SMita aligns. After
a short consultation with Mcos, LMbos introduces the activity (turn 8). After a
series of turns of explanations and answers, in turns 20–41, the coordination of
Mcos and LMbos is evident. Mcos is very active in the explanation (turns 20, 22,
24, 26, 28) while LMbos supports him through a continuer (turn 21), and then
aligns in clarifying the requirements of the game (turns 30, 32, 34, 36 38, 40).
In turn 32, LMbos declares his expertise to reinforce his presentation, however
his position is not coupled with normative expectations. Furthermore, in turn
34, LMbos's self-disclaiming 'but' mitigates such expertise, contributing to shape
his positive self-positioning ('*I am aware that it is hard*'). SMita's support is very
helpful in this coordination, thanks to linguistic forms that signal understanding
(turns 6, 29), active listening (turns 27, 31), and ask for clarifications (turn 25).
His closing turn confirms the success of the decision-making process (turn 42).

(S9)
1. Mcos: ok, so the first game we've planned is Shoes game   [with
2. SMita: [activity 1?
3. LMbos: **yeah**
4. SMita: yeah, activity one
5. Mcos: so, everyone sits in a circle and take the shoes a part, next to, so there's a
            leader and that person gets the shoes, throw it to one person, so that person
            throw it to another one *((continuing to explain))* **do you understand?**
6. SMita: **yeah**
7. *((Mcos and LMbos talk for a while in a very low tone of voice))*
8. LMbos: ok, second game is In the middle of two fires (…) because we have
            basketball field and we have no free area

[...]

20. Mcos: with a rope, we put a rope in a triangle and so in four?

21. LMbos: **yeah**

22. Mcos: in four groups, so one group is inside the triangle and they have to go out the triangle without touching the rope

23. LFola: uuhh. I like it

24. Mcos: without touching the rope and they are always (?)

25. SMita: so you, I didn't understand: you make a triangle with a rope. **And then?**

26. Mcos: one group goes inside the triangle

27. SMita: **yeah** *((nodding))*

28. Mcos: and so they (?) hands and they have to go out of the triangle without touching the rope

29. SMita: **ok, if someone touch the triangle, yeah it's like (?)**

30. LMbos: (?)

31. SMita: **yeah, yeah, just to -**

32. LMbos: **we played something similar on our camp**

33. LFita: yeah

34. LMbos: **but I think this is (hard)**

35. DFita: why? Because if they touch the   [triangle

36. LMbos: [no. no no no. Because we are taking (?)

37. DFita: ah, they cannot?

38. LMbos: touch

39. DFita: so you need maybe mattresses

40. LMbos: I don't think

41. Mcos: we thought like an handicap game, so some people have no hand or like that so

42. SMita: mmm. **Yeah, we should know it in the early morning, to organise an handicap meal, because we want to do a very difficult lunch (...) ok.**

S9 shows both successful coordination of joint presentation (between Mcos and LMbos) and the importance of clarifications and active listening for this coordination: these are dialogic actions which enhance the success of coordination in decision-making processes.

In S10, LFbel and some staff members facilitate and coordinate adolescents' actions, in particular Fcan's self-expression. Initially, LFbel supports Fcan's actions through her request for clarification (turn 2) and helps her in explaining the planning (turns 4, 6). In turn 7, Fcan's self-disclaiming 'but' supports the positive contributions of the participating mates. Then, the staff members ask questions and make suggestions about the materials that will be used (turns 8, 11), supporting the organisation of the activities through cognitive expectations, i.e. expectations of role performances. This support continues when Meng starts presenting another activity which the adults appreciate (turn 14) and positively connote (turns 15, 17). Through requests for clarification, helps in the explanation, friendly suggestions, and appreciation, adults affectively and cognitively support adolescents' participation, achieving with them coordination of decision-making process.

(S10)

1. Fcan: we had to plan activity three on Thursday and we've decided to do a game called Fantasy Island –

2. LFbel: **what's that?**

3. Fcan: erm (..) it's a game where you make your own country and you put your (.) erm (..) –

4. LFbel: **flag?**

5. Fcan: yeah, flag

6. LFbel: **the map and the money**

7. Fcan: the map, the money and stuff (.) erm we decided to play in the gym and the aim of the activity we said that there's (.) no world is perfect so people are going to try and make their world as perfect as they can (??) because **there will be problems in the game but they will solve** (..) and also we are planning this activity because it has to do with cooperation and you need to understand a lot of things so in relation to the theme of the camp (..) erm (..) erm we said that we need a snack (..) chocolate in the middle

8. SMita: for example (05) so, **what material?**

9. Fcan: paper posters and markers

10. SMita: ok

11. SFita: **maybe you can also use** some recycled materials, like plastic boxes and so on

12. Fcan: yes

13. Meng: ok (.) we are doing activity one on Thursday, in the morning, and the general theme is love –

14. Leaders: **uuuuhhhh!!!** ((Meng starts explaining the game))

15. SMita: **I like this game!**

16. ((Meng continues her explanation))

17. ((Applause of the adults))

Both leaders and staff members may support and promote adolescents' presentations through dialogic actions, such as active listening, feedback showing their own level of involvement and understanding, requests for further explanation, questions to foster the adolescents' thinking, creativity and problem-solving, appreciations and positive comments, suggestions and additional proposals, final applauses and thanks. These supportive and encouraging actions seem to be successful in confirming adolescents' self-expression and in contributing to building their trust in adults.

Adults may support adolescents' actions both affectively (appreciation for the proposals, encouragement to participate, helps in descriptions and explanations) and cognitively (requests for clarifications and support for the organisation of activities). In this way, adults' contributions to learning and support of self-expression blend in the interaction, enhancing a social structure which enables the planning of activities through affective support.

4.4.2 Mediation

Coordination may require mediation among different proposals, to help finding a satisfactory decision, without the need of hierarchical actions. Mediation (see Chapter 1) is a third-party coordination of different perspectives, which promotes participants' self-management, satisfying their expectations. Mediators promote active participation, deliberate self-positioning, expression of opinions and emotions.

S11 is an example of mediation. In turns 63 and 65, JMdan invites his interlocutors to self-express (self-positioning), using either interrogative ('*does any have any idea?*') or assertive ('*but if you have any ideas*') forms. In turns 63 and 65, JMdan's self-disclaiming 'but' projects promotional questions, opening to new contributions. In turn 65 it is preceded by JMdan's change of footing from 'we' to 'I', indicating his self-positioning as agent; the new change of footing from 'I' to 'you', associated to a self-disclaimer, opens to new contributions. In his following turns (67, 69), JMdan verbally and not verbally supports LFswe's contributions (turn 66), and LMbra positively positions his conversational work (turn 70). In turns 71 and 73, JMdan explains his proposal, supported by the change of footing towards self-positioning, supplemented with the suggestions of other participants. Then he supports the contributions put forward by his interlocutors confirming them (turn 75, 88), adding information (turns 77, 80, 94), asking for further support (turn 82, 97), and formulating the interlocutors' contributions in order to coordinate them (turn 90). Overall, JMdan's mediation is successful in promoting other contributions (turns 85, 87, 89, 95, 96) which complete the story.

(S11)

63. JMdan: well I'm getting- *((laughing))* erm: **yeah, but** (.) **any: does any have any idea?** if we end up (activity night) just twenty minutes, fifteen minutes up

64. (03)

65. JMdan: ok **we don't know** if they still erm:, **does anyone have plan?** I have, I **mean** for one hour, I I I *((reading and looking at the paper))* have (??) **but if you have any ideas..**

66. LFswe: but, **if we just** end up with like: ten or twenty minutes left, couldn't we just the leaders in the groups keep on making some name games because:

67. *((JMdan nods))*
68. LFswe: probably it's ok just to find out or the kids maybe have some good ideas, because gather them one more time and (translation) with them, all of this (end up) ↓
69. JMdan: **all right,** so I'm gonna explain everything in Danish tonight
70. LMbra: **good, good**
71. JMdan: and: First, first **we're gonna do** (.) the lion hunt, (...) erm:: then it's, we're gonna do Mingo, with (all leaders) and that erm, **I think I'm gonna explain** to people, because well somebody just began singing Mingo, mingo, mingo, and he will like (..) yeah -
72. LMcan: (also the)
73. JMdan: what wrong is going on, **what I need to do,** and then, three groups and then people like (.) <u>erm</u>::: *((opening his eyes wide and looking around, miming being disoriented))* ok, so: **we should mainly -**
74. LMcan: also the kiitos?
75. JMdan: **also the kiitos, yah! erm well**
76. LFfar: the kiitos is at the end!
77. JMdan: the breakfast, erm there were people like, why are we shouting? what's wrong?
78. LMcan: yeah
79. SMmex: <u>hhh</u>
80. JMdan: why are we jumping? why are we saying?
81. LFfar: yeah
82. JMdan: so I think someone should (..) tell them, maybe:, **maybe before dinner?** before we: -
83. LMcan: yeah
84. Other leaders: yeah
85. LFind: **maybe it doesn't need, all the leaders can talk to their delegation**
86. ??:   yeah
87. LFind: **during delegation time, °that is easier°**
88. JMdan: **good**
89. LMcan: **so they can explain**
90. JMdan: **or:!** <u>Everybody, all the leaders</u> **can just talk to their delegation, during delegation time!** *((nodding and smiling))*
91. Many leaders: yeah! *((laughing))*
92. JMdan: <u>erm</u>::, kiitos, (.) do you know?
93. LMcan: no
94. JMdan: (kids)? (..) ok, erm: I was just going (turning around), <u>kiitos is the<thanks for food ></u>, it was delicious! some, and then:, what's first it's "Kiitos ruuasta se oli maukasta" *((singing the first sentence))* and that's something in Finnish, erm I only know Kiitos is (.) thanks, and I think it's (.) thanks for

the dinner, or (thanks) for the food, it was good, (.) and then:, and then it says "tack för maten den var god"*((singing the second sentence))*, thanks for the food, it's good, and then: erm: "vi er alle mette no, ikke no, ikke no, ikke no, men no" *((singing the third sentence))*, we are all full now, but not now, not now, not now, <u>but now</u>! You're jumping and yelling, food inside *((hopping))*, all right, erm (..) <u>now</u>! So, that's basically, and <u>then</u> everybody needs to <u>shout</u>, everybody needs to (.) because it's like, erm: I know it's (blame), I need to catch my breath, erm: when I, I didn't shout anymore, it's like one or two persons on(h)ly be shou(h)ting, and like (.) all the kids were (.) *((looking around))*

95. LMusa: **it's only like (.) one or two people that**   [**they need (words)**]

96. LMcan: [**you get there (.)** (outside)]

97. JMdan: yeah, **and where are we gonna go outside?** (..) This maybe is the easy one, I know what's going on.

JMdan's actions enhance mediation for various reasons,: (1) his turns are systematically coupled with those of his interlocutors, (2) he pays attention to both the interlocutors' self-expressions and to their coordination, (3) his actions promote the interlocutors' deliberate self-positioning, actively contributing to the decision-making process through the joint construction of an alternative story. This interaction shows that mediation is active coordination which requires a great deal of dialogic actions.

4.5   Assessments

Proposals may be assessed in different ways and following different criteria, although generally speaking the use of assessments prevents active participation and self-positioning. Assessments are based on cognitive and normative expectations which aim to determine the experience of interlocutors, i.e. they position interlocutors in a forced and hierarchical way. This may happen in different forms: education, control and judgement, disclaiming and direct use of expertise.

In educational assessments, cognitive expectations are primarily connected with the willingness to direct actions in order to tackle the activity. The speaker aims to impart knowledge and competences to the interlocutors.

Normative expectations may be produced in the interaction through invitations to acquire and respect rules, therefore preserving mainstream guidelines. In particular, camp directors often play the role of controllers, or even "judges", by dictating rules mainly concerning risk management and security matters.

Disclaiming forms of assessment consist in the introduction of doubts about the interlocutors' positions, denying and displacing the interlocutors, thus avoiding attempts to control the interaction in direct ways.

In OMs, the participants' previous experience of CISV activities is considered particularly relevant. This experience may be used to draw a distinction between competent and incompetent adults during presentations and discussions of planned activities and organisational problems. Staff members, mainly camp directors, and sometimes other participants, speak as experts, providing information on management mechanisms, rules, and meanings of the activities, making reference to past experiences. They refer to their CISV past experience, training their interlocutors about organisational matters, practices and values. In the interaction, experienced adults project themselves both (1) into an educational perspective towards less experienced adults, and (2) into a witnessing perspective, reporting past experiences to support their point. In general, these experts provide examples from their past experience to legitimise and support their points or proposals, making them more meaningful in the eyes of other participants. Experts' actions, therefore, project reactions of consent and acceptance. Past experience enables them to take the role of trainers of the interlocutors, focusing on CISV values, rules and methodologies.

These actions correspond to the management of duties, rights and responsibilities related to individual competence. Speakers assert their primacy in competence through assessments and then claim their rights and their social identities. Following Heritage & Raymond (2005), we define these claims as *socio-epistemic claims,* i.e. claims concerning speakers' alleged superior competence in ruling, and giving meanings and objectives to activities. Speakers' distinction between right and wrong, between what is relevant for the interaction and what is irrelevant, depends on hierarchical distribution of competence and rights to be competent. Speakers preserve their primacy in competence by means of assessments, claiming superior rights associated with their roles. In the following sections, our analysis will focus on the ways in which these claims are produced in the interaction.

4.5.1 Educational stances

In S12, as soon as LFnor has introduced her proposal, a staff member (SFisr) intervenes to point out the leaders' role (turn 2), introducing the problem of the thin line which separates the leaders' influence from children's autonomous expression (turns 4, 7), supported by LMmoz and LFusa (turns 5, 6). In turn 9, LFnor tries to postpone the discussion, interrupting SFisr's lesson. However, in turn 10, LFusa does not align with this attempt and projects SFisr's educational positioning. In the next turns (11, 13, 15, 17), SFisr keeps on taking the floor prevailing on the interlocutors and projecting a hierarchical stance on the interaction. Her action has an evident educational purpose: she aims to clarify the meaning of the activity and, in particular, to fix the 'extremely thin' line of the adults' influence, as LFnor ironically says in turn 20, using 'but' as a disclaimer of SFisr's self-positioning.

(S12)
((LFnor has introduced and explained the second activity: "Stereotypes"))
2. SFisr: **the the role of the leaders is very important** also because we cannot say things to the kids or influence them in any way (?).
3. LFbra: a: a: also the leader of the group has to be (.) come on (.) they don't (.) they don't have to let the kids write whatever they want (...) it's very important because (.) (?) (.) like a slap in the face for them (.) not writings that might (.) come on.
4. SFisr: **the line is very very thin** because we on one hand we want them to write whatever they feel and we want people to confront on the (.) ((she cannot pronounce the word in English))
5. LMmoz: prejudice.
6. SFusa: prejudice.
7. SFisr: (prejudice) A:: and from the other hand don't want anyone to, we don't want to (.) make it too hard.
8. (05)
9. LFnor: **ok: we'll talk about that tomorrow** at a (.) quarter to three.
10. LFusa: based on the peace war peace game I would say these kids (have more fun to not care than to care) and that it would be better for me to say (?) things and have a real conversation than to say like a bunch of (.) really (.) non (...) (?)
11. SFisr: what (.) In this sort of game (.) if they write everything that it's right and correct about the country, that all the countries are beautiful, wonderful trees that's not, it doesn't really (?) meaning of the game.
12. LFusa: yeah
13. SFisr: we are looking on the things that can be (.) that we can say this is not true.
14. LFusa: yeah
15. SFisr: And: (.) so (...) they can write whatever they feel to write
16. LFusa: (?) ((noise which covers the voices))
17. SFisr: yes. It is especially for some countries here that can be sensitive about (...)
18. LFusa: (?) ((noises))
19. (04)
20. LFnor: **oh there is a line, but (.) it's <u>extremely</u> thin (.) so yea.**
21. LFusa: ((interrupting)) like for Germany would you say (?) except for one or?

SFisr assumes the position – and societal role (Weizman 2008) – of trainer of the interlocutors. This role positions the interlocutors in a hierarchical way: they can only experience SFisr's action, with the help from LFusa. Apart from LFnor's ironic disclaiming, the interlocutors (LFbra and LFusa) take part in the interaction only showing understanding and uttering continuers (turns 12, 14) which confirm and strengthen the dominant perspective, consequently SFisr's action seems to be successful.

4.5.2 Control and judgement

In S13, LFger introduces her explanation of the cultural activity which is planned for the following day (turn 1) encouraged by LFecu and LMpor (turns 2, 3). She starts stating the topic, the organisation and the place for the activity, i.e. the 'dining hall' (turn 4). DMita reacts only to this last part of her turn, asking whether it is possible to move the activity outdoor because of the heat indoor (turn 5). Given the insistence of LFger to carry out the activity indoor (turn 6), DMita proposes a new solution, i.e. the new kitchen, where it should be forbidden to play activities (turn 7). In the name of children's health and well-being (turn 9) and in the absence of an alternative solution (turn 11), he allows making an exception to the rule (turn 13), but repeats that it is 'first and last time' (turns 15, 17). In turns 9, 11, and 13, DMita's mitigated other-disclaiming ('yes but') underlines the difference between his deliberate and correct self-positioning and his forced and exceptional self-positioning. LFger aligns with DMita's position, also expressing astonishment for his deviant proposal (turns 10, 12), and formulating it to be sure of her own understanding (turn 14).

(S13)

1. LFger: I wanna say only few things about my cultural activity
2. LFecu: **oh yea,** you have too tomorrow
3. LMpor: **come on!** *((speaking with the Norwegian leader; they have a day off together the following day))* We're going to miss two cultural activity tomorrow!
4. LFger: our starting point is the natural condition of Germany, a situation created by a new motorway. We were divided into groups (..) **it will be in a dining room, the dining hall**
5. DMita: **can't you make it outside, because in the dining room is too hot**
6. LFger: hh **no, it's very important to do it inside**
7. DMita: **don't you want to do in the new kitchen?**
8. LFger: we <u>prefer</u> to do there *((it is forbidden to use the new room for activities; therefore, LFger has not asked for it))*

9. DMita: **yes, but for once I prefer you do there than in the old dining room,** **because it's so hot and their noses bleeding because it's so hot** *((some episodes of nose bleeding occurred due to the heat))*

10. LFger: ya, for me it's really cool, after yesterday you said that-

11. DMita: **ya,** because we don't have the possibility to do the activity in that room, **but (.) if there is no other option.** And the cleaning service cleans the old dining hall because the chapter want to do this to close it, so I prefer to do activities outside, or in the other place, there is no solution, and it is erm:

12. LFger: **so we can do in the new dining room**

13. DMita: **ya, but just for this time** because you said in the amphitheatre don't want, **but then I don't want** that for every cultural activity you ask me 'can we use this room?' so this is the only exception

14. LFger: **so we can't use it anymore**

15. DMita: **ya, first and last time** (02). Does anyone agree?

16. Different voices: ya

17. DMita: **first and last time**

DMita assumes the position and the societal role of judge. He allows LFger to make an exception to the rule established inside the village but underlining that the normative expectations still hold for the future. DMita's point of view stands out (*'I prefer, I don't want'*) in this hierarchical interaction, positioning his interlocutors within it. DMita does not care about obtaining feedback, and his final request for feedback (*'does anyone agree?'*) appears as a rhetorical question because of the normative imposition he expressed before. Therefore, his interlocutors can only accept it (turn 16) and DMita concludes with a solemn normative statement (turn 17).

4.5.3 Disclaiming

Disclaiming is frequent in all situations in which other-positioning is forced by the speaker who is hierarchically superior. In some situations, it is the prevalent feature of the interaction.

In S14, turn 1, LFbel is concluding the presentation and asks for feedback, while at the same time underlining the difficulties of the proposal, through a self-disclaiming 'but'. In turn 2, DFita negatively evaluates the proposal, introducing it with a disclaiming 'but', although mitigating it by laughing, while reinforcing it with a vulgar metaphor. LFbel's continuer (turn 3) displays that she has been hierarchically positioned and probably uncertain about the meaning of the stretch of conversation opened by DFita's comment. It is followed by general laughing which seems an invitation to share this comment interpreting it as a joke. At the transition relevant place (Sacks, Schegloff & Jefferson 1974) created by this laughing, SMita takes the turn and tries to support and at the same time mitigate DFita's assessment, by proposing a more refined comment (turn 5). This initial double and differentiated assessment brings LFbel to a self-repair (turn 6), introduced by a self-disclaiming 'but' in defence of her subordinated position, consisting in the possibility to renounce. This is followed by a sort of display of relief (turn 7) and a new collective laughing marking it (turn 8). The tension which has been projected by DFita's negative assessment leads LFcan (co-author of the proposal) to explain the two proponents' concerns (turn 9). However, in turn 10, DFita ignores her two concerns and adds a third one, openly resuming her negative assessment, which projects a silent alignment. She insists on her position, with a doubtful new start which she suspends (turn 12), and which is followed by LFnor's attempt to support the proposal marked by a 'we-perspective' which contrasts with DFita's self-positioning 'I' (turn 13). In turn 14, DFita seems to accept LFnor's proposal though, when LFnor concludes it, she poses another problem, in the form of a new other-disclaiming 'but' (turn 16).

(S14)

1. LFbel: **did you understand? It's not easy but** –
2. DFita: **but it's really a mental masturbation to divide people like this** ((*laughing*))
3. LFbel: **yeah**
4. ((*laughing*))
5. SMita: **it's a different way**
6. LFbel: **but we are not sure** that we are going to do like this because –
7. SMita: **ah!**
8. ((*laughing*))
9. LFcan: **we have two concerns about this.** One is (??). Second concern is that we are not sure how comfortable some of the delegates would be with erm other delegates looking at their work. We are afraid that they can feel that their work has been judged, they might not feel comfortable on someone else coming for that (..) so that's what we've thought
10. DFita: **I think another concern should be** maybe the difficulty for the delegates to understand the paper –
11. ((*Non verbal signs of agreement*))
12. DFita: **I don't know if** –
13. LFnor: **we think that one of the leaders should be there with each group**, in the first just to tell them and (..) make them begin the discussion
14. DFita: **ok**
15. LFnor: and then just have a step back –
16. DFlta: **yes but (..) what about translation?** Maybe –

In S14, DFita repeatedly introduces problems and doubts, creating a climate of negative assessment about the proposal, positioning LFbel and other leaders according to a hierarchical form of communication. DFita continuously moves her position in the conversation, avoiding a direct confrontation on the contents which are presented by the leaders.

4.5.4 Self-positioning as an expert

In S15, DFita repeatedly positions herself as an expert. In turn 115, she declares she has some suggestions for the activities, pointing out their superior cognitive and emotional status. In turns 117 and 119, she begins to describe the activity in details, outlining its development and providing instructions about the debriefing. In her explanation, DFita is supported by LMusa through continuers (turns 116, 118). In turn 121 DFita rejects JMdan's suggestion (turn 120), through a mitigated other-disclaiming 'but', and immediately after that through the use of irony (turn 123). DFita's assessment in turn 123 introduces normative expectations about the structure of the activity: it is not possible to change the game to avoid the risk of jeopardizing the educational purposes, which are well pointed out by DFita (turn 127). DFita proposes an activity that she has already experienced and that she defines, according to her experience, 'very interesting, a cool game' which the children enjoy a lot, 'especially if the leaders are with them and they love it'. DFita concludes her turn trying to promote the leaders' participation, inviting them to self-express. In this turn, DFita focuses on the 'educational curve', introducing the prominence of cognitive expectations in the interaction. Her invitation, however, is not followed by active participation; the only reaction concerns an organisational aspect (turn 128), followed by DFita's indirect confirmation (turn 129).

(S15)

115. DFita: yeah I have a suggestion for activities, like I have some ideas then I guess **(they) are very interesting and I'd really love to do**

116. LMusa: **mhm mhm**

117. DFita: it's called the game of life, or something like that

118. LMusa: **mhm**

119. DFita: and: like the kids have erm: this: (.) life, fake life, where they're supposed to live, and the days go ten minutes ((miming with hands the time that passes)) (...) and ten minutes ten minutes, every ten minutes it's a new day (.) and they have (.) some of them are married, some of them are singles, some of them are kids, some of them are (.) adults ↑, erm: some of them have families right from the beginning (.) and they have to survive in order that every day they have to buy two pieces of food, (.)

one piece of (clothes) for <u>every</u> member of the family (.) so there is gonna be a supermarket where they can be what they need: ↑

120. JMdan: **can I (suggest) wash their clothes?**

121. DFita: **erm:: well (.) yes (.) but-**

122. JMdan: hhh [stand by new (?)

123. DFita: **then (.) [then the stores close with the (?) and (then) people will be unemployed so they have to buy clothes** *((laughing))*

124. JMdan: o(h)k *((tee-hee))*

125. DFita: they: (.) some of them don't have a job, so do have to find a job (.) and: if they can't find a job they can also go to school, (.) learn, and then find a job more easily (.) some of them will be very rich, some will be poor ↓ (.) if they're very rich they can also go on holidays, so the days when they're on vacation they don't have to buy anything (.) 'cause they can just survive being on vacation ↓ (..) and: (..) for that we're gonna (.) if you want to do we're gonna need a lot of (.) help because the leaders have to be in charge of the bank, the stores, the school and: the pharmacy ↑ (.) and there will be, there is also an angel going around the place and: and delivering (.) children, babies *((smiling))*

126. Many leaders: <u>hhhh</u>

127. DFita: and (.) sickness, so when the people get kids, they have, they also have to go to the pharmacy and buy medicines (.) what happens if the most of the kids go (.) broke, they: lose all the money, they spent all the money, they come very poor (.) and they start to erm: <u>ste</u>al money, or steal (.) food or what they need, so we (.) we have also jail and policemen go around and (put) into jail everybody that (.) *((using hands))* steals. Or: kids also <u>die</u> in the game, but they never tell you, they never say that they're dead, because they want to go on playing ↑, and the debriefing afterwards is (.) like the first question I usually ask them is (.) how many of you (.) died? (.) actually died and they didn't tell us ↑ and a <u>lot</u> of them actually do ↑ and then you say erm well <u>what</u> would it be if it was real life? (...) **and that's how they actually start to learn what (.) in real life they (would do) (.) fight for surviving (..) and: it's a cool game that I play twice (.) three times** *((smiling))* **in every mini-camp ↓, they enjoyed it a lot, and especially if the leaders are with them and they love it, (.) but I just want to know if you like the idea and if you think it can be played with** <u>these</u> **kids, at** <u>this</u> **point of the (.) curve, of the educational curve**

128. LMbra: **so we play it in the morning?**

129. DFita: **it will take the whole morning**

In S15, the camp director plays the role of the expert. The cues for expertise are the superior cognitive and emotional status of suggestions, explanations and instructions, rejections of alternative suggestions (prevalently indirect, using disclaimers and irony), normative expectations about activities, and underlined educational meanings of the activities. Finally, expertise projects interlocutors' passivity. During this presentation and explanation of the activity, DFita introduces cognitive expectations which refer to the 'educational circle' upon which CISV programmes have to rely.

4.6   Conclusions

This chapter has focused on two-part sequences which include proposals of planned activities or problems which emerged in the activities (as first part) and reactions to these proposals and problems (as second part). In particular, we have examined the consequences of this kind of sequences for active participation during organisational meetings in CISV villages and summer camps, observing the main contextualization cues contributing to the signalling of expectations, roles and personal expressions.

1. The first part of the sequences (proposals) is successful in promoting participation if it includes the use of the linguistic form of 'asking for' with particular concern for clarification and support, which encourages checking of understanding, and opening to suggestions and discussions. This linguistic form may be considered a cue for the promotion of active participation and deliberate self-positioning: therefore its empirical expressions may be considered *promotional questions*. Furthermore, the self-disclaiming 'but' may be used to promote interlocutors' participation and a change of footing can support personal responsibility in proposing. The first part of the sequence is instead unsuccessful in promoting active participation when it projects normative expectations, which force the interlocutors' positioning in a hierarchical relationship, through the other-disclaiming 'but' and changes of footing underlining the power of 'I' on 'we'.

2. Successful promotion of active participation is based on a combination of affective and cognitive expectations manifested through dialogic actions following as second part of the sequences. After the presentation of planned activities, proposals or problems, the participants can support and promote their interlocutors' actions and positions through dialogic actions such as: (1) checking their understanding, (2) actively listening to the introduced topics and giving feedback to show their understanding and involvement, (3) requesting further explanations about the presentation, (4) appreciating and positively commenting it, (5) suggesting and adding proposals, (6) applauding and thanking for it. Affective formulations seem to be particularly

important in this promotion of empowering dialogue, in the forms of coordination among different contributions and from different positions, and mediation whereby an alternative story is promoted by a single participant who is able to coordinate and empower the others. Sometimes, self-disclaimers and changes of footing, which support agency, help in this action.

3. Participants often position themselves assuming roles of organisers and planners focusing mainly on the management of the village/camp. In particular, starting from this reflexive positioning, the hierarchical roles of staff members, especially of camp directors, prevail in the interaction, although their actions range from direction to coordination. Staff members often introduce suggestions and requests for explanation about the organisation and the development of the activities, and frequently put forward doubts concerning aims and problems, often linked to risk management, through other-disclaimers and changes of footing supporting role hierarchies. Therefore, in the communication process, staff members highlight normative and cognitive expectations through their actions. The hierarchical structure of the interactions is demonstrated by the primacy of staff members/camp directors' *actions* (and deliberate self-positioning) over other participants' *experiences* (and forced positioning). Especially camp directors, and occasionally other staff members and some leaders, try to manage the interaction assuming the roles of trainers, experts and judges, reminding, explaining and fixing CISV activities and their rules, values and methodologies. In this context, assessments of proposals are used to underline expectations of respect for rules and pointing out the different stages and possible results in terms of children's learning, i.e. introducing third order-positioning. These assessments mainly project passive participation and forced positioning, featuring lack of personal proposals, based on the experience of meaningful expert actions.

Staff members, in particular camp directors, assume a decisive position in reminding, explaining and fixing CISV rules and the role that leaders (and adolescents in summer camps) have to take, reporting past experiences to support their perspective. However, their actions may block active participation and deliberate self-positioning in these meetings and reduce a collective decision-making process essentially to a monologue.

Organisational meetings 2
Conflict management

Claudio Baraldi and Elena Gambari

Chapter 5 concludes the analysis of organisational meetings, specifically focusing on forms of conflict management. Normative conflict resolution is identified as a frequent strategy of conflict management emerging in interactions. This is based on hierarchical relationships between camp directors and their staff, on the one hand, and adults who are leading the delegations of children and adolescents on the other. Frequently conflicts are avoided through withdrawals, minimisations, elusions/diversions, mitigations and postponements. Overall, the actions of directors and their staff are frequently oriented to the disempowerment of other participants, who frequently adapt to these strategies. Coordination and mediation are alternative strategies in conflict management, featuring interesting dialogic actions.

5.1 Conflicts in organisational meetings

Conflicts are communicated contradictions (see Chapter 1) which produce insecurity in the interaction and need to be faced through further communication. Conflicts can be analysed observing the communication processes in which they take shape and develop and how these processes enhance second order positioning which questions existing normative expectations of order. In this chapter we shall observe how conflicts affect the decision-making process in organisational meetings (OMs). In these meetings, disagreements may concern the aims and developments of the activities, contrasting or blocking communicated choices. These obstacles mainly arise in situations in which participation is not equally distributed and role hierarchies are evident: as we have seen these situations are usual in the interaction between staff members, especially camp directors, on the one hand, and leaders on the other (Chapter 4).

Conflicts can be classified observing in which ways disagreement is considered in communication, i.e. in which ways coordination between participants' utterances and understanding is managed (Luhmann 1984). During OMs, role conflicts are preponderant, while intercultural conflicts are much less frequent, and very few conflicts concern interpersonal relationships. In role conflicts, contradictions concern role performances, and may be generated by both their different interpretations and by participant's insubordination to hierarchical relationships. These conflicts mainly concern organisational aspects of the activities and less frequently their educational meaning. Organisational and educational roles are specific societal roles (Weizman 2008), and therefore conflicts related to these roles do not concern interactional structures, but their cultural presuppositions. Intercultural conflicts deal with different cultural presuppositions, i.e. they concern cultural incompatibilities about values, objectives, identities, procedural and relational problems, between actors who are observed as representatives of different cultures (Chapter 1). In OMs, intercultural conflicts concern mainly food habits and the use of time.

The opening of conflicts projects different forms of management in the interaction, e.g. attempts to avoid reproducing contradictions, normative solutions, redistribution of participation among the interactants, reproduction of the block until the communication system 'collapse' (participants withdraw from communication). In the next sections, we will analyse the different forms of conflict management in OMs, considering both role conflicts and intercultural conflicts.

5.2   Conflict normative resolution

The opening of conflicts projects attempts at conflict resolution. Conflict resolution requires a *decision* concerning the communicated contradiction. The main form of conflict resolution observed in OMs is conflict normative resolution (CNR), managed by staff members and camp directors and based on the projection of their normative expectations in the interaction. CNR is based on the distinction between right and wrong, which either establishes or confirms positioning and role hierarchies in the interaction. CNR is mostly proposed by staff members and in particular by camp directors. Since staff members have the task of supervising activities, their actions tend to establish rules and assess proposals. Consequently, positioning and role hierarchies are evident and frequent, and conflict resolutions are mainly projected by staff members' actions. These actions do not only state right/wrong distinctions, but also the rules which limit the means for conflicts.

In S1, DMita introduces a problem related to the role performances of 'night angels', i.e. leaders and JCs who are in charge of the surveillance of children at night (turn 80). This projects LFger's defensive position, which indicates that she thinks that DMita is referring to her action (turn 81). In turn 82, DMita tries to postpone the discussion while at the same time confirming his position (introduced by the other-disclaiming 'but'), not aligning with LFger's action. After few seconds of silence, signalling the uncertainty created by this contradiction, LFger reaffirms her point of view, opposing implicitly DMita's perspective (turn 84). DMita ignores her contribution, listing the problems he has observed (turn 85), and LFger withdraws from the interaction. In response to LFphi's expression of uncertainty (turn 86), DMita clarifies the problem in turn 87, introducing it with a mitigated other-disclaimer 'ya, but'. His normative action is followed by many seconds of silence and no further reactions. Nevertheless, DMita continues to call for the leaders' attention in turn 90, not aligning with LMpor's attempt to change topic (turn 89). All participants, except LMpor, passively accept DMita's critique. LMpor tries to mitigate DMita's actions (turns 91, 93, 95, 97), finally disclaiming DMita's position overtly (through a direct other-disclaiming 'but') and immediately leading to a change of topic (turn 97).

(S1)

80. DMita: for the next topic we wrote night angels because in some days they work pretty well, in some other days there is no checking at all. Like to today there was nobody in the gym. The point is that in the gym there's the majority of the kids.

81. LFger: **I was in the gym**

82. DMita: I mean, we can discuss later if you want **but today is not working** (..) because there are angels outside and no one in the gym.

83. (03)

84. LFger: **I was there for all the time and all there was Rob sometimes with me.**

85. DMita: and there was boys in girls room today

86. LFphi: I don't know what to do about that-

87. DMita: **ya, but the point is not that- if you put three piece persons, the point is that the three persons have to be in three different places.** If there are three persons in the amphitheatre and there no kids because the kids are here, in the gym and in the room, we can delete this thing of the day angels and this is the same thing (02) ok? (04) So we (?) supervision.

88. (04)

89. LMpor: °so:° next topic, ya? ((asking for DMita's confirmation))

90. DMita: ok, **so take it into consideration**

91. LMpor: I **think it's worse during the day.** During the night is-

92. DMita: no, during the night is working better, because also yesterday during the night working better

93. LMpor: **it is also because during the day there is dispersion** cause they are <u>all</u> campsite and there's still only two night angels

94. DMita: no, there are three
95. LMpor: erm, **we decided to have the next night angel, so the third night angel**
             <to the night> because all there's nobody else, but to the day
96. DMita: today there was the third one
97. LMpor: **but there's an exception,** because they are in all campsite, so, it's more
             difficult to check them, because they are in all campsite, °so:, so:° (..).
             Cultural activity, Brazil.

The hierarchical structure of this interaction is evident. On the one hand, DMita *can* claim for attention and discipline, intentionally positioning the leaders in a hierarchical interaction. On the other hand, the leaders *cannot* change the course of action, and are compelled to position themselves only through withdrawal and diversion of attention (see § 5.4).

In S2, LFfra criticizes the structure of the activity *Circle of nations* (turn 310), mitigating this critique through a self-disclaiming 'but'. In turn 312, LFfra insists on her positioning, this time through an other-disclaiming 'but' which creates doubts about the interlocutors' positive positions. After some interlocutory turns, in turn 320, DMita asserts the importance of the activity, using a mitigated other-disclaimer 'yeah but'. In turns 321 and 323 however, LFita aligns with LFfra, in-directly contradicting DMita, who reacts by reaffirming his position (turns 322, 324), supported by LFeng (turn 327), although approving a change in the pro-cedure (turn 328). In turn 329, LFita seems to aligns with DMita's decision, al-though her non verbal behaviour shows some concern. In turns 331, 332 and 334, LFeng and LFmex also align with DMita's position, projecting his final normative statement 'that's all' (turn 337).

(S2)
310. LFfra: we was talking before, I know LMspa and JMaus and some people, just
              think that (when we did) the circle of nation we should like just say
              without problems, I mean if we don't talk that mean that everything is
              fine because (..) I think (we're losing) a few minutes saying 'ok my kids
              are fine, ok my kids are fine, (??)' **but I don't know (??) think about that.**
311. DMita: em::
312. LFfra: I mean it's good to see that for example these kids are fine **but you**
              (shouldn't) think that they're fine so -
313. LMpor: yes! it's (??)
314. LFfra: it's (??) the same
315. SMfar: but this (??) it to a little.
316. DMita: what?
317. SMfar: (??) it to a little.
318. DMita: can we lower the-?

319. LFfra: fine.
320. DMita: fine. (04) **Yeah I understand it's the same time (??) but (03) it's very fast and in this way we give time-** we have- we give time for everybody to speak instead of (..) 'does anybody have something to say?'
321. LFita: **I totally agree with LFfra.**
322. DMita: **circle of nation is very important (??)**
323. LFita: just (??) to say my kids are fine!   [**just shut up it's the same**
324. DMita: [**Yeah (??) it's a very important moment.**
325. JMisr: so what?
326. DMita: I don't (??) it
327. LFeng: good, good, good, good, bad, (..) blablabla,
328. DMita: **yeah! OK let's keep it: if you want to say it's good and you pass (..) and it's fast, let's do this. But let's keep the formality, I mean it's important.**
329. LFita: **yeah we can do it this way** ((*bothered*))
330. DMita: yeah it can take two minutes if it's good, good, good, good, good, good, and it's just -
331. LFeng: **ok!**
332. LFmex: **I think it's important to give the time for that (..) (circle).** We don't have to speak or (..) DMita said can be only good, good, good, good, good, but (02) because of the personality of all of us, maybe someone doesn't want to make a special thought in the meeting to say 'I'm bad'.
333. LFfra: what? Sorry?
334. LFmex: yeah. Because of the personality of all of us (02) **you have to give this moment for say 'good, good, good, good, good' maybe bad,** because if you don't do this time, if you don't have this (3) point
335. LFfra: opportunity
336. LFmex: opportunity, maybe there will be someone that feels (04) that is shy and doesn't want to make a break in the meeting to say 'Hey! I'm bad!' (03) I need (tell) with this, I need (tell) with that (02) so, I think we, we, we- that's why I think we should keep that. It can be really fast like 'good, good, good, good, good, good, good, good, bye, that's all' but maybe also like (ok).
337. DMita: **I don't think we waste much time with circle of nation. (..) That's all.**

LFfra and LFita align with DMita's decision withdrawing from the conflict. This hierarchical structure blocks negotiation, and the alliances (LFita and LFfra vs. DMita and LFmex) demonstrate the power hierarchy: only DMita's actions are treated as performative in the interaction and can position the interlocutors.

Insistence can however mitigate the role hierarchy. In S3, SM1ita opens a discussion about food preferences in the village (turn 12), and some leaders declare that they have difficulties in getting used to the new habits, asking for changes, in particular for extending the variety of food (turns 13, 14, 15, 17, 22), while LFger uses a two-part self-disclaiming 'but' (turns 19, 20). At the beginning, staff members are helpful in listening to this request (turns 16, 18, 21, 25), however LMdan's request (turn 29), introduced by an other-disclaiming 'but', first projects a chain of misunderstandings and clarifications (turns 31-38), and then SM1ita's normative reaction (turns 44, 47, 49) negatively assessing LMdan's proposal, particularly for its cultural contents (turn 49). This reaction is expressed through a chain of other-disclaiming 'but'. Furthermore, SM1ita supports his position narrating his cross-cultural experience as an example of adaptation (turn 47). The conflict can be closed only by abandoning its intercultural definition (turns 50-52), which is not accepted by the staff. This abandonment is introduced by a mitigated other-disclaiming 'yes but' (turn 50).

(S3)

12. SM1ita: […] if you don't have nothing else to say about the food and meals (.) we
       go on to the-
13. LFchi: **oh, about the food, also we- we need some salty food**
14. LMdan: **ya, we said that**
15. LFchi: **ya (.) Chinese always need- ((smiling)) need salty food**
16. SF2ita: so you need (??) for breakfast, right?
17. LFchi: **also for breakfast**
18. SF2ita: usually, how many (.) delegations eat salty, Norway (.) ((writing delegation
       names in her notepad)) Norway (.) China (.) Denmark (.) Brazil (.)
       Messico, a:nd Finland and Germany?
19. ((LFger nods))
20. LFger: but I think my kids are fine well, I think they can arrange [(??)
21. SF2ita: [and Finland also?
22. LFfin: (??) **something like ham or (??), only butter**
23. SF2ita: eh?
24. Some voices: butter
25. SF2ita: and there is some delegations that eat salt and sweet? yes, Brazil, Messico
       (..) and your kids eat only salt?
26. LFger: [no, the both
27. LMdan: [no
28. LFNor: [not only, but both
29. LMdan: **-both, but I want to ask if it is possible to have some oatmeal for
       breakfast,** I don't know (.) I think many of my children would have and
       (?) too and-
30. LFnor: me too
31. SF2ita: you talk about what?
32. LFnor: oatmeal

33. LMdan: oatmeal
34. SM3ita: fiocchi d'avena *((oatmeal in Italian))*
35. SF2ita: oatmeal?
36. SM1ita: hot milk? (.) no oatmeal
37. LMdan: oatmeal
38. SM3ita: it's like a cereal
39. LFnor: yes, but-
40. SF1ita: how do you spell that?
41. LMdan: o, ei, t, m, i, ei, el
42. SM3ita: I know, but this is cereal (..) not this one we have-
43. LMdan: it's kind of like (??) but pressed and-
44. SM1ita: **ok, ok, but- ehm, just a point (.) I don't want to:- you are in Italy (..)-**
45. LFnor: -ya
46. LMdan: ya we know
47. SM1ita: -and when I went- **it's not because I don't like Sweden but I went to Sweden and I had some problem with the food** (.) the schedule of the food wa:s (..)   [the centre –
48. SF2ita: [but we will have something salty, for sure *((moves her hands to express finality))*
49. SM1ita: **of course we want you to have to- (.) <u>but just remind</u> that (..) <u>if you came to another culture</u> and so also food-**
50. LFnor: **yes, but we have to get it for** *((touches her belly to indicate intestinal problems))*
51. SM1ita: **ah, ok, that's not culture it's**   [**good health**
52. LMdan: [good health

Negative assessments introduce normative expectations in the interaction and oblige the interlocutors to decide how to react and which risks to take in order to participate and position themselves. Actions based on normative expectations seem to produce the block of participation based on an interactive forced positioning; however, they may also demonstrate that conflicts tend to be unbearable, as the risk of blocking the OM becomes high. CNR may be more difficult than expected if interlocutors do not renounce their perspective. For example, in S3, turn 51, SM1ita convenes that the problem is not in cultural habits but in 'good health', mitigating his position and converging with LMdan. This mitigation derives from the fact that in these OMs, hierarchical order is not legitimised by formal rules. Although there is a formal role difference between camp directors and staff members on the one hand and leaders on the other, CISV democratic and participatory narrative may create problems in establishing hierarchical orders and forced other-positioning.

For this reason, *conflict avoidance* is frequent as a general form of conflict management in OMs. Conflicts are mainly avoided when stable CNR is not quickly available in the interaction. Conflict avoidance reduces the uncertainty and shortens the time of decision-making, resuming the interaction which has been interrupted and completing the decision-making process. Conflict avoidance consists in trying to maintain the consensus in the interaction avoiding the potential effects of contradictions. Specific forms of conflict avoidance are:

1. Abandoning or minimizing contradictions.
2. Ignoring contradictions, above all through the shift of the communication process towards alternative topics.
3. Mitigating contradictions and postponing decisions.

These kinds of actions are frequent in OMs, and their effects are forms of communication like minimisation, elusion and diversion, mitigation, and postponement.

5.3   Withdrawal and minimisation

Withdrawal consists in the participant's abandonment of the interaction, thus avoiding conflicts. In S4, turn 131, LFfar expresses her anger connected to her negative assessment of some JCs's actions and invites the interlocutors to reflect upon this. JMnor aligns with LFfar's critique showing his embarrassment through a continuer (turn 132). JMnor's continuer projects LFfar's further complaint (turn 133). This time, following this insistence, JMnor's reaction is defensive (turns 134, 136). However, in turns 135 and 137, LFfar insists in underlining her critique. In turn 138, JMnor abandons the conflict, confirming LFfar's perspective, and postponing the discussion of the problem.

(S4)

131. LFfar: *((laughter))* (??) (..) I have one more issue before we close this stuff, °we close°, and that is, (..) **we talked about in front of the children, that is bothering me**, (.) I've heard people talking about drugs in front of the children, today (at meal), in front of <u>mine</u> children (..) and **that is pis(h)(h)ing me off** (.) drugs and (.) °it was a Jcs°, so **everybody and Jcs** *((turning toward JMnor))* **use the delegation time today to discuss what is** (.) **appropriate talk about in front of the kids**

132. JMnor: °yeah°

133. LFfar: I mentioned, I said, I told them that erm (.) those people concerning that (.) said that, in front of my kid, and **I was very pissed off** ↑, so they all know, but (.) **I'd like you to talk about it** 'cause like (..) today they were talking about drugs in front of my kids, **I'm not happy** (.) **about that**

134. JMnor: yeah, erm (...) °you know the names, I don't (of us), [like **I don't think
it's intentional-**

135. LFfar: [yeah a kitchen
staff and one of JC was there

136. JMnor: **ok, I don't think it's (.) intentional (..)** like probably   [they speak up, so
(??) probably

137. LFfar: [**but even** yeah,
because: (.) **even if it's: joking, the kids look so much up to you than
they** (..) yeah, because (of that)

138. JMnor: **yeah, ok, °we'll talk about°**

Withdrawals are clearly linked to role hierarchies and forced positioning: in S4,
JMnor, faced with the leader's contestation, abandons the conflict; in other situations, leaders abandon the conflict when they face the opposition of camp directors (see Chapter 4). This demonstrates the relevance of hierarchical structures in
the interaction.

Minimisation is the opposite of withdrawal and consists in reducing the
relevance of the causes and motivations of conflicts. In S5, SF1ita asks for clarifications about the proposed activity (turns 36, 38). LFecu answers in turn 39,
but SM1ita contradicts her (turn 40). LFecu's and LMpor's reactions open a
conflict, based on an other-disclaiming 'but' which mitigates their subordinated
positions (turns 41, 42). In these circumstances, mitigated other-disclaimers
introduce the minimisation of the previously communicated contradiction:
LFecu focuses on the short period the children have to keep the pen in their
mouth during the activity, and LMpor tries to generalise the problem affirming
that kids always put their dirty fingers in their mouth. SM1ita aligns with these
minimisations (turn 43) followed by SF1ita (turn 44), and in turn 45 LMpor
changes topic.

(S5)

36. SF1ita: so there are different stations

37. LFecu: ya, and oh they first do the same things with the hands in order to see the
different tasks how it can be difficult

38. SF1ita: and so did they paint with the mouth?

39. LFecu: **with the markers**

40. SM1ita: **no, because it's dirty**

41. LFecu: **ya but** only a little bit in order to show what does it mean to do everything
without hands.

42. LMpor: Antonio *((SM1ita))*, **I understand you but,** you know, they always touch
everywhere with the hands and then put them like this *((imitating kids
who put fingers into their mouth))*

43. SM1ita: **ya, I know**

44. SF1ita: **ok**
45. LMpor: **ok. Delegation time**

Mitigated other-disclaiming appears to be useful in minimising the reasons for the conflict, if accompanied with explanations concerning the positions of conflicting interactants. In these situations, in contrast with others (see Chapter 4), such mitigated other-disclaimers do not signal hierarchical structures. The case analysed demonstrates that mitigated other-disclaimers may support, oppose or minimise the effects of hierarchical structures, depending on the interactants' self-positioning.

Withdrawals and minimizations are both based on the presupposition of hierarchical structures and both reduce the effects of conflicts, as they prevent hierarchical relationships becoming forms of dominance and avoid forced positioning.

5.4   Elusion through diversion

Elusion is more frequent than abandonment and minimisation. Elusion consists in ignoring communicated contradictions by showing lack of interest, either in the reasons for contradiction or in contradictions themselves. Elusion is based on specific selections, aiming to exclude conflicts and whoever wants to open them; conflicts are not suppressed or normatively resolved, but put aside.

In S6, LFbel is concluding her presentation of a proposal for an activity (turn 14). In turn 15, LMpor puts forward a hypothesis, which is confirmed by LFbel in turn 16. This confirmation projects LMpor's contradiction of LFbel's proposal (turn 17). In turn 18, SF1ita reacts to LMpor's objection with an interlocutory confirmation. Her hesitation is followed by a pause having the effect to drop LMpor's objection, which is not considered by the other participants. In turn 20, LFecu ignores LMpor's position and changes the topic of conversation, showing her lack of interest for his contribution, and avoiding troubles in the interaction. In turn 21, LMspa aligns to LFecu in this change of topic.

(S6)
14. LFbel: it's just asked to each group to erm: when they play the movies erm: just (..) they just act first and then they explained, maybe just why they choose that movie
15. LMpor: **when they see the movie they have to do by the name, by the title**
16. LFbel: **mmh, ya**
17. LMpor: the movie they see, especially if you do it by delegation, every movie they see is doubled. So **there is no way, maybe they know, but they are doubled and they have no idea of what is the title in English**
18. SF1ita: **ya, ok**

19. (03)
20. LFecu: **ok, so who has the activity in the morning**
21. LMspa: me. Well, I need of all leaders and staff

Turn 20 shows lack of interest for the conflict and its reasons. Diversion means moving the focus towards other topics and is the main way to elude conflicts.

In S7, the structure is very similar. In turn 2 LMpor asks a question about the organisation of an activity, in turn 4 he proposes a formulation of LFbel's clarification (turn 3), to check if he has understood it, and in turn 5 he obtains LFbel's substantial confirmation. In turn 6, however, LMpor clearly contradicts LFbel's position, manifesting his expectations and his expert role. LFbel overtly disagrees with LMpor (turn 7), confirming again her perspective in turn 9. In turn 10, LFecu partially contradicts LFbel using a third proposal asserting her authoritative position and changing the footing from 'I' (*think, mean*) to 'we' (*don't have, have*). In turn 11, SF1ita moves to a new topic, ignoring the previous discussion, and LFbel aligns to her diversion (turn 12).

(S7)
2. LMpor: **just a question.** Do you want that a leader has to be in each group, or –
3. LFbel: the kids decide everyone of them, of the planning want to participate they will walk around each group-
4. LMpor: **so the leaders will be in each group**
5. LFbel: **basically yes,** because as they stay in the planning they want to be present during the activity and also as there is a discussion
6. LMpor: **no, because** can the leaders influence- **we can,** **if you want, influence their answers, we can actually usually make (.) what (.) we think it's correct to-** ((SMita shakes his head with an ironic smile))
7. LFbel: **it's just - It's fine if they have to say in a discussion-** it's – if (.) they believe that one the person should stay they should defend the argument why should they choose it. They would say how to come up to a solution, this, this and that. **So it's fine and there's not to be-**
8. LMpor: it's just-
9. LFbel: like the leaders can just give them their opinion, but they don't have to (.) tell the groups "that is the best option"
10. LFecu: actually I think that the fact that they have a discussion, talking a little bit on the various solutions, finding a majority in the group. So for this reason **I think that we don't have to influence in any way their answers because they know how to do, they know,** you know (.) **I mean (..) we have to let them just do this activity and to get a point. We can say "ok, why?"** There's a kind of discussion.
11. SF1ita: ya. (..) **So do you need any materials?**
12. LFbel: only papers and markers.

Elusions are frequently based on diversions, which are announced by a prefatory 'false' confirmation ('*ya*', '*ok*'). These false confirmations make it possible to change topic and consequently erase the conflict from the interaction. The use of these false confirmations turns 'no' into 'yes', and implicitly states that the conflict does not exist. Such confirmations are 'false' because they do not confirm any specific position, as the immediate change of topic demonstrates. Being prefatory of a change of topic, confirmation does not mean consent; rather, it is a contextualization cue contributing to the signalling of diversion.

5.5   Mitigation and postponement

Mitigation is achieved if one party revises her/his position, embarking on negotiation and eventually accepting a compromise. In S8, DFita hinders LMbra's proposal: she wants to be sure that the activity proposed by LMbra is safe for the children (turn 6, 8). Moreover, in turns 18 and 22, she seems perplexed about the aims of the activity: if the aim is trust, there is no reason to use mattresses. LMbra withdraws (turn 23), but DFita insists on her position (turn 25). When LMbra confirms his withdrawal (turn 26), DFita mitigates her position through a self-disclaiming 'but', which opens to alternative opportunities on the one hand, and is doubtful and ambivalent on the other, as it introduces leaders to the possible risks of the activity (turn 27). LMbra confirms his desire to renounce (turn 28), but DFita mitigates her position further, inviting to reflect and expressing her trust in LMbra (turn 29). This expression of trust reaffirms LMbra's participation (turn 30) and DFita mitigates her position for the third time, confirming LMbra's action (turn 31) and making a suggestion (turn 33). In turn 33 DFita also points out adults' duties and responsibilities, proposing normative expectations as a sort of mitigation of her mitigation, obtaining the convergence with LMbra in turn 34 (reinforced in turn 35).

(S8)
2. DFita: is that (.) the Chinese wall?
3. LMbra: yes
4. DFita: that they have to pass the all team to the other side?
5. Lmbra: yeah
6. DFita: **is that safe enough?**
7. Lmbra: [no the- *((miming with hands))*
8. DFita: **[can be safe enough?**
9. LMbra: it's a game where we- *((miming with hands))*, we can put like a -, we can use our (thread) method in the other side

10. LMdan: (thread) method in the other side
11. DFita: yeah
12. LMbra: yeah
13. DFita: but then, then must be in
14. LMbra: mhm
15. DFita: of the game
16. LMbra: of the game?
17. LMdan: [(??)
18. DFita: [to put the mattress there is no aim ((overlapping of voices))
19. LMbra: (??) they have to have-
20. DFita: yeah
21. LMbra: they have to have their (triadic)
22. DFita: and the last one have to jump ((miming)) but (.) the trust issue about (showing) into the mattresses
23. LMbra: mhm ((perplexed))
24. JMsve: put (invisible) mattress
25. DFita: you said like the point in the game is trusting (the team)
26. LMbra: ok, so we don't use them, the-
27. DFita: I don't know, but it's up to you guys, it can be very dangerous, it can be very dangerous (??) trust the children
28. LMbra: all right, so we (make) just activity one
29. DFita: no I don't wanna skip it, I just want to make sure you know what game it is erm (.) well you know your game
30. LMbra: I I I I've already had this game for a couple of times, that's why I just talked over about (it),so
31. DFita: yeah
32. LMbra: usually we just leave the: the grown up (??) for the end, the grown up, the grown up (??) I mean the JCs, so that we adults we are, we just (.) take them, and that's would be ok, so it's gonna be very safe, because they just spare it ((mimes it)), spare them
33. DFita: and maybe, before you start that game make sure that all the leaders are there
34. LMbra: all right, for sure
35. DFita: that's mean adults

In the context of this hierarchical structure, DFita's mitigation of her own normative actions and her subsequent reflexive mitigation (mitigation of mitigation) promote LMbra's action and sharing: without giving up her normative expectations, DFita can approve the proposed planning.

In S9, LMpor repeatedly contradicts LMbra's proposal (turns 22, 25, 29), but mitigates his contradictions, opening his turns with an other-disclaiming 'but' (turn 22) mitigated through linguistic forms which express doubts, reiterated in the following turns (turns 25, 28). LMpor's doubts are supported by LFecu (turn 26), and LMbra aligns with an alternative solution (turn 27), approved by LMpor (turn 28).

(S9)

19. LMbra: everybody wears caps or sunglasses and they're going to make a presentation of their own country with their costumes and things like that. (..) It's a simple but I think that they're going to have fun together and know each other

20. LFger: how long is it? Just to know

21. LMbra: we can do something very quickly but we can also do something which takes the two hours

22. LMpor: **I don't know but maybe** you need an activity in the morning because they can enjoy more (..) **You said that it is a calm activity, but when I talk about a calm one I imagine kids sitting down with their papers and drawing the flags and say this and that-**

23. LMbra: Z. ((*LFleb*)), is it your one calm?

24. LFleb: ya, it's calm.

25. LMpor: **I don't know because** I think that in your activity ((*talking to LMbra*)) they need a lot of materials.

26. LFecu: ya, actually I agree with you.

27. LMbra: ya, I would like to take the afternoon (..)

28. LMpor: ya, **it's just a suggestion because** I think you need to do an activity during the day

Mitigations may produce re-alignments, which consist in renouncing contradictions, avoiding further refusals. While withdrawal and minimisation mainly concern those who are at the bottom of the role hierarchy, mitigations affect the dominant positioning, reducing its impact and allowing its absorption in new and different structures of the interaction. In particular, the conjunction of mitigation and alternative proposals may change the course of the interaction. Mitigation may also lead to postponement of decisions, as a way to avoid conflicts.

In S10, after a preliminary discussion about the organisation of an activity, LFcan invites the participants to vote for one of the two options (turn 24). In turn 25, DFita expresses her opinion, without commenting on the two options. This opinion projects LFdut's doubts expressed through a suspended other-disclaimer (turn 26) and a doubtful suggestion (turn 27). In turns 30, 32, and 34, SMita expresses his perplexity, while leaders encourage him through continuers (turns 31, 33, 35). In turn 36, this position is reinforced by an other-disclaiming 'but' opening to the doubt that 'maybe is too early'. In turn 37, SFbos tries to postpone the decision, but SMita does not align with her proposal (turn 38). In the following turns, SMita's position is rebated and reinforced by some leaders through continuers (turns 39, 41, 46) and active support (turn 42), and this projects his perseverance (turn 47). However, rather surprisingly, in this turn SMita seems to mitigate his position. This projects LFnor's perplexed response (turn 49), which in its turn projects LFcan's final proposal of postponement (turn 50), the latter being followed by the interlocutors' alignment.

(S10)

24. LFcan: so there is two options. One is staying in the group all the time, trying to put them all together and discuss in the group. And then the second option is to divide them in groups and number them in 1, 2, 3, 4, 5, and 6. All the number one after you've been in your group for ten minutes you move into another group so to see what they have done and then come back to the other group. **So one or two?**

25. DFita: **one**

26. LFdut: **I think two would be quite interesting but the concerns –**

27. LMcos: everybody would be looking at everybody's work? It would be like sharing, **what do you think?**

28. *((Staff and leader talk over each other; incomprehensible))*

29. LMcos: what do you think?

30. SMita: **in my opinion your are taking a risk** (.) in this way, 'cause we don't know yet all the kids

31. LMcos: **yeah**

32. SMita: we cannot know if everyone (..) if you are splitting, all of the kids who will belong to a group have to go to another one and express themselves. **Right now we don't have the argue to say "ok, everyone feels comfortable –**

33. LFbel: **mmm**

34. SMita: to put himself in front of the group –

35. LFita: **mmm**

36. SMita: right now. **So in my opinion is for sure more interesting the choice two, but maybe is too early**

37. SFbos: maybe we can decide tomorrow and –

38. SMita: **I think it is not after one day** (..) lucky us if we can decide after one day if we can split them and everybody feels comfortable to express himself

39. LFbel: **mmm**

40. SMita: it's just my personal opinion of course

41. LFnor: **yeah**

42. LFfin: we were thinking the same: it is too early (.) because it's not so easy to express your feelings in front of everyone and there's language barriers and –

43. SMita: yeah
44. LFfin.   and new people and everything so it's –
45. SMita: but at least you are belonging to the group
46. LFfin: **yeah**
47. SMita: and maybe (..) in twenty minutes, half an hour, you can just have a little talk to someone and then you just (..) begin to build the bridge to (??) while after twenty minutes you only jump into another and someone may have difficulties to create relationships keep on jumping (..) about serious matters it might be more difficult (..) **if we all agree to take the risk, we can do it.** Keep in mind that after the activity there's always a discussion, an evaluation of the planning group and we can also develop and work on mistakes so maybe it's gonna be good also for us if we do something that is not correct in this period
48. *((The leaders nod))*
49. LFnor: **how should we work out that?**
50. LFcan: I don't think we need to decide right now, we can see it tomorrow
51. LFbel-LFfin: yeah

What seemed to be asserted as a choice supported by the role hierarchy, is rapidly reversed. Mitigation projects a change in perspective which prevents decision-making.

5.6   Coordination and mediation

Negotiation reflects the CISV narrative regarding the respect of different positions. Negotiation is sometimes concluded with a ballot, but it is more successful when it is concluded with shared decisions based on the coordination of different positions. As we have seen (Chapter 4), coordination is a dialogic co-construction of decisions. In cases of conflicts, it satisfies all the parties involved without a winner/loser distinction. In this form of conflict management, participants present themselves as open-minded and active listeners, they cooperate in the construction of new meanings, and show their trust in the interaction (Lewicki & Tomlinson 2003).

In S11, LFbra expresses her disagreement with previous proposals, here not shown (turn 475).Such disagreement is supported by LFger (turn 476) and LFaus (turn 478), who also remarks the need for a solution. In turn 480, DFcos invites the other participants to take part in the interaction displaying their opinions. In turn 483, LMarg starts coordinating the interaction; he formulates the previous perspectives and at the same time he expresses his perspective. In the subsequent turns (485, 487, 489), LMarg clarifies his perspective as a 'third' position. He is supported by LFger and LFcan through continuers (turns 484, 488). In turn 490, LFcan formulates LMarg's perspective, commenting and adding her own suggestion in turn 493, supported by LFaus (turns 491, 497) and DFcos (turns 494, 496, 498). LFphi partially aligns with it, although reaffirming the importance of the opposite perspective (turn 499), and is supported by DFcos and JFusa through a new formulation in the form of a comment (turns 500 and 501 respectively). DFcos underlines cognitive expectations (leaders should ask questions in order to stimulate reflection), and JFusa suggests a focus on normative expectations (CISV values and beliefs).

(S11)

475. LFbra: **I really don't wanna to talk to my kids about the game,** I think it's good to be a surprise for them because (??) work on this, the thing is 'ok, what do you think about (??), what people know about us' (.) we are talking about the game since the beginning of the camp, 'why we have to do a national night, why we have to teach them something of Brazil' that's why they love the activity for the national night because they are 'ok, so I think that we need to teach them good thing on Brazil' so I don't wanna talk to them about this (..) and we can see, if we make a good debrief, I think there's no problem

476. LFger: is like, that we talk to the kids about the game (??) they will think of things like (??) **so it's not spontaneous**

477. LFbra: yeah, they're gonna prepare for it

478. LFaus: [(??) **expectations to the game and it'll completely change the whole dynamic,** say the German kids (??) and they don't then they might feel (??)

                          [**I think that we need to decide**

479. LFbra: [(??)

480. DFcos: I don't know, what do you think

481. LFcan: [(??) I'll go for ice-cream *((laugh))*

482. LFaus: [(??)

483. LMarg: **I'm in the middle** because **on one hand** I really think it's better to -, I don't know, to be spontaneous, right, whatever you want **but on the other hand** I feel like my kids are not really much sure enough, but like C. *((LFger))*, it's not going to change if we do it tomorrow or at the very end of the camp

484. LFger: **yeah**

485. LMarg: it's like that and they're not much sure, especially B. *((M1arg))* and G. *((M2arg))*, they're very (childish) and I'm not expecting them to write something

486. LFphil: (??)

487. LMarg: yeah, <u>seriously</u>, nor tomorrow nor the last -, nor the very last day of the camp so, as LFger says, it's the same, for me doing tomorrow it's a good idea, I really see a lot of kids mature and prepared so (.) but if I don't really tell them anything before, I'm afraid they like don't really get to understand the (??), the seriousness?

488. LFcan: **yeah**

489. LMarg: seriousness of the game and of the activity *((LFcan raises her hand))*

490. LFcan: well, maybe we should talk about it today (??) because that way, if they feel they need to discuss something (??) seriously is not a good idea, but if you're worried (??) other expectations and stuff so maybe we should do it in the morning after cleaning, we get to delegation, we talk [(??)

491. LFaus: [yes, we translate (??)

492. LFita: before starting the game?

493. LFcan: well, this meeting will be with our own and then they'll go to the gym (??)

494. DFcos: and also the thing is that you're gonna be with your delegation

495. LFcan: yes

496. DFcos: so you can like, whenever or something didn't comes up then you're gonna be there <u>all the time</u> with them

497. LFaus: yeah

498. DFcos: so you can (??) the situation

499. LFphil: actually, if I -, **if I can make a suggestion like maybe -, and correct me if I'm wrong, maybe it would help if you just** -, just give them a little (??) in general when I said that I mean like guys just to remind you that we're having a lot of fun, you know, just to remind them why they're here, you know, ask them how they feel about, you know, meet someone of another country for the first time and, you know, in a (??) thoughts about that country before maybe (??) thing, just give them a little (grammar)

500. DFcos: **yeah, it's not about <u>explaining the game</u>, tell them how it's going to be, it's just exactly, to question -, make questions that are gonna help them to think about -, a little bit about it, but not telling them that this is gonna be the things that tomorrow**

501. JFusa: **just remind them (what CISV is for)**

This decision-making process is based on cooperation among LMarg, LFcan, LMaus, DFcos and JFusa; in particular, DFcos aligns with the turns which demonstrate coordination among the participants. This coordinated process avoids polarized alliances and promotes changes of opinions until a co-constructed decision is arrived at. Coordination requires multiple voices chained in a sequence of reciprocal encouragements. Staff members, including camp directors, may participate in coordination with their interlocutors and in these cases the hierarchical structure of the interaction is dissolved.

Coordination may also be promoted through *mediation* (see Chapter 1 and 4). Mediation promotes positive treatment of diversity and non-violent conflict management, i.e. alternative co-constructed stories.

In S12, LFbel introduces her interpretation of the adolescents' activities in the summer camp (turn 1) asserting her position through a change of footing from 'I' (*think*) to 'we' (*have to do*). In turn 2, referring to this topic, LFnor suggests the planning of basketball or football tournaments. SMita objects to LFnor's proposal that sports are not good practices for CISV (turn 3). As LFnor insists (turn 4), SMita interrupts her with an explicit negative assessment (turn 5). Lfnor, however, insists again (turn 6) with an overt other-disclaiming 'but' and projecting LFbel's support (turn 7), through an indirect other-disclaiming 'but', which denies SMita's position. Indirectness here mitigates LFbel's conflicting but subordinated position. In turn 8, SMita continues to contradict this position. In turn 9, LFbel tries to force coordination, deviating the meaning of SMita's turn. At this point, SMita is forced to increase the level of conflict (turn 10) and LFbel is forced to negotiate a solution with him (turns 11 e 13), although she tries to maintain her authoritative position through a new change of footing (turn 11). In turn 14, LFdut assumes the role of mediator, both declaring her understanding for LFbel's position, and opening to an alternative solution. Interestingly, LFdut's opening is mitigated by an other-disclaiming 'yes' ('*yes the theme is important*') plus 'but', which probably explains why her position is immediately approved by SMita (turn 15). Consequently, in turn 16, LFdut can formulate a plan which can satisfy both parties involved in the conflict: with a self-disclaiming 'but' which enforces her position, she supports it further in turn 18 in response to SMita's question (turn 17), and she receives LFbel's indirect support through an echo (turn 19). SMita aligns with this proposal (turn 21), and LFdut reinforces it referring to children's needs (turn 22). This projects a dyadic interaction between LFdut (turns 25, 27) and SMita (turns 24, 26, 28) which displays the harmonious effect created by mediation. Finally, DFita approves the proposal (turn 29) projecting general consent (turns 30, 31) and closing the interaction with a normative recommendation (turn 32).

(S12)

1. LFbel: I think that maybe it's normal that they chose some activities of the village, because it's the only thing that they have done before this camp. And I **think** to grow to summer camp activities **we have to do** that, to do that step between the two camps and to erm in village we have also erm activities like the activities of this night and we have some debriefing of the kids also sometimes. So maybe for me erm it's normal to do that step before erm the

summer camp activities and erm during that moment they can understand how to plan an activity and when they know how to do it they can practice activity more difficult maybe or with discussion about the theme

2. LFnor: I think the kids also would like to have like basketball game or football game and would also like to make like championship or something

3. SMita: **they are not CISV activities,** I think in a summer camp they have to plan activities on the theme of the camp, I don't think that basketball can -

4. LFnor: **I think it's nice** if we can just put together -

5. SMita: **in my opinion. In the free time they can do**

6. LFnor: **but they don't have that much free time** […]

7. LFbel: this camp I know that, well in the guide all the activities have to be related to the theme, **but I think that if we do that all the time the kids get bored about it**. They have to make some activities to have only fun -

8. SMita: **we have running game**

9. LFbel: **yeah. For example basketball could be one**

10. SMita: **I don't agree very much with you**

11. LFbel: **I think that we can do something like competition** or I don't know and with some teams, they can play together like this and it's maybe more funny […] so just for their fun

12. SMita: mmm

13. LFbel: **one time, they can do sport**

14. LFdut: **yes, I understand your point and yours erm I think that yes, the theme is important, but at the same time it's not always** (??)

15. SMita: **yes yes I agree with this**

16. LFdut: **and I have a suggestion to make, not very original but maybe can combine two or three points**. You're saying it should be theme related, you're saying it should be fun (..) olympics? Olympics are about an integration and that people come together. it's about competition, **it's sport obviously, but it's also that we can organise that through sport people get to know each other as well** (??) maybe we can do something on the Olympics, like making -

17. SMita: on what on what on what please?

18. LFdut: the Olympics

19. LFbel: olympic games

20. LFdut: so there's knowledge and -

21. SMita: **yes I was thinking about something similar**

22. LFdut: yeah, I don't know. **I know from my kids that they need sports**

23. LFbel: yeah

24. SMita: **yes yes, I understand, I agree with you,**   [but

25. LFdut: [also I want to say that (…) there should be more free time from tomorrow (…)

26. SMita: **I really agree that they need sport.** I only didn't agree with sports like basketball and football: there's two competitions and also a lot of guys would be excluded. **But if we organise with them an activity like Olimpiade I think it's ok**
27. LFdut: and it will probably involve many sports
28. SMita: **yes, not only sports but also like erm staffetta** – *((relay in Italian))*
29. DFita: I think it's not a matter of theme or not theme, CISV activities or not, I guess. **We need to create a group (??) and about Olympic games I agree but they have to be not individual games**
30. *((Approval))*
31. LMcos: yes, sure sure sure
32. DFita: **and we also have to make them feel as a group**

LFdut's proposal projects SMita's alignment with LFnor's proposal through an interpretation which is satisfactory for both: through her mediation, LFnor's proposal is modified and SMita can waive his objections, i.e. both change their positions to interactive positive positioning.

In the lines preceding S13 (not shown), LFmex has introduced a problem concerning the children's possibility to ask for food either to the kitchen staff or to the leader. LFnor suggests a procedure to solve this problem (turn 9), which projects diverging perspectives (turns 10, 11, 12). In turns 14, 16 and 17, SM1ita and LFger cooperatively propose a third position, combining the previous two: the duty is given to the kitchen staff with the supervision of leaders. In turns 18, 19 and 20, their mediation is approved and in turn 22, LMdan confirms the general agreement.

(S13)
9. LFnor: **ok (.) should we then just tell the kids to sit down a:nd talk to the leader or could they go up (.) and talk to the kitchen staff?**
10. LFmex: **I think they can go**   [**the kitchen staff**
11. JMbra: [**let's both (.) let's both**
12. LFbra: **I think we can go to the kitchen staff** (.) and the kitchen staff- they just after- we have something (??)
13. LFnor: yes
14. SM1ita: I think that the leader (.) in the table should take care of the situation (.) if they see too many people like walking up for nothing ok (.) just ask them what are you doing (.) where are you going
15. LFnor: yeah
16. LFger: they should ask the leader   [if they can get up or doing something?
17. SM1ita: [ya they should first ask the leader
18. LFnor: yeah
19. LF(?): yeah

20. LFusa: yeah
21. SM1ita: so:
22. LMdan: **so ask the leader before doing anything**

S14 concerns adolescents' bedtime in a night in which leaders are out and other volunteers are supervising them. In turn 17, SM1ita opens the debate, overtly expressing his position about bedtime, which he confirms in turn 21. In turn 22, LFbel contradicts him, using her expertise as an argument, and opening the way to conflict (turns 23–24). LFita's ambiguous comment in turn 25 puzzles LFbel (turn 26). In turn 27, DMita makes a proposal which mediates between the previous two, which is no longer objected to. In this turn, some self-disclaiming buts mitigate positions which have been introduced in the first clauses, reinforcing the proposals in the second clauses. After some further explanations (turns 29, 32, 34), in turn 36, DMita proposes the ballot and his suggestion is successful. Finally, he negotiates further small changes with SM1ita (turns 39, 40). The lack of opposition to DMita's proposal is not explained in terms of hierarchy, but depends on his mediation.

(S14)
17. SM1ita: **ok me.** Yes, my idea is, I agree with Lorenzo *((DMita))*. **It's quite a suicide to tell them to go bed at 11.30 this night** that we aren't here and we have here guys that are here for the first time. And also I think that in these two days we have seen some changes, we have not seen the same situation of two days ago, in my opinion. Also from some people that are, that were (.) the problem. I saw a lot of changes. And I think it's also (?) for them yes
18. LMcos: (?)
19. SM1ita: no (..) I don't know the word also in Italy, so –
20. DMita: like to to to to to make a kind of prize because (??) anyway
21. SM1ita: yes, this is my idea. **It's stupid to send them to bed at 11.30**
22. LFbel: **I don't think so, well my position is because before leaving I was erm my sister was in a summer camp also** and there was the leaders' night out just the evening before leaving and they asked me to come with a friend. We were two, only two and forty kids, and the lights off was at 11.30 and (.) we have to do it –
23. SM1ita: **but we have a particular team of guys**
24. LFbel: **yes, it was also a particular team**
25. LFita: **it's always a particular team**
26. LFbel: **yeah (..) So -**
27. DMita: well, my suggestion is: yesterday and the day before we sent them in bed (?), so we should (.) it's a suggestion **but** (.) move a little bit the bedtime saying in a pretty way that we saw that you, some of you at least, are doing something to change in a good way (.) **but** not all the goals that we put are achieved. So today you can go to bed at midnight (.) if you want to have

something more (.) you have to achieve the other goals that we have. So in a kind of way they won't be frustrated because they are doing in a kind of way something good (.) **but** if they have no feedback from us, **but** since they are not that good they won't go to bed at 2.00

28. LFdut: so you will say, I'm not sure if I have understood. Erm so we say (before bedtime it's midnight and you mean if they behave well tonight but in the future). But the only thing that we save is giving them half an hour extra tonight

29. DMita: yeah, half an hour, five minutes, we have to decide it. **But give them a little bit because they were on time this morning**, they (behave) in the right way, so they are changing a little bit. Other things have not changed so they have to achieve what they are supposed to, so little by little (??)

30. SM1ita: I have to say something in Italy to him, sorry

31. ((They speak in a very low voice))

32. DMita: by the way, now of course we're gonna take the decision and we're gonna tell them during the delegation time and (.) ah, please, be very clear with them that they ((the people in charge of the camp)) have our telephone numbers, in case not of emergency of course, but if they have to call us because they are not respectful with them or we have to come back because they are not manageable, that means 11.00 from today till the end of the camp (??)

33. LFdut: but can we tell them during the delegation time this night?

34. DMita: no we have to (?) this night, but for sure is that if they have to call because they are unrespectful and (.) we as a staff we gonna take the decision (??)

35. SM1ita: what are the choices?

36. DMita: **so they choices are**: first go to bed as usual, 11.30. Second one at 2.00. Third one, in a middle way, like 12.00, 12.15 or something like that. **Ok, let's vote** for the first one: 11.30

37. ((They vote for the three options))

38. DMita: so we're gonna send them at midnight in bed, lights off

39. SM1ita: **12.30?**

40. DMita: **12.15**

In the cases examined, mediators' *transformative formulations* express a synthesis of previous antagonistic perspectives, and mediators' *suggestive narratives* project new proposals. Transformative formulations do not simply reflect and interpret the gist of previous turns; they also transform this gist, creating a new narrative. In the case of mediation, the interaction opens with two partial and not con-cluded narratives, which are contradictory and unstable, and closes with a third narrative, leading to a new perspective. Promotion of active participation and deliberate reflexive and interactive self-positioning is crucial in this movement. Staff members, including camp directors, may abandon their hierarchical stances and participate in coordinated decisions, from a mediating position.

5.7   Conclusions

During organisational meetings, staff members may react in different ways to problems and differences emerging from the interactions: they may try to avoid conflicts, to guide discussions making use of hierarchies, and to promote alternative stories through coordination and mediation.

1. Avoiding conflicts is frequent, in interactions in which elusions, diversions, re-alignments, minimisation and mitigations are successful. The final result is ignoring or quitting conflicts, while at the same time avoiding forced positioning determined by hierarchical structures.

2. Conflict resolution is frequently produced in hierarchical forms (conflict normative resolution). Camp directors, staff members and, less frequently, most experienced leaders express their normative expectations, trying to guide the interaction, and ascribing to themselves the responsibility of decisions, recurring for this purpose to changes of footing and other-disclaimers which assert their authoritativeness. Consequently, many conflict resolutions are characterised by non balanced possibilities of expression, and by forced other-positioning. Amendments are proposed by staff members and highlight role hierarchies; staff members' actions generate the alignment of their interlocutors, and block their participation and eloquent silences. However, the perseverance of leaders and JCs in maintaining their perspective may lead to mitigation of hierarchies.

3. Coordination is a form of conflict management which requires cooperative active participation and interactive positive positioning. Coordination can transform contradictions in decision, although it involves only some participants. In particular, coordination through mediation promotes equal and balanced participation in the interaction and satisfying solutions for all participants. Mediation is promoted by a third party's dialogic actions empowering both conflicting perspectives, projects their deliberate self-positioning, which can be enhanced through self-disclaimers, and at the same time produces an alternative narrative, i.e. a 'third' proposal including previous proposals' most relevant aspects. Coordination and mediation can be enhanced exploiting all positions, including those of staff, camp directors, leaders, and JCs in villages, or adolescents in summer camps. They can promote the co-construction of new narratives in the interaction, such as new ideas about bedtime, new relationships between children, kitchen staff and leaders during lunch, introduction of sport activities in summer camps.

4. The forms of conflict management are reflected in the recurrent use of positive openings (*yes, yeah, ok, interesting,* etc.), which are transformed either

into mitigated other-disclaimers, or into changes of topic. The tendency to avoid a direct confrontation based on negative assessment of positions is not associated with appreciation. Negative assessments of positions are clear evidences of hierarchical presuppositions and create risks of insistence in dissent, while positive assertions are associated with avoidance and elusion of conflicts. Chains of active supportive turns give life to coordination. Finally, transformative formulation and suggestive narratives are the main expressions of mediation.

These forms of management concern mainly role conflicts, although some intercultural problems can emerge, for example concerning food preferences and the use of time. Intercultural conflicts emerge only when there are particular problems concerning personal life in villages/camps (e.g. inadequate food, need for silence and rest, etc.). The rarity of conflicts concerning cultural differences is an important sign that adults working at CISV initiatives share a global perspective on organisation and make many efforts to maintain it. These efforts, however, expose the interaction to role conflicts. The final result is that conflict management is mainly related to role hierarchies and performances.

Activities 1
Promoting participation

Monica Bonilauri and Elisa Rossi

Chapter 6 investigates the interactions between adults and children/adolescents in villages and summer camps, considering if and in which ways adults' actions promote children's/adolescents' participation and involvement in decision-making. The analysis reveals that in villages communication processes between children and adults are primarily structured as educational disempowering monologues, while a systematic promotion of children's participation seems difficult to achieve, and ambivalences and oscillations are recurrent in interactions. In summer camps, where disempowering monologues and ambivalences are less frequently produced than in villages, a variety of adults' dialogic actions succeeds in promoting and supporting adolescents' self-expression and active participation, but it frequently fails to create effective coordination among adolescents' contributions, chiefly promoting communication just between adults and adolescents.

6.1   Education and promotion of participation

This chapter analyses interactions between adults and children/adolescents in villages and summer camps, considering if and how adults' actions promote children's and adolescents' participation, self-expression, and involvement in decision-making and negotiation of meanings.

The CISV narrative of education relies on children's active participation (Banks 1999; Van Agt 2001; Kankaslahti 2004). Promotion of intercultural citizenship is seen as the outcome of autonomous and responsible participation to intercultural communication; children learn to be citizens through their participation in practices that make up their lives. As we have seen in Chapter 1, however, education implies hierarchical relationships, cognitive and normative expectations about role performances, and roles of experts who should mould personalities. Children/adolescents are expected to adhere to this perspective and adults assess their contributions in terms of correct/incorrect performances. We have also seen that recent sociological approaches to childhood suggest that education does not sufficiently consider children's agency and active participation, when this takes the form of a monologue.

In villages, we have analysed educational activities such as cooperation, trust and simulation games, which require the greatest amount of verbal communication among participants. In these interactions, children's participation is supported through adults' management. Different ways of leading children's activities can be observed, with different consequences for children's opportunities to actively participate in the interaction. In summer camps, we have observed activities concerning the planning of games, trust/cooperation/simulation games, discussion/cultural activities, debriefing sessions, and camp meetings. While the whole typology aims to promote adolescents' participation, planning groups and camp meetings seek specifically to foster their active involvement in decision-making, i.e. to promote their agency and empowerment. In particular, camp meetings give the chance to launch proposals and make decisions in order to change some organisational aspects (e.g. daily schedules), although not main rules, which cannot be modified.

Our analysis aims to map out a broad picture of adults' interventions inside groups of children and adolescents, in order to identify communicative conditions and forms of participation. We will analyze which forms of communication are created in the interaction, and which are the consequences for children's and adolescents' participation.

6.2   Monologues: Focusing on tasks and normative expectations

Our analysis reveals that communication processes between children and adults are often structured as educational monologues.

In S1, children are working in small groups and are asked to make a poster concerning what they think peace might be. JFbra tries to guide the interaction towards a specific goal (turn 1), inviting the children to adapt to her cognitive expectations (finishing the work) and to respect her normative expectations (stick to the allotted time). In turns 2–9, the children try to organise their work in order to adapt to these expectations. However, JFbra interrupts their work (turn 11) to direct their actions to the right way to accomplish the task, implicitly assessing their previous contributions as not proper (*'that would be better'*). The opening of this distinction between a right way and wrong way of doing produces a paradox in communication: the doubtful content (*'maybe'*) is contradicted by the emphasized tone. In fact, JFbra does not accept the children's choices (turns 12–15): she treats them as not being able to make autonomous choices and normatively imposes a new organisation (turn 17). JFbra's action requires the children to conform to predefined ways of doing, thus preventing their involvement in the decision-making process. She projects the cultural relevance of children's perfor-mances in the interaction, and the children adapt to it (turns 20-25). However, the performance is blocked in a conflict between two groups of children, which is visible in MBra's non-verbal reaction (turn 26). JFbra glosses over the problem and keeps on telling the children what they are expected to do (turn 27); her ac-tion focuses on the results of the activity, rather than on the ongoing interaction.

(S1)

1. JFbra: **boys you have five minutes to finish and put it (out)**
2. Mfar: ok now the paper -
3. Mswe: the paper -
4. Mfar: can someone of you make to (repair) the paper?
5. Mcan: we need to do all the things on the wall?
6. Mswe: yeah, we'll put up   [there on the wall
7. JFbra: [now
8. ((*Confusion of voices*))
9. Mjor: do we stuck the (pole)? Because the pole is supposed to be here [pointing at the poster]
10. Mind: yeah just stuck all of this   [and (??)
11. JFbra: [**maybe** some of you can fix and some of you can start cleaning the mess, [**that would be better**
12. Mswe: [I can fix
13. Mjor: I can fix
14. M(??):   yeah
15. Mfar: I will fix in
16. ((*Confusion of voices*))
17. JFbra: Ok I think is funny because none of you is fixing besides Z. ((*MJor*)) and S. ((*MFar*)) and if one else has to clean, everyone is start fixing! **Guys, ok, split! Half of you clean, half of you fix**
18. ((*Confusion of voices*))
19. JFbra: Ok T. ((*MTai*)) **you fix, erm** J. ((*MSwe*)) **cleaning, and you three fix** ((*pointing at MJor, MInd, MFar*)), (.) F. ((*MBra*)) **fix it, no clean it!**
20. Mind: you see all the pen, <u>all</u> this, all <u>this</u> ((*he shows the colour pens*)) (material), (hold the pen)
21. Mfar: just all the paper, you just leave the paper we have, because you are cleaning and-
22. ((*Children in charge of cleaning start to pick up the papers*))
23. Mfar: <u>hold</u> please! ((*looking at MBra, who is throwing away some papers*)), <u>There is a paper</u> who is supposed to fix, don't put the-

24. Mjor: we're done *((To MSwe, who snorts))*
25. Mfar: J., F. we're supposed to fix them!
26. *((MBra throws the paper he has picked up at MFar))*
27. JFbra: **yeah, well, <u>now</u> (you concentrate the works)** *((To the group of children who are in charge of fixing the work))*

JFbra systematically ignores the ways in which the communication process may affect children's interactional uptake, focusing on the task and on children's performances. She focuses on cognitive and normative expectations, never appreciates children's actions and never checks their perceptions.

In S2, which is the continuation of S1, JFbra insists on calling for the children's performance (turns 29, 34). The children show their disorientation about what JFbra is expecting from them (turns 31–44). JFbra's reaction stresses the hierarchical structure of the interaction: in turn 45, JFbra presents herself as an expert who cannot be wrong, because she is the only knowledgeable person and treats the children as incompetent individuals, who are normatively asked to adapt to her requests ('*you* did it, not *me*! I'm not cleaning for you!'). By emphasizing the word pronouns *me* and *you*, JFbra stresses the role hierarchy, negatively assessing the children's ability to participate in the communication process as autonomous individuals. This kind of action projects the children's passive alignment: they ask for permission before taking action (turns 46, 47) subordinating their self-expression to JFbra's normative expectations. JFbra confirms this hierarchy in turn 48 by giving orders to the children.

(S2, continuation of S1)
28. *((Children are keeping on cleaning and fixing the work))*
29. JFbra: **cleaning, <u>cleaning</u>! the paper off**
30. *((Children keeps on cleaning the room))*
31. MJor: we have to present (that)?
32. Mswe: you have something more *((to Mind))*
33. *((Confusion of voices and noise))*
34. JFBra: **you have only** (??) everything I gave to you
35. Mswe: *((while showing MFar some pieces of paper))* (Do you need this piece on)?
36. M(??):   you have to sit down!
37. Mfar: clean every paper *((to MSwe))*
38. *((Confusion of voices))*
39. Mfar: who told-? *((to JFbra))*
40. JFbra: what?
41. Mfar: did you tell anybody to throw (the paper)?
42. JFbra: why did I do that?
43. Mfar: J. *((Mswe))* who told you to-?
44. Mswe: (she) told us bin, where it is

45. JFbra: <u>me:?</u> <u>I told you to clean</u>, I didn't told you to, to: (.) throw your job away, <u>you</u> did it, not me! I'm not cleaning for you!
46. Mswe: so can we (use this)? *((to MFar))*
47. Mind: can we (??) *((to JFbra))*
48. JFbra: put the paper on, put all the (pen) in the box!

S1 and S2 exemplify a frequent structure of the interaction between adults and children during the activities: a monologue in which children's participation is subordinated to adults' direction. In these cases, adults preserve their primacy in competence by means of assessments, which are associated with a role hierarchy and preserve their socio-epistemic claims (see Chapter 4) in distinguishing right and wrong, relevant and irrelevant topics, fixing a hierarchical distribution of competence and rights of access to competence.

We can notice, however, a difference between S1 and S2 concerning the organisation of turns and the prevailing forms of expectations. In S1, children never select JFbra as their principal interlocutor, while JFbra self-selects five times as next speaker (turns 7, 11, 17, 19, 27). In S2, children tend to select JFbra as their interlocutor (turns 31, 39, 41, 47), while she self-selects herself only once (turn 45). In S2, the interaction between JFbra and the children mostly takes the form of a question-answer pair, in which children ask for clarifications and JFbra answers confirming the role hierarchy in place (turns 31–34, 39–40, 41–42, 47–48). We may consider this as the children's reaction to the communication block engendered in the last part of S1. While JFbra glosses over this block, the children try to manage it, but the hierarchical structure of the interaction leads them to make requests to the 'expert': children look to JFbra as the person in charge of directing their actions.

S1 and S2 show how hierarchical structures are constructed in the interaction. JFbra starts fixing primary expectations. She confirms them during the first part of the interaction, ignoring the children's difficulties, and then acts as an expert who is directing the interaction. JFbra's actions may be interpreted as normative attempts to improve the children's abilities and autonomy in doing their job. JFbra focuses on tasks, rather than on the communication process, and this prevents her from empowering children to act.

In S3, which is about the game *Life Boat*, the adult's socio-epistemic claim is not associated to assessments. Children are working in small groups, each child representing a particular character, and each group deciding which characters should be thrown out of the boat. There are three characters left: a pregnant secretary, a single young doctor, and an old governor, married and with two daughters. Leaders have asked children to save one of them. LFmex coordinates the interaction. Her assertion in turn 1 can be interpreted as follows: it is easy to make a choice either because (a) there are only three characters left, or because (b) its cultural presupposition is clear. Her statement initiates a monologue, which does not leave space for children's expression: Mecu's attempt to introduce his perspective in the interaction (turn 3) is rejected by LFmex (turn 6), and this projects Fpor's alignment (turn 7).

(S3)

1. LFmex: well, we have to choose one to be alive, **it's easy**, we choose the one who has to stay alive
2. Meng: eh:: the one who stays alive is she *((pointing at FMex, the pregnant secretary))* I think
3. Mecu: I did'n- I think (you're right) because the person (??) is not important, she's a secretary and she can't survive alone 'coz she can no- she can't do lot of things
4. LFmex: eh tenemos –
           eh we have to -
5. Fmex: pero si la matas
           but if you kill her
6. LFmex: **tenemos que (??) (cuidar) cada vida** (02) a ver
           ***we should (??) (take care of) every life** (02) let's see*
7. Fpor: **it's ok**

LFmex aims to propose a single set of cultural values. Her use of code-switching shows that she wants to be sure that Mecu and Mmex understand the meaning of the game, which is to demonstrate that killing people is not the right thing to do. This narrative is normatively made explicit, and made linguistically clear when Mecu seems to deviate from it (turn 3).

Monologues are often constructed through the use of particular rituals, which are repeated every day during the activities. These rituals employ standardized formulae, which are left incomplete to elicit children's predictable choral completions. One of these rituals is the emphatic and cooperative pronunciation of the word 'CISV' in a specific form of adjacency pair. In S4, LFnzl starts the word pronouncing the first phoneme (turn 1), but the children do not provide the expected emphasis (turn 2), and LFnzl reinforces the rule repeating the phoneme in a much louder voice (turn 3). In turn 5, she assesses the children's new attempt as positively aligned to her intention.

(S4)

1. LFNzl: C I!
2. Children: S V! *((in a low voice volume and an annoyed tone))*
3. LFNzl: C I:! *((in a much louder voice))*
4. Children: S V:! *((with a higher voice volume))*
5. LFNzl: that's better

This ritual is repeated in villages to re-establish social order through (1) the reproduction of the 'we-village' community identity (Chapter 3), and (2) the reproduction of hierarchical structures, as only adults are allowed to initiate the adjacency pair ('*C I*'). As a result, as we can see in S5, children's participation is strictly regulated, although some deviation is still temporarily possible.

In S1 and S2, children act primarily on the basis of expected role performances (cleaning, fixing). The interaction is oriented towards the goals established, while children are not asked to participate in the construction of their meanings. The result is a competitive form of communication, which favours conflicts between children, and passive alignment to adult's perspectives. In S3 and S4, adults ask children to adapt to specific cultural monologues. The unpredictability that may arise from children's empowerment is controlled, stressing CISV basic rules and values and avoiding conceding opportunities for children's agency.

In villages, children are progressively led to learn the meanings of correct actions. They can express their dissent refusing to act in the expected way, but adults' normative interventions can easily restore the social order and strengthen the consensus about CISV basic values. Children's alignment to their leaders' claims and assessments recurrently reproduce the primacy of normative expectations and role hierarchies.

While this can be useful for the regular development of activities and the accomplishment of tasks, the analysis shows that a systematic use of educational monologues restricts children's opportunities of active participation.

In summer camps, monologues are less frequent than in villages. At the beginning of summer camps, leaders and staff members provide explanations and presentations for adolescents, concerning rules and procedures. They explain and present contents and topics in extended turns, while adolescents simply listen to them, or to their leaders' translations. These interactions, which highlight hierarchical structures, are somehow expected. In this sense, we can distinguish these *accepted* monologues, in which adults are expected to illustrate rules and organisational aspects, and to explain useful contents for the activity, from *imposed* monologues.

Monologues are imposed when, especially in debriefing sessions or in camp meetings, leaders and even staff members either take their turns when they are not supposed to do it, or do not involve adolescents in communicative processes, selecting only few participants as interlocutors and failing in distributing equal opportunities to talk and in supporting a generalised self-expression. Moreover, monologues are imposed when adults introduce cognitive and normative expectations in the interaction, emphasising their role as experts, negatively assessing adolescents' contributions, and directing their reflection.

In S5, LFdut, who is supposed to facilitate the planning group, engages in a long monologue (turn 1) in which she judges as partially inadequate the preparation and presentation of the previously planned activity, introducing the distinction "right/wrong way of doing things", through an other-disclaiming 'but'. In addition, she emphasises the importance of achieving the task and *saving her face* (Goffman 1967), i.e. her reputation in front of the other camp participants (*'I felt I was doing a bit too much the presentation for the activities and that's probably because we didn't plan it, because we said "do that, that's fine" but we didn't try it'*), with another disclaiming 'but' coupled with a change of footing (from 'I' to 'we'), which signals the negative involvement of adolescents, rather than focusing on the communication process. Finally, she complains about this process, through a self-disclaiming 'but'. Moreover, LFdut's action shows a contradiction: she underlines her wish to take a step back from the interaction and the planning process, but at the very same time she maintains the turn and anticipates 'what to do and how to do' it, with the consequence of controlling and limiting adolescents' self-expression. LFdut's educational monologue blocks adolescents' participation. She ignores Mcan's attempt at making a proposal and continues to guide the interaction (turn 3). Adolescents remain silent and thus withdraw from the planning process; LFdut confirms her concern for saving her reputation as leader (turn 5) through a 'but' which works as an indirect other-disclaimer, implicitly referring to the adolescents' responsibility.

(S5)

1. LFdut: ok. Well, I just feel that, I mean **I thought it was great and I think people enjoyed it, which is pretty good, but I do think that the preparation could be better.** Because we were stressing about (?), no it's not your fault *((looking at the Finnish girl))*, I'm not saying it, I'm saying that we were stressing about it and you know *((to the Belgian girl))* I asked you to do to do the presentation and you had no idea, you didn't know *((the Belgian girl seems to agree))*, right? […] **I mean** next time maybe **we should, today we should plan a bit better, so that you can all explain this game really well** […]. **I think that's quite important,** because I think you are the planning group, ah? You are, it's not me and **I felt I was doing a bit too much the presentation for the activities and that's probably because we didn't plan it, because we said "do that, that's fine" but we didn't try it.** I mean *((looking at the Italian boy))* you didn't feel comfortable with the explaining, did you? **But maybe if we have done it before,** if we had tried, we have exercise, we have practice, maybe next time it's easier (??) ok? Somebody needs to present the game. So who wants to do that? Explain the game to all and somebody that has to do the discussion afterwards *((the Finnish girl looks frightened))*

2. Mcan: what we can do is take up four or five questions and use those to (??) (..)
3. LFdut: so I need volunteers: I need somebody to present the game and to explain
to everyone and I need somebody to lead discussion
4. (04)
5. LFdut: I know it's hard **but I don't want to be in the same situation of today**

In S6, while adolescents are negotiating some proposals (turns 1-9, 11-13) during a camp meeting, SFita takes a hierarchical stance and claims that the staff is responsible for the final decision (turns 10, 14), marking her position with a disclaiming 'but'. In turn 10, a self-disclaiming 'but' reinforces her role, while the 'but' in turn 14 has an other-disclaiming function. This action deprives adolescents of their decisional power and projects both the disappointment of their affective expectations (self-expression and autonomous choices) and their adaptation to the adult's normative perspective.

(S6)
1. M1can: someone else? (..) ok. We have a proposition for tonight: sleep over
2. *((Someone applauds, someone else asks to sleep over the following night))*
3. F1dut: just one thing. Erm we want to do tonight because tonight there's one
delegation leaving and tomorrow night there are already three delegations
gone so –
4. Group: yea!
5. F2eng: yeah, sleep over tonight *((someone says yea!))* and tomorrow *((someone
says yea!))*
6. M1can: everyone agrees on that?
7. *((Someone applauds, someone raises the hand))*
8. F2eng: yea, everybody is agreeing
9. M1can: ok *((giving the turn to the staff member))*
10. SFita: you have to keep in mind that tomorrow will be a really hard day. We have
to clean up everything and also we planned to stay awake all the night all
together, yeah without Finland, **but (.) yeah I think that it will be too
much don't sleep for two days.** We will have a great evening tonight, we
will visit the bell of peace and we will come back late. So, I don't know.
We can discuss it in the staff meeting and leaders meeting but (.) *((smiling
a bit))* **I'm not so sure that you can don't sleep tonight.** Maybe we can
make something with our friends from Finland but not don't sleep, **I
don't think so** (…)
11. F2eng: yea, it's our final night of the whole camp and yea, you are supposed
to spend it all together, so we can't just do it tomorrow without three
delegations
12. F1dut: I make erm I have a suggestion. What we may do is that we stay awake
until Finland has left (…) so we all spend as long as we could all together

but we can also sleep. And if we also sleep on the bus I think we can manage just to have enough sleep for cleaning tomorrow. And then we have sleep over tomorrow too

13. *((Discussion among adolescents goes on and leads to several proposals as well as to some decisions))*

14. SFita: *((seriously))* I already said that we have to think about it with leaders and staff. **You are not allowed to take a decision about the bedtime.** So, we'll try to do our best **but please don't (..) repeat always the same stuff**

In S7, SF2ita imposes her decision on the adolescents, blocking their participation and therefore any further possibility to discuss the issue (turns 1, 3, and 5). In turn 5, a self-disclaiming 'but' enhances SF2ita's role, introducing her self-positioning as responsible member of the camp staff.

(S7)

1. SF2ita: one thing (.) ahm (01) since we hear from you that you are tired, tired and tired and tomorrow we have a hike and you are gonna wake up at 8, **tomorrow sleep time will be at midnight**

2. SMita: tonight

3. SF2ita: so don't be (.) today, today. **So there won't be anything to discuss about**

4. F1arg: we were talking (??) I have been the last two days I've been going to sleep at 11.30, 12 and   [I'm-

5. SF2ita: [it's, it's not, **it's something we decided.** I don't, you take the decision, **but if we see that so many people get sick,** it's something for the security of you and your health and tomorrow you are going to walk in the mountain, so we don't want to see anyone fainting or things like that, **so we have to take this decision as a staff.** Ok?

To sum up, in villages and summer camps, monologues tend to be based on:

1. Turn dominance, frequently adopted in debriefing sessions and discussions during the activities;
2. Unequal distribution of participation;
3. Negative assessment of children's and adolescents' contributions, especially during activities and their planning;
4. Role hierarchy and power stances, emerging especially in camp meetings in summer camps.

Monologues restrict the possibilities for adolescents' full and active participation: adults' actions primarily project their passive adaptation to cognitive and normative expectations and their marginalisation in the interaction especially when differences in linguistic competence, viewpoints and choices are not seriously taken into account.

6.3   Empowering dialogue

6.3.1 Summer camps

In summer camps, empowering dialogue is particularly visible during activity planning, when leaders are asked to facilitate negotiations of proposals among adolescents, coordinate their decision-making, and mediate their conflicts. In these cases, leaders' actions display their intention to foster and support adolescents' active participation and self-expression in the interaction.

In S8, F1arg's personal expressions (turns 1, 4) are supported by LFgre's continuers and acknowledgement tokens (turns 3, 5), which stimulate F1arg's checking of the leader's understanding (turn 8). In the subsequent turns, LFgre seeks to improve her own understanding of the planned activity through questions which invite clarifications (turns 11, 14, 16). In these turns, LFgre's formulations make the adolescents' proposal explicit through promotional questions (turn 11, 14) and a hypothesis (turn 16). This is an example of how a leader can follow and support adolescents' expression of proposals, although LFgre does not act to involve the rest of the group.

(S8)

1. F1arg: ah for example (…) ah:m he can't see ah we put like an activity that he, he, he (?) can't do, only he can do and I need to (.) to: (.) to cross ahm one place without ahm falling with some objects and the other ahm, the other participants in that group have to tell him what   [where he have to go

2. M1dan: [where he can go

3. LFgre: **mm mmm**

4. F1arg: so that he doesn't fall and in that way they are helping him

5. LFgre: **yea**

6. F1arg: ahm although she can't see

7. F1ita: ok

8. F1arg: **do you understand?**

9. LFgre: yea, I understood

10. M1dan: I also   [have

11. LFgre: [**but there, there are gonna be six groups and the six groups are gonna do something at the same time?**

12. (02)

13. F1arg: no, no! they are gonna be in different places

14. LFgre: **yea, so they are gonna be in different places at the same time doing different things?**

15. F1arg: yes and then they are going to (.) change, like to go around

16. LFgre: **so every group has to go to every –**

17. F1arg: every situation yea

In S9, LMcos supports adolescents' active participation and self-expression. Firstly, he stimulates their ideas and preferences through promotional questions (turns 1, 10, 14, 18, 20), sometimes referring to their past experience of CISV activities (turns 8, 12). Secondly, he appreciates their proposals (turns 5, 8; in turn 8 the appreciative function of '*ahhh*' is remarkable). Thirdly, he shows affective closeness through non verbal actions (turn 12). Fourthly, he actively listens using continuers at the beginning of the turn (turns 10, 18, 23). Fifthly, he actively proposes personal ideas (turns 3, 10), leaving the participants free to choose and decide on the basis of their preferences and previous experience. Finally, he performs linguistic mediation (turn 18). In turns 21–23, the achievement of coordination between the leader and adolescents is demonstrated by a triple echo ('*picture game*').

(S9)

1. LMcos: **is there any song you would like to sing or -? Do you have any to suggest?**
2. Mcos: no
3. LMcos: **ok** (.) let me think, **it's like a sing, dance, energizer –**
4. Ffin: (??)
5. LMcos: **yea yea!** "One, two, three, four"!!
6. Ffin: "five, six, seven, eight"!!
7. *((The leader simulates the energizer together with the Finnish girl; the Dutch girl suggests something that is inaudible))*
8. LMcos: **ahhhh!!!** The chain of love. **Do you remember it?**
9. Fola: yea
10. LMcos: ok, so (..) activity. **We can have activity** (03) ok let's start with (03) **would you like to run, or would you like to do some arts and crafts, or would you like to do some drama – ?**
11. (05)
12. LMcos: *((putting his hand on the Finnish girl's shoulder))* **do you remember any activity from your** (..) **from your** (..) **minicamp?**
13. Ffin: I don't remember
14. LMcos: **you don't remember?**
15. Ffin: no
16. LMcos: **all right** (..) *((to his delegate))* **E. do you remember the activities you liked?**
17. *((His delegate answers something in Spanish))*
18. LMcos: **ok. Erm** (.) **in a summer camp we did this activity that he is talking about** *((he describes the game in Spanish))* **Do you think you like something like this?**
19. Mnor: yea
20. LMcos: **how should we name it?**

21. Mnor: *((smiling))* **picture game**
22. Mcos: **picture game**
23. LMcos: **picture game. Ok, let's make like (..) erm bigger ideas and then we start**

In S10, LFcan stimulates adolescents' reflection with promotional questions (turns 1, 5), she distributes equal opportunities of self-expression, trying to give voice to males, and fosters active listening through echoes (turns 3, 13). Finally, the leader promotes acknowledgment of diversity formulating the different proposals and giving adolescents the chance to decide autonomously (turn 11). Although F1bra tends to prevail in the interaction (in turn 6 she steals the turn from M1dan), LFcan's actions succeed in getting the boys involved, in promoting the expression of their ideas, and also in activating some exchanges between the adolescents (turns 6–7; 14–15), achieving dialogic mediation.

(S10)
1. LFcan: **what do you think? (03) Your idea was to have two, like you would say maybe commoner and something else?**
2. F1bra: ah::m I, I was thinking special
3. LFcan: **special/perfect**
4. F1bra: yea special and it doesn't have to be perfect, we are perfect as we are
5. LFcan: **what do you guys think? Did you hear what she said? Hh did you guys listened to that?**
6. F1bra: is perfect, but (.) he's perfect but we are also perfect, like for us we are perfect
7. M1dan: we are perfect selves
8. *((LFcan smiles))*
9. LFcan: ok
10. F1bra: but the commoners (?) it
11. LFcan: **so we have two ideas: we can call it special/perfect or the common-commoner (03) it's up to you guys, whatever you think**
12. M1ita: special/common
13. LFcan: **special/commoner?**
14. M1dan: let's do that
15. F1bra: yea::hhh

In S11, LFgre's actions facilitate F1ita's understanding and participation in the activity planning. F1ita's proposals (turns 1, 3, 5) project firstly LFgre's continuer (turn 2) and secondly her check of meanings (turn 4). This stimulates F1ita's check on understanding, which is addressed to F1arg (turn 5), and promotes a dyadic exchange (turns 6–7, 11–14). LFgre supports this exchange formulating the meanings of F1ita's proposal (turns 8, 10), and F1ita confirms the meaning of LFgre's formulations (turns 9, 11). The effects of LFgre's dialogic actions emerge in turns 12 and 14, when F1arg displays her understanding of F1ita's proposal, which has been mediated by the leader.

(S11)
1. F1ita:	yea but we can do the: (.) they (02) we can ahm no they can: use another, another sense, because the eyes are, must use
2. LFgre:	**mm mm**
3. F1ita:	you must use
4. LFgre:	**because it's night you mean? we must use them?**
5. F1ita:	yea, we must use (both the eyes) (??) you understand?
6. F1arg:	no
7. F1ita:	but
8. LFgre:	**they cannot see**
9. F1ita:	yea
10. LFgre:	**so they must use another sense**
11. F1ita:	*((nodding))* another sense
12. F1arg:	ahh! I understand
13. F1ita:	yea. And we can ahm I don't know do: ahm a (?) or (?)
14. F1arg:	ah I understand! I understand what she's saying

To sum up, leaders promote equal opportunities of participation and facilitate adolescents' reflections mainly in two ways.

1. Asking promotional questions (S8, turns 11, 14; S9, turns 1, 8, 10, 12, 14, 18, 20; S10, 1, 5). S12 is a short example focused on promotional questions (turn 4).

(S12)
1. SF1ita:	so we – erm: this was supposed to be only to introduce yourselves, so: after they find the solution for example 'Philippines', you know, maybe you can say-
2. LMpor:	your name
3. SF1ita:	I'm George and something of you and in the same way all of us and this is the introduction and then: (..) after that?
4. LMpor:	**what do you think? (3) do you have any ideas for games?**
5. (04)	
6. Mecu1:	no running games
7. LMpor:	no

2. Inviting them to self-express and reflect through continuers (S8, turns 1, 4; S9, turns 10, 18, 23), acknowledgement tokens (S8, turns 3, 5), echoes (S10, turns 3, 13) and, less frequently, direct incitements as in S13 (turn 5), S14 (turn 4), and S15 (turns 1, 3).

(S13)
1. F2por: I think that it's a good idea
2. F2bra: to mix (.) both the situations (.) like the ones who – ?
3. F2por: *((whispering))* yes, because it gets more (.) ideas
4. (03)
5. LMspa: **come on girls (..) come on girls**
6. (..)
7. F2bra: *((to F2ita))* try to say what do you think in English and I can help you with the Italian

(S14)
1. LFecu: I don't know if we can do water games
2. SF2ita: maybe mini mini mini banana without water
3. LFecu: ok (.) and-
4. LMbra: **wait, wait, wait. Simon** *((M2phi))* **wants to say something** *((M2phi didn't speak very much during the whole camp))*
5. M2phi: when we will get the lunch?

(S15)
1. LFgre: **just say whatever you have in your mind**, don't ahm you know, ahm keep it
2. M1dan: yea
3. LFgre: **just say**
4. M1dan: yea, it could be a good idea (…) just thinking what we could do with it

Moreover, leaders support adolescents' self-expression in three ways.

1. Appreciating their contributions (S9, turns 5, 8). S16 is a short example focused on appreciation (turns 1, 4).

(S16)
((The planning group shows the trust game))
1. LFcan: <u>**That's so cool! It's amazing!**</u>
2. F2dan: that's a real trust game!
3. F(?):   I wanna do it everyday!
4. LFcan: **That's <u>awesome</u>**
5. F2dan: then we are going to do, we are going to –

2. Formulating the meanings expressed by them (S8, turns 11, 14, 16; S11, turns 8, 10). S17 is a short example focused on formulation (turn 4).

(S17)
1. F2ita: a group of person (02) –

2. LMspa: ya?

3. F2ita: talk together (..) and another group (..) with (..) book or: another thing (..) but don't do together the two group (..) so (..) –

4. LMspa: ya. **So, there is a group of people which talk together, but there are other group of shy, probably** (.) with less people which are a bit a bit apart (.) so: they look at the most talk like together and having a lot of fun and the shy just can't join because they are shy. (..) Do – do you mean that? In that way?

5. F2ita: ya

6. F2bra: maybe we can do like a for example here. Two groups of two talkative and two shy. And the two talk together and the two shy they just stay there and without talking to each other

7. LMspa: ya

3.   Formulating differences between their positions (S10, turn 11). S18 is a short example focused on this kind of formulation (turn 10).

(S18)

1. M2ita: can guys shut up, please? (.) Booga lu, the shark one-

2. F1phi: train of love

3. Different voices: no: no: *((F1phi smiles))*

4. M2ita: ok, the other one, the "pollo" one and another one.

5. M2spa: pelota de ping pong.

6. F2por: *((singing))* pelota de ping pong y boto, boto, boto por todo mi salón, si te toco botas

7. M2spa: we all have to do this.

8. M2ita: erm: *((very self-confident))* so we have to choose three or four warms up-

9. M2spa: five

10. LFecu: **so we have the booga lu, we have the shark one, the pollo –**

Finally, leaders actively suggest actions, without imposing their perspectives, rather introducing alternative narratives (S9, turns 3, 10). S19 is a short example focused on this kind of suggestion (turn 3).

(S19)

1. LFgre: mm mm, a game

2. M1ind: (it can be a game or not?)

3. LFgre: yea *((shrugging her shoulders))* (02) we can, you know some games (?) from your countries, from CISV and maybe **we can use these games or maybe we invent a game** a:nd ah:m find some ways to relate that to the theme (02) do you, do you have anything in mind like a: game that might

be something like that but not exactly? What maybe we can make it? (.) I, I go to take a chair

4. (13)

5. LFgre: mm?

6. (09)

7. F1arg: ahm a:hm because when we made the activity, the cultural activity (we do it in Argentina) we have to do it like ahm related to that country, what flows under the city of Buenos Aires (and all that) so now it's, it's like very ahm general the theme *((LFgre is nodding))* (.) ahm we can't relate it to a country in special or something like that because it's very –

The analysis presented in this section shows leaders' dialogic actions which succeed in promoting and supporting adolescents' self-expression and active participation. Leaders may also act as mediators able to improve adolescents' understanding and get them more involved in decision-making. In these situations, adolescents are treated as autonomous individuals who can express their personal emotions and ideas, whereas cognitive/normative expectations and evaluation of role performances are not important. However, leaders' promotion of participation may fail in creating effective coordination among adolescents' contributions, promoting only adult-adolescent interactions, especially when their dialogic actions include only, or mainly, promotional questions and cues for active listening, while effective adults' mediation is not frequent.

6.3.2 Villages

In villages, during activities with children, adults' dialogic actions are much more infrequent.

In S20, children must decide the plot of a short drama. In turn 1, LFeng proposes the organisation of space to guarantee equal distribution of opportunities for children's active participation and self-expression. In the subsequent turns, LFeng recurrently confirms and supports children's contributions, appreciating their actions and experiences, ignoring role performances and cognitive expectations. She recurrently uses continuers ('*ok*', '*yeah*') and promotional questions (turns 3, 5, 7, 9, 12, 18, 25, 29). She also invites into the conversation children who appear to be less active (turns 27, 31), and, less frequently, she makes short positive comments about children's ideas. This appreciation is expressed as personal attitude ('*I like*' in turns 27, 39). In turns 14 and 16, LFeng formulates children's previous turns in order to clarify their meanings. This action has a twofold effect: giving linguistic support to Mdut and showing interest for his action, thus encouraging him to maintain his active participation. Finally, LFeng asks children to decide autonomously (turns 39, 41). LFeng treats all children's contributions as equal, guaranteeing their generalized active participation. LFeng's actions enable children's involvement in co-constructing knowledge, and their self-selection as participants. This is particularly effective in turns 32–38. In turn 33, some children help Mfra in finding an English term, hindering LFeng's contribution (turn 34). In turn 35, Mecu tries to formulate Mfra's proposal, producing a multilingual turn in which he uses the French word for "door" ('*porte*') to make it more comprehensible for Mfra. The series of turns (32–36) about the translation *door/porte* shows the effective cooperation between the children and the adult in enhancing shared meanings, and promoting the inclusion of Mfra's perspective, who can express his ideas about the story in French without any problems (turn 37) or interruptions. At the end of turn 37, Mfra's laughter projects the other children's sharing of it (turn 38), which displays affective expectations, thus stressing the importance of participants' self-expression and leaving aside their performances. Finally, in turns 39–41, LFeng coordinates this process towards a shared conclusion, including Mfra's contribution among the possible choices. In this way, a narrative has been created through a coordinated negotiation process. This is confirmed by FMex's introduction of a personal variation in the story (turn 43), which is accepted by the other participants (turn 44).

(S20)

1. LFeng: Ok, let's go round the circle, everyone say their idea, ok so F. *((MEcu))*
2. Mecu: <u>ok</u> like you said if (there's) someone going to act like the lemon said "I am the lemon" and just (..) and or he or she have it (.) and someone be the (??) (the only character) and there was a- in the door there was a thing that said no kids and they work it. So they enter and they find a spider web with a (.) a spider. And (..) then that's the problem that they got catching the spider web
3. LFeng: <u>ok</u>, **ok**
4. Mecu: and -
5. LFeng: **that's good**, at least it's one idea. Anybody else has got some idea?
6. Mdut: there were three kids and they were looking for that bottle with (.) magic water and
7. LFeng: **ok**
8. Mdut: they go to, with a bus
9. LFeng: **ok yeah**
10. Mecu: ah yeah
11. Mdut: to a house
12. LFeng: **yeah**
13. Mdut: and (..) (they (.) don't allow kids)
14. LFeng: **so the house says "no kids allowed"**

15. Mdut: yeah
16. LFeng: **for the magic water's inside the house**
17. Mdut: yeah
18. LFeng: **ok,**   [ok
19. Mdut: [and they have (..) And they have a (lemon)
20. Fmex: yeah::!
21. Mdut: and they find a spider web and beyond the spider web there's the bottle with magic water and they (throw) the lemon to destroy the spider web
22. Mnor: [and take
23. Mdut: [and then -
24. Musa: yeah.
25. LFeng: **ok,**   [ok
26. Mita: [and when we take the magic water (.) we drink (02) and we can fly
27. LFeng: **ok ok ok! I like that idea** OK! **what's [your idea?** *((pointing at MNor, who nods))*
28. Mnor: [(??) (leaders)
29. LFeng: **ok, your idea?**
30. Mnor: no – *((pointing at MDut))* his::
31. LFeng: **you like that one, ok! And A.** *((MFra))*?
32. Mfra: the: (02) example (..) Is indoors, one (..) carpet? No. porte *((door in French))*?
33. Some Children: door
34. LFeng: one door, door
35. Mecu: yeah one door on (??) [He takes the symbol of "No kids allowed"] why not (..) no (..) yeah, when: the porte *((door))*
36. LFeng: uhm
37. Mfra: il est (??) in (??) the porte eh: mis (it is (??) in (??) the door eh: put) on door and: (the people) and no kid and they (give) yes and when: ticket, bus ticket and: no: no kid and: and no (??) *((laughter))*!
38. Everybody: *((laughter))*
39. LFeng: ok well it's good, good, good start. **I like the house idea** so, ok? (.) do we want to go with P. *((MDut))*'s idea?
40. Some Children: yeah!
41. LFeng: do you like? Between the two, A. *((MFra))* and P. *((MDut))*'s idea of the house with the no kids sign and stuff, ok so?
42. Mita: P. *((MDut))* is a::
43. Fmex: yeah but the story begins with a (??) and a (lemon)
44. All children: yeah!

LFeng's actions are focused on the communication process, rather than on its results. She promotes dialogic mediation, treating the participants as autonomous individuals, who are able to express their personal choices. The focus is on children as persons, rather than on their roles, and children's actions are never assessed. These dialogic actions enhance a co-constructed narrative in the communication process; this kind of co-construction needs empowering dialogue, centred on children's personal expressions.

6.4   Ambivalences

In villages, a systematic promotion of children's participation seems difficult to achieve, while ambivalences are recurrent in the interaction, in two forms: (1) oscillations between monologues and dialogic actions, and (2) person-centred forms of education. In both of these forms, adults alternate different forms of action, projecting uncertainties in children's actions. The recurrence of this ambivalence in adults' actions is confirmed by the children's narrative of their experience (see Chapter 3).

S21 was recorded during the game called *Peace War Peace*. The groups of children involved have the task to build a 'perfect city'. In turn 1, LMpor teaches children how to draw a road, testing the effects of his action, and finally substituting children in the task. This kind of action is reproduced in turns 4 and 6. The ensuing hierarchical relationship provides a stable orientation to which children can refer in their actions: they make proposals that the adult-expert assesses according to her/his educational goals. In turn 8, LMpor addresses the children as persons, inviting them to take autonomous decisions ('*you can do whatever you want*'), but also stressing his role as expert, telling them what to do ('*and also you can go out of this paper, no?*'). Uncertainty is evident in Mdut's reaction in turn 9 and in the subsequent children's turns (10–13). Mjor tries to find a solution (turn 14), but LMpor stops him (turn 15). His normative action projects Fphi's self-selection (turn 16) before the first transitional relevant point, thus violating the turn-taking mechanism as LMpor has not concluded his turn yet. When LMpor moves away from the group, children become more active (turns 17–21), showing affective expectations which enhance appreciation for others' contributions (turn 21). LMPor's return is marked by normative assertions (turns 23, 26, 30), disclaiming them (in turn 23, through an other-disclaiming 'but'). However, in turn 33, he softens his normative expectations ('*Wait wait! You have to cut it*'), opening up opportunities for participation through a self-disclaiming 'but' ('*but that's a good idea*'). This opening is immediately contradicted by a new normative assessment which conveys a negative assessment of children's performances (turn 35). This sudden shift from dialogic action (end of turn 33) to monologue (turn 35) creates the conditions for a new block, which is visible in children's long silence, followed by embarrassed laughter (turn 37).

(S21)

1. LMpor: ((to MJor)) yes:, if you do a road, draw on use this paper to draw on the road, you (??) **do you understand?** the car, I mean (??) F. ((Mjor)) you can (??) ((the leader takes the pen that Mjor was using and he starts to draw instead of the child)) you (have to) do like this

2. Fita: °(??)°

3. M(??):   °(??)°

4. LMpor: you draw all the roads   [you put the cars here

5. Fphi: [I know I did a house

6. LMpor: you know? and then you can draw: a different back scores and stuff ((he keeps on drawing on the sheet of paper))

7. Mdut: but like we did few of (??) ?

8. LMpor: yes, you can do, **you can do whatever you want** ((he stops drawing and stands up)) (02) **and also you go (out of) this paper no?**

9. Mdut: **(I don't know)**

10. LMpor: bigger city

11. Fphi: it's really small!

12. LMpor: what?

13. Mdut: eh: th- I mean this   [(city)

14. Mjor: [no: are we gonna make like this here, we can-

15. LMpor: continue   [here you

16. Fphi: [I can make a house here (??) (02) now any (??)

17. ((LFjor comes into the room and LMpor moves away to talk with her. Children resume work at the 'city'))

18. Mjor: no no! it's a car! (??)

19. Fjor: (??)

20. Mjor: we can make a (car-shop) there

21. Fphi: yeah! it can be the (??)

22. ((LMpor goes where the children are))

23. LMpor: **but first I think you should draw the roads**

24. Mfra: (??)

25. LFjor: F. ((Mjor))! ((She takes a picture of Mjor))

26. LMpor: F. ((Mjor)) **you draw the roads, you do and helping her**

27. Mjor: ok

28. ((Confusion of voices for 20 seconds))

29. Fjor: (can) (??)?

30. LMpor: **no you can't**

31. Musa: (??) for that (??) ((he gives a sheet of paper to Mjor))

32. Mjor: I can (??) tape that. (02) You do it (??)   [because
33. LMpor: [wait wait! you have to cut it,
         but it's a good idea F. ((Mjor))
34. Musa: oh ok
35. LMpor: **continue to draw the road!** (03) A. ((Musa)) you (??) you can start (02)
         you can do A. ((Fita))
36. ((10 seconds of silence; the children stop working))
37. Children: ((laughter)) ((they look embarrassed))

The main result of this ambivalent form of communication is uncertainty of expectations and contributions. Adults' ambivalent actions project children's uncertain reactions, affecting the cultural presuppositions of the interaction and blocking the communication process. This process re-starts only when the source of the ambivalence disappears. The conclusion is that ambivalent sequences of dialogic and normative actions block children's active participation. The only way for the process to start again seems the shift to a stable form of communication.

The second ambivalent form of communication is person-centred education. In person-centred education, children's self-expression is considered central, but children are guided to the fulfilment of normative and cognitive expectations. It follows that the interaction is simultaneously based on affective and cognitive/normative expectations.

S22 concerns an activity which is called *Media game*. In the first phase, children have been divided into small groups and leaders have given to each group a newspaper, with photos and articles, saying that somebody stole the flag of the village. Children have been asked to discover who the thief is. Each group has been provided with a different newspaper with different pictures leading to a different suspect (leader, JC or staff member). In the second phase, all groups are provided with all newspapers, to compare them and find out who really stole the flag. S22 concerns this second phase. DMita promotes an ambivalent interactional structure. On the one hand, he formulates what children have said or done before, as a stimulus to project their reflection (turn 1, turn 32 first part). He also confirms children's previous contributions, through echoes (turns 8, 10, 21, 50) and formulations (turns 3, 17, 61). Finally, his linguistic support promotes children's participation (turns 63, 65). Through these actions, he shows his acceptance and acknowledgement, positively connoting the children. On the other hand, DMita continuously use questions and invitations to act, which direct children's attention to some elements that he has selected as important in understanding the "real" meaning of the activity (turns 5, 13, 23, 32 second part, 34, 36, 38, 40, 67), trying to adapt children's participation to his own perspective (turns 34, 36). For eight times, he invites them to look at pictures and newspapers and order them.

Such repeated invitation reveals his intention to lead children to a particular conclusion, which they are expected to discover 'by themselves'. Moreover, his feedback actions clarify the meaning of children's contributions and the cognitive consequences they have for the interaction (turns 15, 19, 42, 55, 57).

(S22)

1. DMita: ok. I want to say something. Ehm - the four groups read one newspaper and the conclusion were (.) two groups voted for F. ((*SFita*)), one for B. ((*SMfar*)) and one for S. (*(LFeng)*). **Take this into account**, I mean (..) just know that we have four- three suspects, B, S. and two times F.,
                            [so
2. Meng: [maybe it's M. ((*JMaus*))
3. DMita: **and for you is M.**
4. Fjor: yes we voted (??) new, like it's a new newspaper so we have more (pictures)
5. DMita: more (pictures). **So if you read them all and you see, and you watch at all the pictures –**
6. Fjor: I see F. ((*SFita*)) in one, (even in those)
7. Meng: M. ((*JMaus*))?
8. DMita: **you see F. and –**
9. Fphi: F. is in all the pictures
10. DMita: **F. is in all the pictures**
11. Fjor: she's in all pictures but (??)
12. ((*LFfra comes into the room to ask DMita if the group already has all the newspapers*))
13. DMita: the others they all left - the newspaper. Ok! (..) **what you- do you get more from the new - the other newspapers?**
14. Fjor: that F. went all around the school with gloves and a bucket
15. DMita: **are you saying that F. - what do you say?**
16. Fjor: F. is going around the all school with a bucket and gloves
17. DMita: **ok so F. is on- in all the newspapers**
18. Meng: but   [maybe
19. DMita: [and she's going around with that bucket and the? flag inside? no in the gloves, in glove   [and bucket
20. Meng: [maybe she was cleaning!
21. DMita: **maybe she's cleaning**
22. Meng: because the:: right
23. DMita: **what she's doing there?**
24. Meng.   [(??)
25. Fjor: [well I saw a glove beside the flag pole, yesterday
26. Meng: maybe M. ((*JMaus*)) has used it, or someone else has used it for - everyday is like they (??) F. ((*SFita*)) Could anyone (??) the glove

27. Fusa: maybe   [ehm: F.
28. DMita: [(??)
29. Fusa: (??) cleaning so much maybe, like maybe em - she was cleaning a lot and nobody was paying attention to her so maybe -
30. DMita: so ehm -
31. Meng: but why M. (had to) stay there?
32. DMita: **ok, we have F. in all the pictures, in all the newspapers, she's going around the camp with eh: with a flag. Maybe she's cleaning and she's- maybe she wants everyone for cleaning. This is. Now ehm - (..) let's, let's e: see how the story went, from the newspapers, how is the story?**
33. Fjor: you can do the story by holding all
34. DMita: **maybe the pictures have an order**
35. Fjor: yes
36. DMita: **ok, let's put them in order**
37. Fjor: over here I think it's the same as - [here
38. DMita: **[which is the, from the stealing thing which is the**
                                                    [first
39. Fjor: [S. *((LFeng))* and B. *((SMfar))* are (??)
40. DMita: **what is the first picture of the - stealing history?**
41. JFpor: it's in the morning probably
42. DMita: uhm. What did you say F. *((Fjor))*?
43. Meng: I think that is after, because L. *((DMita))* (??) just be not killed
44. (03)
45. DMita: hopefully he didn't kill me!
46. Everybody: <u>hhhh</u>!
47. DMita: lucky! eh: so
48. (02)
49. Meng: we know it's not S. *((LFita))*
50. DMita: **you know it's not S.**
51. Meng: well, I know (it's not S.)
52. (05)
53. Fjor: and why did she went no - why did she go on frontback door?
54. Meng: because possibly she was sleeping (??) or a lot people tonight
55. DMita: **are you chois- are you coming back to S.? you're going to back to S.?**
56. Fjor: yes
57. DMita: **oh ok! ok!**
58. Meng: she was going to graduate, wasn't she. That's when she was going back, possibly
59. Fmex: yes
60. Fjor: [or maybe the flag is in

61. DMita: [and G. *((Fmex))* is - she agrees
62. (03)
63. DMita: D. *((Mpor))* ven, ven aquì! vieni! mi- mira - em - (02) come si-
              come, come here! Come! Lo- look – em – (02) how do you- how do you say
              newspaper?
64. JFpor: *((She speaks in Portuguese))*
65. DMita: quieres traduccion? (..) no? sì? Dai!
              Do you need translation? (..) no? yes? Come on!
66. JFpor: *((She speaks in Portuguese))*
67. DMita: ok. The question you have to - to ask yourself is what do you get more
              from the newspapers

DMita's actions show interest and appreciation for children's active participation and reveal his attention for their self-expression. Consequently, children actively contribute with personal proposals. They are free to make single choices, but they are asked to follow a normative procedure (i.e. to compare the pictures and get a complete view of the facts). Children are expected to reproduce the 'right' meanings which are predefined by the adult-expert, who does not negotiate them with children. The adult-expert simply helps children to 'discover' them in the interaction.

In normative monologues, children's actions are exclusively treated as role performances, while in S22 the adult's actions are more attentive to children's personal expressions, which are considered useful contributions to communication. However, this approach frames children's personal autonomy with pre-established cultural presuppositions concerning the meanings of the interaction. This creates a paradox in the interaction: children's actions must be both autonomous personal expressions and guided role performances. The paradox is hidden by cognitive expectations, which avoid stressing normative requests; the explicit expectation is that children learn something from their experience of the interaction. Children are observed as incompetent individuals who need to be guided by an expert to learn how to participate in a proper way. In these paradoxical conditions, adults show the intention to guide children's construction of autonomous choices through their own actions, reducing the opportunities for children's active participation.

Similarly, in summer camps, especially during camp meetings, adults frequently display ambivalent actions: on the one hand, they allow adolescents to manage spaces and opportunities for their own empowerment and agency, leave them to discuss, vote and make decisions; on the other hand, they control the decision-making processes by imposing their perspective, when they believe that adolescents' negotiated choices do not fit their expectations. In S23, while apparently leaving the decision to adolescents, LMarg is dictating normative conditions. In turn 1, LMarg seems to coordinate a reflection on the consequences of a choice. However, in his subsequent turns, he forces participants to be responsible for and respect the decision they have made (turn 8), by menacing to adopt sanctions and punishments in case of violation (turn 6). LMarg does not consider adolescents autonomous and responsible, and makes reference to the role hierarchy. Adaptation and passive alignment characterise adolescents' participation in this interaction (turns 4, 7, 9).

(S23)
1. LMarg: (thinking) about consequences <u>think</u> **so which decision you take?**
2. F1arg: that if we are late we have to go to bed earlier
3. LMarg: **ok**
4. M2bra: everybody or just the people?
5. (?):   shhhh!
6. LMarg: **if you don't respect this rule**, I mean, if we say ok tomorrow we will go ten earlier and we tell you to go to bed and you make a mess upstairs (…) **the first time that happens we go back to the old rules –**
7. M1nor: yea
8. LMarg: **and we come back a lot more harsher than now. Yes? So it's up to you to respect this new rule that you put. Ok?**
9. (?):   yea

6.5   Conclusions

The analysis conducted in this chapter has highlighted four main forms of communication, which are recurrently produced during activities in villages and summer camps.

1. Normative monologues based on mono-cultural values (adults' perspectives and decisions), to which children are expected to conform. In this framework, adults prevent or block children's and adolescents' expressions of personal choices, restricting their active participation to role performances, with the implicit aim of reducing unpredictability, expressions of diversity and possible conflicts in the interaction.

2. Dialogic promotion of active participation, particularly in summer camps. Adults' dialogic actions enhance opportunities for active participation, above all for adolescents' self-expression in the interaction. Empowering dialogue enhances equal opportunities for participation and mutual support, based on affective expectations. Sometimes, adults' dialogic actions promote dialogic mediation, i.e. they coordinate children's and adolescents' actions.

3. Ambivalence between monologue and empowering dialogue, particularly in villages. This communication process takes an unstable form, where children are observed alternatively for their role performances and their personal expressions. This fluctuation projects uncertainty and creates blocks in the interaction, which can re-start only by shifting to a more stable form of communication.

4. Person-centred education, particularly in villages. Dialogic actions are used in order to achieve predefined educational goals. Children are considered for their personal expressions, while they are not free to express autonomous choices, because they are asked to adhere to predefined cultural presuppositions.

In general, monologues restrict the opportunities for participation, submitting children's and adolescents' actions and experiences to adult's assessments, controlling their verbal and non-verbal actions and determining who can speak, when and how. By contrast, when adults' dialogic actions encourage self-expression, children and adolescents actively participate in the construction of meanings, expressing personal views and supporting their interlocutors. Empowering dialogue seems to be a fundamental condition for promoting children's and adolescents' active participation. However, when dialogic actions are coupled with normative and cognitive educational purposes, children renounce expressing their personal views, adapting them to predefined cultural presuppositions.

As expected, adults mostly deal with children as dependent on educational monologues, while they act in a more differentiated way with adolescents, promoting empowering dialogue more frequently or leaving them free to choose, but also rejecting those choices which do not fit CISV cultural presuppositions. The general purpose of helping children and adolescents to learn the meaning of participation in intercultural communication seems difficult to achieve without promoting their agency. The main obstacle for children's and adolescents' empowerment seems to be adults' opposition to unpredictability: the promotion of different expressions in the interaction is often treated as a problem for the reproduction of communication, instead of a possible source of new meanings.

Activities 2

Coordinating reflection

Federico Farini

Chapter 7 deals with the debriefing sessions which, after the conclusion of cooperation and trust games, stimulate children's collective reflections on their previous experience. Debriefing sessions are supposed to promote appreciation of the ways in which sociality is constructed, and acknowledgement of a deeper common ground in terms of fundamental values, on the basis of which intercultural citizenship can be established. Thus, a crucial question is: how is reflection sustained in debriefing sessions? Reflection is often the outcome of a disempowering monologue relying on competence-related hierarchies between adults and children, where adults try to control the interaction. The promotion of creative forms of reflection, where children's active participation brings about new meanings, is evident only in few interactions.

7.1   Reflection in educational activities

Among educational activities in villages, debriefing sessions deserve particular attention. Debriefing sessions are communication systems in which leaders promote children's reflection on their experience of activities. These sessions follow cooperation and trust games, which are scheduled in the second half of the village, when interpersonal relationships are expected to evolve towards cooperation and reciprocal trust. After the conclusion of cooperation and trust games, debriefing sessions stimulate children's collective reflections on their experience of these activities. Debriefing sessions are accomplished by means of interviews, which are set up according to CISV guidelines.

Reflection is a communication process whereby a social system interrogates itself about the meaning and the consequences of its internal processes, exploring causal relationships between structures and processes, attributing motives and scope to social action (Luhmann 1984). By means of reflection, the internal structure and processes constituting the 'reality' of the social system are considered as a *unicum*, becoming in this way an object of knowledge. Reflection during debriefing sessions is the most important component of the intentional educational process which relies on the hierarchy of role performances and cognitive expectations. Debriefing sessions display the organisation of a specialised turn-taking in which hierarchies between adults (leading the interaction) and children (learning from the interaction) may be observed. This chapter aims to observe how reflection is managed in debriefing sessions.

Reflection is expected to provide children with the opportunity to recognise both common and different aspects in their perceptions. Debriefing sessions are supposed to bring about appreciation of the ways in which sociality is constructed, and acknowledgement of a deeper common ground in terms of fundamental values, on the basis of which a peaceful intercultural citizenship can be created. In debriefing sessions, the cultural presuppositions of CISV education are visible through specific contextualization cues, which enable participants to make inferences about their interlocutors' intentions and goals. Through these linguistic cues, the cultural presuppositions of the interaction become visible.

Promotion of reflection requires that adults observe children's active participation as a resource for their upbringing. If adults observe children's active participation as a risk, they will rely on social hierarchies in order to make children's participation compatible with their educational goals and expectations. These cultural presuppositions are not compatible with children's active participation, as they enhance monologues. However, monologues are not the only form to support reflection. Promotion of reflection also relies on empowering dialogue. Empowering dialogue requires that educators leave pre-planned activities, accepting that children tackle important issues, even if these issues are not present in their agenda, and promoting expressions of concern and support in response to interlocutors' actions. In particular, the systematic appreciation of children's actions allows their personal emotional involvement in the interaction. Empowering dialogue implies the dissolution of the role hierarchy between expert adults and incompetent children. Adults are required to take into account that children's creativity plays a role in shaping the trajectory of the interaction, even if children's actions are not aligned with their expectations and goals.

Crucial questions for analysing debriefing sessions are: How is reflection sustained in the interaction? Is reflection the outcome of either children's active participation or hierarchical relationships between social roles? Do leaders' actions promote children's autonomy and responsibility?

7.2   Hierarchical structures

Turn-taking is the basic mechanism in the organisation of debriefing sessions, as for all other types of interaction: after each completed turn a speaker arrives at the point of a possible speaker change (Sacks, Schegloff & Jefferson 1974). The hierarchical relationship between leaders and children in debriefing sessions is visible in the organisation of turn-taking: there is little opportunity for children to take any initiative, while leaders maintain control over the trajectory and the agenda of the interaction. Leaders distribute opportunities to talk among children by means of two standardised practices: (1) calling the name of a child either before or after asking a question; (2) enacting the 'first-raise-hand-talk' rule.

Both these practices are shaped by a specific cultural presupposition: since leaders have the task to impose constraints on children's contributions in the interaction, they control the sequence of turns. The leaders' control is an inherent feature of debriefing sessions.

In S1, turn 3, LFeng selects a child, M1por, as the next speaker, asking him to provide an explanation for the actions performed in the group during the activity. After M1por's response in turn 4, the co-coordinator of the debriefing session (LMusa) selects another speaker (Liam) to answer the question by calling his name (turn 5).

(S1)
1. LMusa: what kind of colours did you send? and why did you send that?
2. Children: blue
3. LFeng: you guys were sending blue every single time, why? (.) **Luis?**
4. M1por: (to score) more points
5. LMusa: **Liam, why?**

In S2, LMdan explicitly enacts a "first-raise-hand-talk" rule in turn 1, applying it systematically during the interaction to select the next speaker after each child's response, in turns 3, 5 and 7. Once a child has completed her/his turn, the leader takes the turn again, at least to select the next speaker; only LMdan holds the right to select the next speaker; this confirms the leaders' control of the distribution of opportunities to talk, that is the opportunity to act.

(S2)
1. LMdan: We're ready (.) anyone has: (..) anything to answer about, **raise your ha:nd** anything has to say about it? (..) take turn! (04) ((*selects F1Tha as next speaker*))
2. F1tha: I feel (...) this: I think it's not fair, because: (.) If you want to teach us, you should (...) do everybody poor and rich

3. LMdan: *((Selects F1bra as next speaker **by indicating her))***
4. F1bra: I think), I think erm it was (so much) fair, and: another thing I didn't
             like it, the: then erm we were poor in the evening, I just discovered that
             erm: when you're poor, you're (.) not, erm: how do you say, not selfish,
             you share with the other persons, and: erm: you share a lot more than the
             rich, then the riches
5. LMdan: someone (else) raised the hand? (..) **raising your hand** so
6. F1usa: °yeah°
7. LMdan: **Robbie?** *((selects F1usa as next speaker))*

Deviances from these procedures are overtly sanctioned. Children's selections of
next speakers are uncommon and systematically treated as deviant cases. In S3,
M1bra selects another child as the next speaker at the first transition-relevance
point (turn 3), that is after providing a sufficient amount of data to satisfy LFusa's
request for information (turn 2). By doing this, M1bra substitutes the leader's
right to distribute children's opportunities to act. This kind of action is deviant, as
it appears clearly by the fact that LFusa takes the turn of talk without hesitations
(turn 4), after M1bra's response, overlapping with the unexpected second part of
turn 3 (where M1bra selects the next speaker). The competition for the right to
talk is easily "won" by LFusa who sanctions M1bra's action, reiterating her role of
gatekeeper of children's participation.

(S3)
1. M1hgk: I think: (.) our group (.) we didn't collaborate
2. LFusa: so: didn't you↑(.) **Lucas?**
3. M1bra: <u>No</u> No we: collaborate: a l(h)ot   [m: Mi(h)ki hhh?]
4. LFusa: [**Chen, do you agree with-**]
             hey: <u>hey</u> next is: Chen m: (.) **let's keep it ordered**, ok?

In debriefing sessions, the basic adjacency pair involves the leader's question
and the child(ren)'s answer(s). Leaders' questions project children's answers:
this reflects role performances and cognitive expectations which are the cultural presuppositions of the sequential order of interaction. Consequently,
in debriefing sessions, participation is mostly restricted within a question-
answer framework.

The structure of conditional relevance is visible when an unexpected second
part of the adjacency pair has particular consequences in the interaction, e.g. a
question which follows a previous question (Arminen 2007). In these particular
phases of debriefing sessions, unexpected second parts of adjacency pairs violate
the principle of conditional relevance and project negative evaluations.

In S4, LMusa expresses a harsh negative assessment of M1usa's action in turns 8 and 10, excluding the child from the interaction, and selecting another speaker (turn 12).

(S4)

6. LMusa: m:? someone didn't respect the rule? Aaron, why did you say someone didn't: respect the rule?

7. M1usa: *((addressing M1spa))* hh (°no: no; before°) (.) *((addressing LMusa))* shall we have JC shop be before lunchtime, tomorrow?

8. LMusa: **hey hey that's: (odd) I asked you something, m:**

9. M1usa: °bu:[t°

10. LMusa: [no:o listen usually people asked are supposed to answer, **isn't it such a bad thing do not answer to a question**

11. Musa1:   °o:h sorry° (.) well (.) [I -] °o:h°

12. LMusa: [Nat] *((addressing M2usa))* (..) did someone cheat?

LMusa's reaction to deviance from the normative expectations concerning the adjacency pair question-answer reveals the features of social structures. The adjacently positioned second turn is the *locus* where a speaker shows that s/he understands and reacts to the previous turn. The acceptance, or refusal, of aligning to the expectations which are projected by the first part, highlights the cultural presuppositions of the interaction.

In order to avoid negative assessments, children systematically align with the first part of the question-answer pair, meeting leaders' expectations, which they are able to infer relying on the progression of the ongoing interaction. In these cases, the organisation of adjacency pairs is biased towards preferred responses. Preferred responses, that is acceptances, tend to be immediately produced (see turns 2 and 4 in S5).

(S5)

1. SM1ita: yes (.) and what do you get about information? for example, from your life (..) does it happen often that you: have just: too information, then after sometimes you get more information and you change your mind?

2. M1jor: **yes**

3. SM1ita: any: any:: episode? like, even in the camp, from the beginning to now (.) that is similar to this activity (.) eh?

4. F1fra: **>yes, oh yes<**

Dispreferred responses and refusals tend to provoke delays, e.g. with the insertion of additional speech particles and explanations/reasons for refusal (see turns 2 and 4 in S6). In turn 4, M1bra's self-disclaiming 'but' enhances his positive self-positioning.

(S6)
1. LMpol: you mean that: after all: cooperation is not important?
2. M1bra: °it's (1.2)   [that he: -°
3. LMusa: [you said you like competition to be: like: first (.) the only
            number one, m:?
4. M1bra: m::: (1) no: (..) m:: well: it's: it's: (.) ok: I like competition **but** it's not I
            don't like cooperation

As can be seen, debriefing sessions are characterised by role hierarchies between leaders and children. These hierarchies are expressed in terms of opportunities to participate in the interaction, and are signalled through the recursive chain of three-part "Question-Answer-Assessment" (QAA) sequences. The structural components of this kind of sequences are:

1. The leader's question, addressed to a specific child or to the group (turn 1);
2. The children's answer to this question, which is normatively expected as the second part of a "question-answer" adjacency pair (turn 2);
3. The leader's assessment (appreciation) of the answer (turn 3).

The structure QAA is similar to the structure "Initiation-Response-Evaluation" (IRE) sequences described by Mehan (1979), which is recurrent in classroom interactions where the third turns assesses children's learning. Educational monologues are generally realised through this kind of triplet. However, QAA and IRE are different, with regard to both their functions and sequential properties. While in IRE sequences teachers generally ask questions to which they already know the answers, to test (or extend) students' competence, in debriefing sessions, children are asked to express their personal meanings, that is to provide information that the questioner (the leader) is not expected to know. While in IRE sequences, positive assessment suggests that, given the correct answer, there is nothing more to say about the current topic, thus making a change of topic relevant, in QAA sequences positive assessment or appreciation do not exclude that a different answer to the same question will be positively assessed or appreciated. Debriefing sessions are "competence-in-progress" processes, where the adult may be surprised by any contribution. In QAA, positive assessments produced by adults in turn 3 do not mean that the current topic has come to an end; adults may choose either to change topic or to elicit new contributions to the current topic. Explicit questions may become relevant after positive assessments in turn 3 of QAA sequences.

In S7, LFusa, after the positive assessment of F1bra's answer, which represents the first part of her turn of talk (turn 3), selects another responder to her question, thus eliciting the prosecution of the discussion about the topic firstly introduced by LFhgk's question in turn 1.

(S7)
1. LFhgk: do you think that work together as a group helped group two to win?
2. F1bra: yes
3. LFusa: °yes° (.) *((addressing M1hgk))* **and you, Chen?**

In QAA sequences adults are distributors of rights and duties to speak among children; their selection of next speakers surrogates the repetition of the question opening the sequence. In S8, having been selected by LFhgk's as next speaker (turn 7), M1swe provides an answer (turn 8) that is different from the one provided by F1bra in turn 6, which received no assessment. Similarly to IRE sequences, when adults do not react to responses, children's prosecution of the search for answers is elicited. LFhgk's selection of the next speaker in turn 7 coincides with the opening of a second sequence, connected to the previous one.

(S8)
5. LFhgk: so: ple:ase raise your hands if you have something to say about it, ok? we saw that group two won, m:: so: why do you think group two won?
6. F1bra: because there was (.) was: Paulo he was good in °pone-° put the water in the cup
7. LFhgk: **Bjorn?**
8. M1swe: m: they take only a little water so they wasted less water than us

7.3   QAA sequences and socio-epistemic claims

What is significant for the analysis of reflection in debriefing sessions are the ways in which (a) cooperation is achieved and (b) different participants' perspectives about the meanings of activities become aligned through leaders' actions.

As we have seen, the structure of education implies a hierarchy between competent adults and incompetent children, who need to learn in order to become able to participate in the most significant social processes. It follows that a major concern for education is the management of rights and responsibilities related to competence. Most debriefing sessions are characterised by role hierarchies between leaders and children. These hierarchies produce differences in opportunities to participate in the interaction, and are signalled by QAA sequences, which are by far the most common in our data.

In QAA sequences children have scarce opportunities to take any initiative, while leaders hold control over introduction and change of topics, and hence over the "agenda" of the interaction. The leaders' ability to control the trajectories of actions in QAA relies on differences between social roles: children's participation is based on the social structures of education and this presupposition is evident in the sequential order of the interaction.

S9 and S10 are two examples of leaders' control over the interaction, which is a feature of QAA sequences. In both sequences, the leader's selection of different speakers (turns 9, 11, 13 and 15 in S9; turn 3 in S10) makes the occurrence of different answers possible (turns 10, 12, 14, 16 in S9; turn 4 in S10). Once the answer which meets the expectations of the leader is offered by a child, the leader's positive assessment works as a termination act. Leaders' selections of next speakers, most often realised by simply calling their names, make different responses to the original question possible. These are treated as repetitions of QAA sequences. In S9, the lack of LFusa's assessment of M1swe's response (turn 12) elicits the children's prosecution of their search for answers. After LFhgk selects M1swe as next speaker by calling his name in turn 11, M1swe provides an answer that is different from the previous one provided by F1bra in turn 10, which did not receive any assessments. The same structure is repeated in the next turns. Both positive assessments in S9 (turn 17) and in S10 (turn 5) close QAA sequences, selecting M1usa's answer in turn 16 (S9) and F1bra's answer in turn 4 (S10) as the correct ones. In S9, turn 17, the positive assessment ('*good*') is followed by a formulation which reinforces its normative meaning.

(S9 continuation of S8)
9. LFhgk: so: ple:ase raise your hands if you have something to say about it, ok? we saw that group two won, m:: so: **why do you think group two won?**
10. F1bra: because there was (.) was: Paulo he was good in °pone-° put the water in the cup
11. LFhgk: **Bjorn?**
12. M1swe: m: they take only a little water so they wasted less water than us
13. LFusa: **Inga?**
14. F1pol: e: they are good
15. LFhgk: **Brad?**
16. M1usa: they help each other so: they were so: effective
17. LFhgk: **good (.) so: cooperating is very important**

In S10, the positive assessment closing the multiple QAA sequence (turn 5) is reinforced through a repetition of the leader's appreciations such as '*excellent*', '*you guys got it*', '*that's a good job*' etc., which assert the meanings that the children were expected to get from reflection on the activity. In this way, this QAA sequence is cognitively, rather than normatively, supported.

(S10)
1. JFusa: Ok, my last question is how does this activity resemble different cultures around the world?

2. LMcan: CISV is the, it's an example of the game, so if you are, we have no: (.) common language, so English, it's will be a big big problem to make some (??) how to live and: the complication of working

3. JFusa: **Ana?**

4. F1bra: e: each game is a co-, it 's a erm country, could be a country, erm the rules erm is the rules of the country, erm because you don't - when you go to a country, maybe you don't know the rules, there, so you need to learn, erm erm (..) erm stay with erm according to the rules (.) there

5. JFusa: **that's excellent, you guys got it.** Any other (.) answers? No? That's it? (.) Ok, **that's a good job guys, you're awesome**

6. ((*Applause*))

After the closing of a QAA sequence, the leader is expected to take the turn to start a new course of action. Leaders usually employ markers to indicate that the current topic is closing, and a new one is starting. In S11, turn 5, SF1ita, after the positive assessment of M1ger's answer, marks the beginning of a new topic by means of the adverb 'So'. 'So' is often used as marker for changing topic, because it preserves the impression of coherence among the different topics composing debriefing sessions. The new topic in S11 includes a change of footing from 'we' to 'you', which identifies a specific group (of children) and implicitly introduces SF1ita's negative assessment of the group's destructive attitude.

(S11)

1. SF1ita: ok, Aaron?

2. M1usa: it was : interesting that the: the people that was most (.) committed in building the city were also the ones that were: were most destructive

3. SF1ita: right, Philip?

4. M1ger: we were angry (.) because some children loved destroy other countries

5. SF1ita: good (.) **So:** (.) the next question **we** already touched on, but not really (.) if **you** did destroy, why **you** did it?

During debriefing sessions, sequential markers signal that something new is going to happen in the interaction, urging children to raise their level of attention, in order to maintain their competent participation in the interaction, e.g. responding appropriately to the leader's questions related to a new topic of discussion introduced by the sequential marker.

In debriefing sessions, the leaders' right to distinguish what is right from what is wrong, what is relevant from what is irrelevant for the discussion, largely depends on the hierarchical distribution of competence and rights of access to competence in educational communication. It follows that a major concern for education should be the management of rights and responsibilities related to competence. In debriefing sessions, leaders assert their primacy in competence by using assessments to claim their rights and social identity. These socio-epistemic claims are claims to hold a superior competence in ruling, giving meanings and setting goals for the activities by virtue of the rights embedded in the status of educator.

Leaders preserve their primacy in competence as they preserve their capability to make children's contributions an object of assessment (Heritage & Raymond 2005). In the following sections, our analysis will focus on the ways in which these claims are produced during debriefing sessions.

7.3.1   Use of candidate answers within questions

Firstly, leaders' socio-epistemic claims are achieved in debriefing sessions through the production of candidate answers within their questions. According to Pomerantz (1988), offering a candidate answer allows the speaker to guide the interlocutors towards giving particular information. By means of a candidate answer within questions, the speaker leads the interlocutors to respond in a certain way, suggesting not only what should be important in the following answer, but also what the following answer might be (Arminen 2005). Therefore, the proposal of a candidate answer within a question implies an anticipated evaluation of the following answer.

In S12, LMbra's candidate answers within his questions (turns 1 and 3) lead children to align with the meanings that he expects them to get from reflection. Children align with LMBra's expectations (turns 2 and 4): their participation is oriented by his expectations and is limited to an expression of agreement.

(S12)
1. LMbra: **have you ever think that maybe the: best way to help yourself is to help the others?**
2. Children: *((nodding))*
3. LMbra: if I don't think "it's a problem, how can I work it out" but "how can we work it together? **Maybe if I help her ((*F1jor*)) then she will find ways to help me I wouldn't think about (.) M:h?**
4. M1ned: °yes°

By virtue of its interrogative syntax, a question including a candidate answer projects an assessment in the next turn. In this way, this kind of questions project the meanings which children should use in their assessments, reducing the risk of actions which might hinder the interaction (Raymond 2003). These forms of questions are the first part of a monologue, as they project the "correct" answers.

7.3.2 Use of interrogative negative questions

Secondly, an important interactional resource for leaders to preserve their socio-epistemic claims is the use of interrogative negative questions, exemplified by interrogative turn-initial components like '*Isn't it..?*', '*Doesn't this..?*' and '*Don't you..?*' (Heritage 2002).

By asking questions in a negative form, leaders assert a more extensive competence in the topic and/or a right to assess it (Raymond & Heritage 2006). By projecting a "yes/no" answer, this action asserts the control of the terms that may be used by the interlocutor in her/his assessments (Raymond 2003). Finally, interrogative negative questions strongly invite agreement (Heritage 2002), as contradicting such assertive questions would mean questioning the social status of their performers.

The strength of interrogative negative questions in controlling the trajectory of actions comes from their mixed format: interrogative negative questions combine the import of a declarative assessment with the sequential implicativeness of an interrogative form, using both to project next speaker's initiative.

In S13, in turns 7 and 9, M1bra aligns with LMnor's claims of competence regarding the way in which M1bra should feel during the activity expressed through interrogative-negative questions (turns 6 and 8). Negative-interrogative questions project the alignment to speaker's stance, opinions or assessments as preferred action in the next turn, hiding their coerciveness behind the interrogative format.

(S13)
4. LMnor: what do you think of the activity? Did you enjoyed it? Paulo?
5. M1bra: it was funny
6. LMnor: **didn't you feel bad when your countries: (..) were destroyed?**
7. M1bra: o:h °yes°
8. LMnor: **wasn't it sad that you worked a lot and in a minute everything was destroyed?**
9. M1bra: °yes° (.) I: I didn't want to say it was funny to destroy

7.4   Children's reactions

7.4.1 Children's downgrading of their own competence

The leaders' authority may be confirmed in the interaction also by children's downgrading of their competence. This downgrading confirms the role hierarchy between the expert and the incompetent participants.

In turn 2 of S14, F1pol downgrades her claim of competence attributing it to LMpol, and in this way she marks her leaders' epistemic primacy, which involves the right to assess what the correct behaviour is.

(S14)
1. LFusa: You just say that group one won because they found like a: method to bring water from one side to the other
2. F1pol: we collaborate (.) e: **Karel** *((LMpol))* **said** you have to help the others in your life
3. LFusa: yeah that's: that's a good point you got it

A second way for children to downgrade their claims of competence is the use of tag questions. Downgrading tag questions are used in educational interaction mainly as requests for clarifications.

In S15, turn 2, M1mex downgrades his competence by means of a tag question in the second part of his turn, thus submitting the validity of his assertion to LFbra's confirmation. A significant interactive achievement in S15 is that M1mex's tag question makes his participation subject to assessment, which follows the standards of the expert leader.

(S15)
1. LFBra: how do you (.) feel (.) when you saw the leaders asking you to destroy?
2. M1mex: I feel like: if they don't care (.) let's destroy (.) their city (.) I mean I knew (.) it was an activity: (..) **was it?**

7.4.2 Cooperating in the management of rights and responsibilities

The positioning of assessments in the interaction may be associated to the socio-epistemic claim that they imply. The relationship between positions of assessments and socio-epistemic claims is evident when a first-position assessment implies the claim of a primary right to express competence. However, in some cases, incompatibilities may arise between the rights that a speaker wishes to claim and the position of her/his assessment. In these cases, participants work to manage the relationship between rights to assess and positions of assessments. Leaders can claim their access to competence also in a second-position assessment, through a "confirmation-and-agreement-token" turn format. Confirmation and agreement token turns disengage the second speaker's opinion from agreement or conformity with the first speaker's opinion.

In most cases, leaders' responses react to children's tag questions asserting a claim of limited or precarious competence concerning the meaning of activities. Children's downgrading tag questions are "yes/no" questions that project "yes/no" answers as first components of responses (Raymond 2003). An agreement token ('*yes*') placed after the partial repeat of the children's assertion separates the action of agreeing from the action of confirming.

In this way, leaders' confirmation and agreement tokens confirm children's contributions, rather than simply agreeing with them. By confirming the assessment before responding to the question, leaders give priority to their claim of competence rather than to the agreement with children. Confirmation and agreement token turns are indications that leaders' opinions are relatively independent from the ongoing interaction.

In S16, LFbra's "confirmation and agreement token" (turn 3) is projected by M1mex's "assertion and interrogative tag" (turn 2). In most debriefing sessions, this practice is achieved smoothly, as speakers align to a definition of their rights to assess. In these circumstances, role hierarchies are preserved in the interaction in a relatively mild way.

(S16)
1. LFbra: how do you (.) feel (.) when you saw the leaders asking you to destroy?
2. M1mex: I feel like: let's destroy (.) their city (.) I mean I knew (.) it was an activity: was it?
3. LFbra: **it was an activity (..) yes it was: (.) ya, good**

In S17, LFswe's "confirmation-and-agreement token" format in turn 6 separates the confirmation of F1hkg's assessment from the agreement, which is postponed until the end of the first part of her turn, before a long pause that marks the separation between the two parts. This first part of her turn shows that LFswe is aware of the impossibility that someone would let a friend fall down without catching her/him, independently of F1hkg's contribution. In the second part of the turn, after the pause, LFswe seems to show her competence in analysing and discovering the psychological attitudes of F1hkg, introducing it with a mitigated other-disclaiming 'yes but'. The interrogative negative question projects a second assessment, in the format of a "yes/no" answer. The interrogative negative question gives to LFswe the opportunity to project both F1Hkg's "yes/no" answer that legitimises the leader's role as primary meaning giver, and F1Hkg's alignment to the meanings of her personal experience as proposed by the leader.

(S17)
1. F1hkg: when I was in the middle I was afraid becaus- (.) I was the first but (.) eh:
2. LFswe: m:
3. F1hkg: but if I was the second or the third I wouldn't be afraid
4. LFswe: ah-ah
5. F1hkg: no >because I would see that no: no one leaves you fall< it's like: impossible

6. LFswe: it's impossible that no one leaves someone else fall, **yes (1.2) but** (.) how
can you be sure about it? **Isn't it because you trust the ones around you?**

7. F1hkg: eh: (.) ok (.) m: °yes°

7.4.3   Resisting socio-epistemic claims: Non-type conforming answers

In some cases, children refuse to align with the expectations of "yes/no" questions, i.e. they avoid providing "yes/no" answers. These episodes are signs of disagreement with the cultural presuppositions of the "yes/no" question. Children
produce non–type conforming answers highlighting that the leader's question is
problematic (Raymond 2003).

In S18, M1ned's actions produce meanings that are not consistent with the
educational goals of the debriefing session. LMbra's chain of questions (turns 4,
6, 8) projects a step-by-step alignment of M1ned with the meanings the child is
expected to gain from his participation in the debriefing session, namely the appreciation of the value of cooperation. M1ned weakly aligns with LMbra in turn
9, but, when LMbra produces another interrogative negative question in turn 10,
in order to assert the value of cooperation, M1ned refuses to affiliate with LM-
bra's meanings, avoiding compliance with the conditional relevance projected by
the question, i.e. avoiding providing a "yes/no" answer, and offering a non-type-
conforming answer (turn 11).

(S18)

4. LMbra: **you think that helping each other can be good but also dangerous?**

5. M1ned: yes:

6. LMbra: **do you think only for yourself when you are in trouble?**

7. M1ned: yes

8. LMbra: **wouldn't be better help each other to join: your forces (..) two is stronger
than one, isn't it?**

9. M1ned: °yeah°

10. LMbra: so: **isn't it the better way to help yourself (.) I mean (.) to help the others,
m:?**

11. M1Ned: **I was afraid, in some points, to fall off the chair**

M1ned partially withdraws from his previous alignment through a non-type conforming answer and in this way the leader's socio-epistemic claim is indirectly
disclaimed.

7.5   Question-Answer-Appreciation sequences

The achievement of cooperation among different participants' perspectives about the meanings of activities does not necessarily require the reproduction of a role hierarchy. In some sequences it is possible to appreciate that the leader addresses children as competent interlocutors, taking into account their perspectives and supporting their self-expression. In these interactions, competence is considered a result of communication where leaders and children hold equal opportunities to participate, children may play an active role as meaning-producers, and leaders promote their participation showing interest in their self-expressions. These sequences are examples of empowering dialogue which may be defined Question-Answer-Appreciation (QAAp) sequences.

QAAp sequences display the same formal features of QAA sequences. The specificity of QAAp sequences consists in the systematic appreciation of children's contributions in turn 3. In QAAp, leaders always appreciate children's contributions. In other words, leaders' appreciations do not depend on the placement of children's contributions on the positive side of the educational distinction between correct and incorrect answers; leaders unconditionally appreciate children's contributions as expressions of their autonomy and willingness to take responsibilities in acting.

In S19, LFarg and LMusa systematically appreciate children's contributions (turns 3, 5, 7, 9) by means of explicit appreciation markers ('*ah-ah*', '*good*', '*ok*', '*very good*'), although these contributions express different and sometime contradictory meanings (turns 2 and 4). In QAAp sequences, leaders appreciate children's participation itself, rather than the content of children's second turns.

(S19)
1. LFarg: ok, so death was who had the hardest job (.) who do you think had the easiest job?
2. F1nor: **the death, but no one can help it**
3. LMusa: **ah-ah, good,** *((addressing Mjor))* and you, Alì?
4. M2jor: **the plague because there was only one death, but many hunters, foxes and: rabbit to catch**
5. LFarg: **o:k good** and you think that in your life the same situations of the game happen or it just a: fiction?
6. F1jor: in the family, the youngest brothers and sisters are the rabbits, they had to do anything and they don't they don't: had anyone to boss around
7. LFarg: **go:od** in the family, **nice one**
8. M1bra: at schools, students are like rabbits, teachers are like foxes, they can catch them to take from them all they know
9. LMusa: **o:k** (.) I see there's some catch, in some points (among) you (..) **ve:ry good**

The differences between QAAp and QAA sequences emerge by comparing S18 and S9. As we have seen, in S9 both LFhgk and LFusa fail to offer systematic appreciation of children's contributions. Absence of feedback for children's contributions makes the provision of different answers relevant, until the preferred one is provided by M1usa. In this way, educational communication reaches its goal, that is to inform children about the 'correct behaviour' which they should learn through their participation in debriefing sessions. However, is leaders' inattentiveness to appreciate children's action an efficient means to empower children's active participation in the interaction?

In QAAp sequences, leaders may use continuers to promote reflection. The use of continuers is much more common in QAAp than in QAA sequences, i.e. it represents a sequential feature of the former. In S20, LMusa's continuers express his attention to M2bul's actions (turns 3, 7 and 9). Through continuers, LMusa supports M2bul's active participation, allowing him to take an active part in the joint production of reflection. If uttered at a transition- relevance place, where a change of speaker is a significant option, continuers are minimal turn construction units used to signify that their utterer is willing to pass her/his turn of talk, in order to permit further topic development by her/his interlocutor. In QAAp sequences, continuers realise a *perspective display* (Maynard 1991), that is they elicit the interlocutor's expression of her/his own perspective, showing attention for it. The effect can be observed in the way M2bul's participation evolves from a mitigated other-disclaiming 'but' (turn 2), through a disagreement (turn 6) to an autonomous contribution (turns 8, 10).

(S20)
1. LMusa: you have something to add, I see, maybe I'm wrong hh °as usual° you don't agree ((with me)), isn't it?
2. M2bul: No: **Yes** I agree **but** I think that we have to cooperate in life, anyway and: and:
3. LMusa: **yes**
4. M2bul: you can't cooperate and:
5. LMusa: you say you can't cooperate because it is hard to cooperate, don't you?
6. M2bul: No No I mean it is not you can or can't it is that you always cooperate
7. LMusa: **m:**
8. M2bul: if you: you are walking on the streets, someone's fighting, in the front of the school, someone starts fighting (.) you see they are cooperating
9. LMusa: **m:**
10. M2bul: like here! We can also disagree, but we cooperate anyway because we communicate

In QAAp sequences, differently from IRE and QAA sequences, turn 3 may be used as a resource to promote children's active participation far beyond their institutional roles of passive observers of leaders' action. The interactional function of educators' turns after children's answers does not rely on their sequential position (they are always placed in turn 3), but on their cultural forms, which are features of either educational monologues or promotion of social participation.

7.6   Conclusions

The interactions which produce reflection in debriefing sessions following activities present an ordered sequential organisation, which is structured through specific expectations about children's participation. This sequential order is mainly based on adults' questioning and assessments, which lead to both a Question-Answer-Assessment structure and a series of structures which construct the adults' socio-epistemic claims of their educational roles.

The analysis of debriefing sessions shows that often the reflection on the meanings of activities is the outcome of a monologue relying on competence-related hierarchies between leaders and children, where leaders try to control the interaction. Empowering dialogue, which promotes equal distribution of opportunities for children's active participation and self-expression, seems to be less frequent than role hierarchies and adults' socio-epistemic claims.

Promotion of children's active participation requires that leaders take into account that children's creativity and issues may shape the trajectory of the interaction, even if they are not aligned with their expectations and goals. Empowering dialogue represents a risk as it implies the abolition of differences between competent adults and incompetent children. In debriefing sessions, this risk is particularly evident. Consequently, leaders often avoid the risk of empowering dialogue, appreciating children's active participation above all when it is consistent with their goals and expectations. This tendency matches a widely shared idea among leaders (Chapter 3): in order to make activities significant, it is necessary to emphasise normative and cognitive expectations proper to CISV educational narrative, as children are observed as incompetent persons, needing support to participate in activities.

Apparently, the forms of communication which derive from leaders' questions and assessments reduce the possibility of surprises and difficulties during activities. However, this reduction is what makes the interaction ineffective in promoting children's active participation. In the frame of their monologues, leaders act as gatekeepers of children's participation, which is subject to adherence to pre-established goals. In this way, it is very difficult to achieve the 'creative learning' which should be based on the experience of intercultural communication, and which is at the core of CISV educational theory.

The effectiveness in promoting creative forms of reflection is evident only in some interactions, where children's active participation brings about new meanings.

Activities 3

Conflict management

Vittorio Iervese and Elisa Rossi

Chapter 8 focuses on the relationship between participation and conflict, and between conflict management and decision-making during CISV educational activities. During activities, conflicts between children and adults are modest. When educational interactions take the form of conflict, the problem is how to reproduce them and through which kind of contributions. The chapter observes: (1) if and in which ways it is possible to ensure the reproduction of the ongoing communication process, dealing with conflicts in interactions between adults, children and adolescents; (2) the different patterns presented by conflict management, namely conflict avoidance and prevention, conflict normative resolution, request and assessment of understanding, coordination and mediation. Overall, the analysis shows that conflict management is rarely based on dialogic actions assuring effective mediation.

8.1   Conflicts in educational activities

The topic of this chapter is the relationship between participation and conflict and between conflict management and decision-making during educational activities in CISV programmes. As conflicts contribute to inserting elements of insecurity into communication processes, when a contradiction is mentioned and some participant notices that the interaction takes the form of a conflict, the problem is how to carry out education and what kind of contributions can be made. We will observe if and how it is possible to ensure the continuation of the ongoing communication process dealing with conflict in the interaction.

During activities in villages, conflicts between children and adults are rare and modest. Interpersonal conflicts are nearly absent, while role conflicts and intercultural conflicts are slightly more noticeable. Children rarely contradict either adults or their peers, and when they do it, stable conflicts are very rare. During activities in summer camps, although the communicated contradictions are more frequent than in villages, conflicts are not as recurrent as one might expect in a setting where the promotion of adolescents' opinions, ideas and preferences should prevail over adults' monologues.

What are the reasons for the infrequency of children's and adolescents' contradictions? Which are the ways in which the transformation of these contradictions into conflicts is made unlikely? These two questions introduce the two main issues dealt with in this chapter: participation and decision-making, and their relation with conflict management.

Conflict management presents different patterns:

1. Lack of interest in conflict and participation (conflict avoidance and prevention).
2. Attempts to bring participation into forms which are necessary for activities (conflict normative resolution, CNR).
3. Requirement of children's efforts in understanding activities, and consequently of adjustments in children's participation (CNR).
4. Request and assessment of understanding.
5. Coordination and mediation.

8.2   Conflict avoidance

We will focus firstly on the forms of conflict avoidance, which create the conditions for the lack of contradictions and/or display carelessness about emerged contradictions.

In the previous chapters, CISV structures and narrative supporting the system of activities have been clarified. In particular, in Chapter 3, it has been clarified that the CISV narrative hides a complex set of strategies aiming to create a sense of community based on respect of differences and at the same time search for shared perspectives. In the transition from abstract perspectives to activities, we can notice search for coherence between principles and empirical forms of participation. The activities proposed in villages and summer camps should be the *medium* to achieve this coherence. The success of these activities (the respect of forms, times and planned dynamics) often becomes the main aim of adults' contributions.

In villages, as we have seen in Chapters 5 and 6, during activities we observe a generalised structure including (1) adults' explanations and questions, (2) children's executions and answers, and (3) adults' remarks, such as assessments, appreciations, continuers, formulations and so on. Each of these parts of the interaction presents recurrent forms which define children's opportunities to participate.

Successful activities must respect times and expected forms of communication, and children's participation which tends to deviate from these expected times and forms is discouraged. As a result, conflicts are not considered opportunities for participation, but obstacles to the achievement and fulfillment of planned activities. This means that forms of contributions are selected in the interaction.

In particular, a search for coherence between abstract guiding values and effective forms of contributions can be observed in the recurrent instructions that are provided by adults, before and during activities. Adults provide a lot of detailed instructions concerning how activities work (rules, phases, purposes, etc.). Here we focus especially on those instructions concerning the activities which select children's forms of contribution and are connected to some kind of contradiction. It is possible to observe these selected forms of contribution through the repetition of expressed guiding values, and cognitive and normative expectations.

In S1, M1ita first asks for clarification (turn 2) and then expresses his relevant doubts about the game through an other-disclaiming 'but' (turn 4). LFita subordinates these doubts to the respect of game rules (turn 5), and LMdan subordinates them to group cohesion (turns 10, 15, 16, 20). M1ita's objection is not taken into consideration, as it appears an unnecessary digression. LMdan's imperative actions in these turns are probably emphasised by the aims of the game. They are a vivid example of the frame required for the activity, which LMdan tries to preserve through an operational agreement implying the end of divergences (Goffman 1963) through the reference to a We-identity – a reference which is recurrent in interactions between adults and children, although not always in this emphasised way.

(S1)
1. LFita: here there is the prison. When you touch one of the other team you must bring him/her here, and they will <u>draw</u> (?) you a line.
2. M1ita: can we go in their prison?
3. LFita: yes. If they catch you, then you go to their prison.
4. M1ita: **but it is stupid this game, if one catch you then -**
5. LFita: **you have to try to be not caught.**
             ((LMdan arranges the red team into two lines))
6. LMdan: we've got two lines. Alright?! Jenny there, Gianmaria here. Ok guys. Listen up! You are red team! You are the red team! <u>Act as a team</u>!
7. (?):   ea!
8. LMdan: Don't run around screaming (..) Red Team!
9. (?):   yea.
10. LMdan: <u>act as one</u>! **Allright?! So when we move we move together!**
11. (?):   yea.

12. LMdan: ok?!

13. All together: yea.

14. (?):   <u>yea</u>!

15. LMdan: **so you better start marching! Get in line guys!**
    ((Children come back in line))

16. LMdan: **all ready guys?! Move it! Left! Left! Left right! Left! Left!**

17. LFita: Excuse me, why do they do all these things? *((she refers to the children's
          march looking surprised))*

18. Researcher: I have not any idea

19. M1ita: also my father were soldier.

20. LMdan: **come on guys! Pick up the pace!** Ok, these are our eggs ok?! We have four
          eggs on our team, right?! I'll be placing them around here the area and
          these are the ones you are supposed to protect, one of these eggs are the
          golden egg. We don't want any of these eggs caught by the other team.

This is a recurrent case of conflict avoidance based on guiding values. The emphasis is on the value of the single action in its coordination with other actions (turn 10: '*Act as One*'). This value can be understood if we refer to certain
idiomatic expressions, like 'to be in tune with' or 'to be in unison with', which
are linked to musical narratives. The metaphor of the tuning in and harmonisation of sounds indicates the attempt to coordinate harmoniously the different
voices of participants. Following this metaphor, dissonances or discordances
must be coordinated to reach agreement. Besides the call for group cohesion,
this kind of action gives value to the fact of 'being together' as presupposition
for agreement, and permits the avoidance of the communicated contradiction.
The 'community logic' can be described as the participants' knowledge of making the same thing, all together (Goffman 1963). Coordination and cooperation
are values to respect rather than forms to practise through the comparison of
different perspectives, and this leads to avoiding conflicts in case of doubts or
deviating suggestions.

   However, this guiding value is not always effective. S2 is taken from a phase
of the game *River by river*, which has the purpose of encouraging group cooperation. LMswe's and LFger's incitements and instructions to cooperation and
reciprocal help (turns 1, 3, 4, 6) assert the 'operational agreement' on which
CISV programmes are based. However, these repeated calls for cooperation occur within the context of a competitive game. This combination of cooperation
and competition creates a paradox: the operational agreement consists in asking for participants' contributions which confirm a common guiding value, explicitly declared at the end of S2 (turn 7). Children do not follow the paradoxical incitements, as they are involved in the competitive game (turns 2, 5), and

consequently ignore adults' incitements. Adults' repeated reactions to F1arg's turn (2) seem ineffective.

(S2)

1. LMswe: **you have to cooperate, ok?**
2. F1arg: **yeah, yeah (.) pass here, pass here!** *((she is trying to overcome another group))*
3. LMswe: **careful, be careful. You have to organize it better, ok? More cooperation.**
4. LFger: **c'mon and help each other, help each other.**
5. M1usa: **keep things going, keep things going.**
6. LFger: **help each other, help each other**
7. LMswe: **things go well when you help each other**

The repetition of guiding values is used to pre-select children's possible contributions during activities, avoiding conflicts, with alternate success. Moreover, as we can see in S2, cognitive expectations provide indications on the ways of treating possible divergences, in their combination with amusement. Activities aim to show the important aspects of the CISV narrative in the form of amusement. Consequently, learning and amusement are balanced in activities. The exaltation of amusement motivates participation, while cognitive expectations improve performances. In this case, however, amusement negatively influences children's listening to their leaders' incitements. These two factors (repetition of guiding values and expectations of learning and amusement) contribute to avoiding conflicts.

In summer camps, conflict avoidance is rare and may be observed when either leaders change topic or remain in silence when adolescents express contradictions, or when leaders do not select (pick up from the communication flow) the issues of cultural or personal diversity coming out spontaneously in the ongoing interaction. In these cases, leaders avoid exploring and widening the topic of diversity with adolescents, while they emphasise the values of tolerance and respect, and underline the importance of avoiding disagreements, or they suggest the possibility to melt cultural differences, creating shared cultural forms. The ambivalence of this transcultural paradoxical narrative of reproducing and overcoming personal and cultural diversity, which coincides with the education to the guiding values in CISV narrative, is prominent in conflict avoidance.

In S3 and S4, leaders' contributions include some dialogic actions: (a) active listening through continuers (S3, turns 4, 6) and echoes (S4, turns 15, 17); (b) formulations (S4, turns 8, 10); (c) alternative narratives (S3, turns 8, 10; S4, turn 12); (d) checking adolescents' understanding (S3, turn 10). However, in S3, LFgre's normative transcultural narrative, enhanced by a self-disclaiming 'but' (turn 10), projects F1arg's alignment with the leader's contribution in turn 11.

(S3)

1. LFgre:	what's the aim of the activity. What do you want the rest of the people to understand after we do that activity
2. (04)	
3. F1arg:	the differences we have. The differences (?) that we showed in (the other) activities before
4. LFgre:	**mmm**
5. F1arg:	the: we, we have already showed that we are different
6. LFgre:	**yea**
7. F1arg:	and I don't know what others
8. LFgre:	**maybe we can show it in another way**
9. (10)	
10. LFgre:	**oh maybe not just stay at the differences** (..) we are different we know that, we come from different countries, **but we are here altogether now**, we are talking about the same thing. We are all peo(h)ple and maybe try to find a way to see that through our differences we can make one thing together (03) **do you understand?**
11. F1arg:	°yea°

In S4, LFbra's echoes and normative formulations (turns 8, 10) guide adolescents' reflection and assess their learning in terms of important values, such as tolerance, listening, respect, openness, thus preventing a different treatment of differences.

(S4)

1. LFind:	so what, the aim of this activity was to show you that everybody has different points of views, sometimes you have ahm the same points of views ahm you can agree on the same things and most times ahm you have different points of views, different (?) on your background, the way you grew up, the culture around you, your education and ahm the things that influence you in your life (.) would anyone like to comment on the activity that we have just been doing. Do you think that it was that? It helped you realize those things?
2. Group:	yes
3. (??)	
4. LFbra:	so, can you explain me (..) the why? Why did we do this and what are we doing? (..) yea ((*pointing at a participant*))
5. F2arg:	we have to tolerate other opinions
6. LFbra:	guys! ((*confusion*)) let's... ahm?
7. F2arg:	(??) that we tolerate each other and others' opinions. The, the opinions of the others
8. LFbra:	**then, then we have to be tolerating the other** and (.) and?
9. (?):	accept

10. LFbra: **accept the other** *((nodding))* ok
11. (??)
12. LFbra: **that we are all individuals**
13. F1arg: we are all different
14. F1fra: listen to others and to respect the ideas
15. LFbra: **listen and respect ideas**
16. F1ind: you have to be open minded with things
17. LFbra: **open minded with things**

In both villages and summer camps, the guiding values of sharing, cooperation and tolerance are used in the interaction above all as a way of avoiding and preventing conflicts.

8.3   Conflict normative resolution

During activities, some conflicts cannot be avoided, although they remain at a low intensity level. These conflicts mainly arise either from lack of understanding about activities' rules and objectives or from the refusal of proposals and choices. Although these conflicts may also be reproduced without adults' interventions, we will examine only the cases in which there is some kind of conflict management. Frequently, adults seem to treat these conflicts as unnecessary, as they break the peaceful and normal course of activities. Therefore they treat them as obstacles, adopting CNR strategies, which imply role hierarchies and expressions of power in the interaction, combined with the adult's imposition of rules or perspectives.

8.3.1 Villages

In villages, participation is bound by activity forms and by the ways in which activities are built. Games requiring the mere execution of instructions leave less space to children than activities requiring creative contributions. In the latter, conflicts among participants, as well as the need to control children's participation, are more frequent.

S5 shows the relationship between promotion of participation and risk of conflict. The structure of this dyadic interaction is a regular sequence of turns between leader (LFslo) and child (F2gua):

1.   LFslo's opening questions (turns 1, 7, 17) and comment (turn 13).
2.   F2gua's responses (turns 2, 8, 14, 18).
3.   LFslo's corrections (turns 3, 9, 15, 19).
4.   Fgua's claims (turns 4, 6, 10, 16, 20).
5.   LFslo's normative closing turns (turns 5, 11 and 21).

This interactional structure is repeated until Fgua2's final acceptance of LFslo's protective perspective and the consequent repression of her participation (turn 22).

(S5)

1. LFslo: **what do we use to carry Cinderella?**
2. F2gua: it's easy we use the car we use for the food
3. LFslo: **it's that we don't want no one to be injured**
4. F2gua: but we are careful, we know how to use it
5. LFslo: **it's not something you can be sure of**
6. F2gua: but we tried
7. LFslo: **you mean you used it?**
8. F2gua: and no one was injured
9. LFslo: **do: not do it again it's dangerous**
10. F2gua: but: how do you know it we tried it   [we: -
11. LFslo: [no more
12. F1gua: o:h °ok°
13. LFslo: **and: food goes on it**
14. F2gua: a:h no problem there is no food, they are: empty
15. LFslo: **.hh but there will be food (.) food in a few hours**
16. F2gua: but we find a lot of   [these –
17. LFslo: [where?
18. F2gua: ehm in the: [kitch–
19. LFslo: [did you go in the kitchen, you can:nnot do it
20. F2gua: **no no (.) not in the: kitchen outside the kitchen**
21. LFslo: hh where they were ready to carry food hh so **don't use them**
22. F2gua: °**ok**° ((she goes away))

In this case, the legitimacy of the leader's worry is not in question. The conflict concerns forms of contribution which are different from those considered acceptable in the activity. The strategies to regulate children's contributions basically consist in assertions of indisputable rules and consequent requests of adaptation. Conflict resolution starts with explicit requests which initially are not accepted by the child, it continues with recommendations, and it is concluded with normative closures.

In some cases, CNR is quicker, in other cases the attempts to fix rules produce conflicts which exclude some children from participation. In S6, it is possible to observe a recurrent escalation which makes the activity unmanageable in coincidence with restrictive regulation. S6 concerns the construction of a story about Cinderella. JMtur introduces the character in turn 1 and M1ita immediately starts refusing and diverting his attention (turns 2, 3). In turn 6 M1fin proposes to play the role of Cinderella, and repeats his proposal in turns 13, 16 and 19. This proposal is initially ignored and then openly stigmatised by JMtur (turns 7,

15, 17, 20). In a long series of turns (5, 7, 10, 11, 22, 24, 26, 28), JMtur essentially tries to regulate participation resuming his turns of speech and the hierarchical structure of the interaction. This effort, however, is futile and counterproductive, because the consequence of M1fin's exclusion is his escape from the activity and his search for an alternative activity which becomes antagonist to JMtur's proposal, thus provoking its failure (turn 41).

(S6)

1. JMtur: **Cinderella backwards. Does everybody know Cinderella?**

2. M1ita: **I don't like! Ecco la mia attività preferita.**
     Here is my preferred activity

3. *((He jumps on the mattresses in the room and lays down))*

4. F1ger: I will go to speak backwards?

5. JMtur: **no no, I don't know. The goal is to -**

6. M1fin: **I'm Cinderella!**

7. JMtur: *((with an astonished expression))* **you are Cinderella?! Ok, if everybody knows the story of Cinderella, we are going to do (...) Cinderella played from backwards.**

8. F1ger: *((interrupts JMtur))* We have got (..) we have got three sisters, we have got the mother, we have got the prince -

9. (...)

10. JMtur: **ok let's start. Can everybody come here? Let's make a circle.**

11. JMtur: **yea, who wants to be the first?**

12. M1ice: who wants to be Cinderella?

13. M1fin: **here.**

14. *((Laughing))*

15. JMtur: **come on L.!**

16. M1fin: **I'm Cinderella.**

17. JMtur: **you want?** *((pointing at F1ger))*

18. F1ger: ne!

19. M1fin: **no! I'm Cinderella.**

20. JMtur: **L.** *((M1fin))* **come on! Come on!**

21. M1fin: **I'm Cinderella!**

22. JMtur: **this story starts from backward so we are going to start with the end, the end of story is going to finish happy so we are going like that and we are going to walk (..) Don't (..) No no no** *((pointing at the participants who do not listen to and jump on mattresses))* **I'm going to tell the story! There is one girl called Cinderella -**

23. F1gre: we need the others.

24. JMtur: **ok, we need a stepmother and two sisters.**

25. F1ice: I want to be the stepmother.

26. JMtur: **ok. You want to be a sister?**
27. F1ger: yea.
28. JMtur: **ok. Cinderella is always cleaning, always doing like that and the sisters -**
29. F1ger: ninininini *((she blows on a raspberry))*
30. *((M1fin climbs the wall bars))*
31. JMtur: come on L.!
32. *((JMtur grabs Mifin by the legs and puts him on his shoulders))*
33. JMtur: come on guys!
34. *((the other children are laughing))*
35. JMtur: CI -
36. *((M1fin is dancing on JMtur's shoulders)).*
37. JMtur: help me god!
38. *((JMtur grabs M1fin, but he grips his shoulders)).*
39. M1fin: <u>noooo</u>!
40. JMtur: come on! come on kids!
41. *((In the room there is great confusion. M1bra climbs the wall bars and after few seconds M1fin climbs them again))*

Promotion of participation works only until it is interrupted by regulatory reminders and attempts to recover CNR. S5 and S6 demonstrate that CNR works when it (1) avoids the repetition of conflicts, interrupting alternating shifts among the children, (2) replaces this alternation with sequences opened by monologues, and (3) obtains children's adaptation. These purposes can be achieved in different ways, but the adult's authoritative intervention is the most frequent. Less regulative forms are based on the principle of the majority (e.g. ballot), or chance (e.g. counting rhymes).

S7 is the continuation of S6. JMtur shows his conviction that only a female can act the role of Cinderella. Consequently, the three participating girls decide that a counting rhyme will be used to choose who will play the role. The participants cannot find efficient coordination, in spite of the attempt to decide through the game. The paradox is that none of the three participants wants to win because none of them wants to play the role of Cinderella. The loser has to play the role of Cinderella, while JMtur interprets the game in the opposite way. In turns 47–54, the dispute between F1nor and F1ice concerns the identity of the loser. In turn 55, JMtur indicates the supposed winner (F1ger) as the candidate to play Cinderella. This misunderstanding projects F1ger's silence (turn 56), while the following misunderstanding (turn 57) projects her refusal (turn 58).

(S7 continuation of S6)
42. JMtur: let's make rock, paper and the scissors.
43. M1ice: who lose are gonna be Cinderella.
44. F1ice-F1nor-F1ger: one, two, three.

45. F1nor: yea!!!
46. JMtur: you two. *((pointing at the winners))* L. and A. Again.
47. F1nor: **yea (…) but she *((F1ice))* lost.**
48. F1ice: **nooo!**
49. F1nor: **she lost**
50. F1ice: **nooo!**
51. F1nor: **yea!**
52. JMtur: **she lost?**
53. F1nor: **yes.**
54. F1ice: **no::**
55. JMtur: **ok, ok, ok! So you want to be Cinderella?** *((asking F1ger)).*
56. *((F1ger does not answer)).*
57. JMtur: **ok! L. *((F1ger))* is Cinderella.**
58. F1ger: **no:**

These forms of CNR may be inefficient because regulatory interventions can produce multiplication of objections and abandonment of active participation. Adults' regulatory interventions are often the origin of interruptions and incomplete sequences. They project side sequences and complicate coordination, delaying decisions.

8.3.2 Summer camps

In summer camps, CNR becomes evident when leaders and staff members take a hierarchical position towards adolescents, by deciding who is right and who is wrong in the disputes. This strategy closes the conflict without involving the parties either in a proper clarification of their positions or in an effective coordination of their different perspectives. CNR may concern adult-adolescents conflicts, as well as disputes among adolescents in which leaders and/or staff intervene for their settlement.

In S8 in turn 1, LFdut presents her position as better than others (‘*I like the group more*’, ‘*I think it's better*’), asking the group to agree with her (‘*Do you agree? Yeah?*’), legitimizing her choice with her expert knowledge and past experience in CISV programmes. Moreover, LFdut expresses the wish to involve adolescents in the final decision (‘*shall we do this game?*’), at the same time, however, she expects them to align with her perspective, thus creating a paradoxical and mitigated form of imposition. A change of footing from ‘I’ to ‘we’ indicates that the leader's authoritativeness prevails over the collective We. In turns 2–4, a contradiction between LFdut and Ffin arises: the girl expresses a different opinion, which is denied and rejected by the leader through an other-disclaiming ‘but’ (turn 3). However, in turn 4 Ffin puts forward her idea again, challenging the adult. Conflict develops in turns 5–12, where the attempt to clear up and negotiate the meaning of the two different versions of the game is influenced by LFdut's persuasive strategy. In turns 9, 11 and 13, the leader assigns 'right' and 'wrong' to herself and the girl respectively, imposing her normative expectations in a persuasive way. In turns 9 and 11, the other-disclaiming 'but' supports this distribution. Ffin looks blocked in her participation (turn 10), marginalised in the planning process and forced to adapt to the leader's version of the game (turns 12, 14 and 16).

(S8)

1. LFdut: ok. I know this game slightly different, I like this one better. I know it in drawing a peaceful place, so you just draw happy place (??) **but** it's more individual, **I like the group more, I think it's better.** Ehm **from my experience** ehm **shall we do this game? Do you agree? Yeah?** We've got two hours
2. Ffin: **there's also that kind that someone cannot use colours or someone cannot use tape and like that**
3. LFdut: **but I think that's a different activity, do you know** (??)
4. Ffin: **it's almost the same**
5. LFdut: isn't that game about ehm rich and poor? Some groups they can have all the materials and they can build something easily and some groups have very few materials or not so many and it's difficult
6. Ffin: it's like one group have colours, one group can use tape and so the war is easier to make
7. LFdut: why is it easier to make in this way?
8. Ffin: because someone don't have colours and they have colours and they do not have tape and another group have tape
9. LFdut: **but** then why do they have war? **They have to talk to each other right? They have to cooperate, don't you think?** I don't know, I don't know this part
10. Ffin: ok
11. LFdut: **but did you do this part of this activity? Yes? Can you remember that?**
12. Ffin: **yea, I don't know, I think it was also the same kind**
13. LFdut: it isn't the same kind, right? So I think it's more about (..) ehm differences in general ehm rich and poor, **it's more about that and about cooperation, whereas this one isn't about cooperation.** This one is about war really
14. Ffin: **ah, ok** ((smiling a bit))
15. LFdut: ok. Would you like to do this one?
16. Ffin: **yea**

In S8 the leader exploits the role hierarchy and produces a normative resolution of the conflict: she avoids involving the rest of the group in order to prevent any further and potential enlargement of the conflict; she denies the perspective (considered 'wrong') expressed by Ffin; finally she imposes her own perspective (considered 'right') to the adolescents, who can only passively align to it.

In S9, M1ita refuses a proposal coming from the girls. Both SM1ita and LMarg (turns 4, 8, 10, 18) try to make the two conflicting parties (boys and girls) realise that one option does not exclude the other, because everything they choose is feasible in different ways and times, according to their different preferences. The subsequent turns show how refusals and oppositions project further refusals and oppositions (turns 5, 7, 9), whereas LMarg's promotional actions (turns 10 and 12) succeed in involving F1ita in the process of decision-making and conflict management (turn 13). However, F1ita's proposal stimulates a new opposition by M1ita (turn 14). LMarg's actions therefore show a mitigated form of CNR: (1) he establishes "how to decide who has to plan what" (turn 16); (2) he treats the girls' position as "wrong" and the boys' position as "right", imposing this distribution and asking for the group's adaptation to it (turn 20); finally (3) he mitigates his imposition by acknowledging the girls' creativity and producing an inclusive move towards them (turn 23). This form of CNR seems to satisfy both parties, projecting the de-escalation of the clash and a more relaxed atmosphere. Nevertheless, what should be noticed is the expression of an ethnocentric form of treatment in turn 32, which highlights that the conflict has been partially transformed but not concluded.

(S9)

1. M1ita: it's the same that we planned!
2. SM1ita: but you can do
3. M1ita: <u>no</u>! <u>No</u>!
4. SM1ita: **you can do it in different ways! You can do it in different nights!**
5. M1ita: <u>no</u>! <u>No</u>!
6. F1bra: <u>yea</u>
7. M1ita: <u>no</u>! <u>No</u>! <u>No</u>! Two times the same activity no!
8. SM1ita: **but it's not the same! It's a disco and it's a casino night!**
9. M1bra: <u>because the activity is casino-disco night</u>!
10. LMarg: **can we talk seriously?**
11. F1ita: I'm talking seriously
12. LMarg: yes? (04) **What do you wanna say?**
13. F1ita: you do the disco night and we do another funny night with dancing, so [why not two?
14. M1ita: [it's the same thing!
15. F1ita: <u>yes</u>! But so we can [have fun
16. LMarg: [you can do it differently. Did you wrote (..)?
              <u>What did you write in the</u>: in the   [paper?

17. F1ita: [nothing!
18. LMarg: **nothing. What did you write?** *((irritated))*
19. M1ita-M1bra-M2bra: casino-disco night!
20. LMarg: **so you are doing** the [casino-disco-night
21. F1ita: [ok
22. SM1ita: **[you are doing the party**
23. LMarg: and you are doing another thing, [**you have got millions of idea**
24. F1ita: [ok. Party night!
25. (?):   [a party!
26. LMarg: you guys, you do a casino-disco night (…) Go and plan it! Go and plan it!
            Go away!
27. Girls: bye!
28. M2ita: casino-pyjama-disco night!
29. Girls: by:e!
30. LMarg: bye! Come on!
31. F(?):   by:e! You too P. *((SM1ita))*! Bye!
32. F1arg: **our is going to be better!** *((smiling and joking a bit))*

In S9 we can observe how CNR can lead to adolescents' restriction of participation and adaptation, but also to (re)production of some ethnocentric forms of treating differences.

In S10, M1bra and F1nor are disputing about the meaning of the summer camp experience (learning *versus* fun and relaxation). The clash concerns time for sleeping. In turns 13 and 15, M1bra turns to dialogic actions. However, SF1ita and SF2ita introduce normative expectations in the interaction (turns 19, 20, 24, and 25): instead of facilitating the reciprocal understanding and the coordination of the conflicting parties, this normative regulation blocks adolescents' dialogic actions and self-management of the conflict. S10 ends with the imposition of staff members' perspective and their negative assessment of participants' behaviour (turns 25, 27), considered disrespectful.

(S10)
12. F1arg: I just want to sleep. One day. I sleep and then we do the activities
13. M1bra: **but why the whole day?** I like we finish that
14. F1arg: because we need!
15. M1bra: why you don't finish the activity and go to the bed? **I understand what
            you are saying**: we wake up early, (?) everyday but -
16. F1bra: ahm just ahm if you are so tired why when you finish the activity don't
            you go to bed and you stay here like I'm tired I'm tired I'm (cool) I'm
            staying here and have fun with the others why don't you go to bed because
            you know that tomorrow will be a hard day?
17. F1nor: yea, but lights turns out about

18. F2ita: 1.30
19. SF1ita: **no! Lights turn off at 12!**
20. SF2ita: **lights turns off at 12** *((annoyed))*
21. F1nor: yea 12, but the activity ends at-
22. SF1ita: **you have 9 hours to sleep every night** *((annoyed))* **9 hours**
23. F1nor: but we can't, we can't sleep with lights on! And everybody downstairs yelling and running around
24. SF2ita: but it's not-
25. SF1ita: **you have 28 days for sleep every night from 12 to 9. Nine hours in every day, every night** *((very angry))* **You have to decide what to do,** [it's up to you. Respect –
26. LFgre: [and (?) **everybody is yelling is you**
27. F(?):   yea
28. LFgre: **is not someone else, that everybody you say is yelling is some of you** (01) **you deal with it**

8.4   Requests and assessments of understanding

In villages, we have observed some attempts to manage conflicts improving children's performances. Usually this occurs through the request of understanding and/or through the request to find efficient strategies of problem solving. The purpose is to promote a transformation of participation in order to adapt it to the purposes of activities. In these cases, we observe the assessment of contributions, which are compared to those expected.

In S11, M1ita, M2ita and F1ita are disputing, while LFita unsuccessfully invites them to agreement (turn 4). In turn 9, LMmoz suggests a work strategy and in turn 11 LFita introduces an explicit request of cognitive performance. This turn stops the exchange among the children, and projects a sequence that matches leader's action and children's reactions (turns 12–15). Initially children's objections (turns 16, 18) make the debate possible. However, leaders' assessments stops the discussion and are accepted by children (turns 21, 23, 25). The leaders' actions change children's actions without attributing specific meanings to the contradictions, as the origin of conflict is observed in children's lack of understanding. For this reason, adults provide further information and explanations on the activity.

(S11)
1. M1ita: look! She doesn't do anything.
2. M2ita: Give me the crayon.
3. F1ita: <u>nooo!</u>
4. LFita: **please agree yourselves.**

5. F1ita: look, we are stupid, we are poor stupid.

6. M1ita: it's true.

7. M1ita: we are poor incapable.

8. M2ita: give me the crayon!

9. LMmoz: **decide who make the continents and the work!**

10. F1ita: I'll make the sea.

11. LFita: **who knows how many are the continents?**

12. M2ita: **me.**

13. *((M1ita raises his hand)).*

14. M1ita: **they are 5 (..) 1, 2, 3, 4, we are only in four we can't do anything.**

15. LFita: **well. Do you know what are the continents? Tell me what are the continents.**

16. M1ita: <u>no no no! No no no!</u> No one can guess all the continents.

17. LMmoz: can I-

18. M1ita: <u>no no no!</u> Then you don't make anything!

19. LMmoz: can I tell you a thing? Can I tell you a thing?

20. M1ita: you can't you can't-

21. LMmoz: **Good Morning! Good Morning everybody! Before to start drawing find the way to agree everybody, ok?**

22. M2ita: then-

23. F1ita: ok! Then (…) there is a continent there, there another one, there another one, there another one *((pointing at the flash card))* (..) Ok?! **Draw them!**

24. M1ita: then (..) The Asia is there, the Europa is there (..) The America is there, the Oceania is there -

25. LFita: **ok. Look: you must try hard!**

26. F1ita: we have understand everything -

S12 concerns a debriefing session of the activity *Peace-War-Peace*. The sequence starts with LMita's check on children's feelings (turns 1, 4, and 6). Following this phase, LMita attributes lack of understanding to children concerning the meanings of the activity and the importance of the concepts discussed. The puzzled and sometimes derisory tone (turn 13), the corrections (turns 15, 19), and the explicit check on their understanding (turns 23, 25) project children's justification of their positions (turns 14, 16, 20). Following this discussion, M1ita initiates a self-repair (turn 30). He aligns with the framing introduced by the leader, and his contributions are progressively made compatible with the objectives of the activity. M1ita's preoccupation to be misunderstood and consequently assessed in a wrong way (turns 34, 37) is a cue indicating that the interaction is based on cognitive expectations which prevent the expression of children's opinions and hence their active participation.

(S12)

1. LMita:	**how do you feel now?** -
2. F1ita:	now?
3. M1ita:	how do you feel now?
4. LMita:	**now (.) after we have done this activity**
5. M1ita:	me: ehm, i feel, more social, so -
6. LMita:	**why?**
7. M1ita:	because: the game was; do the things together, paint together; then a game where we do everything together and now I feel more social, no
8. F2ita:	sad
9. LMita:	because they have destroyed the city^
10. M1ita:	oh, why are you so sad?
11. M2ita:	but it was also fine
12. F2ita:	write good, fine, sad, and social?
13. LMita:	((to the researcher)) **do you know how they have answered? They good, she is sad and he is happy because he has socialized with more people** ((derisory tone))
14. M1ita:	**no it's not true:!**
15. LMita:	**eh, but what have you said? You have socialized with more people**
16. M1ita:	**how I feel! Not how I have done!**
17. LMita:	and how do you feel?
18. M1ita:	e: more social!
19. LMita:	**but social is not a feeling, no?**
20. M1ita:	**e: c'mon, it's as I feel (.) You said that I've socialized better**
21. LMita:	no: that this game will allow you in future to socialize in a better way! No? Yes? I've misunderstood?
22. M2ita:	but he says that he socialized mow, and also that:-
23. LMita:	**but have you understood the game?**
24. M2ita:	yes, but:-
25. LMita:	**when have you destroyed the city what did people cry?**
26. M2ita:	a:h
27. M1ita:	war
28. LMita:	a:h, they cried "war", no aah:
29. M2ita:	ah, war?
30. M1ita:	**just because you feel a fondness you're building the houses?**
31. LMita:	ah, I understand (..) but later, later that we've destroyed it-
32. (…)	
33. LMita:	but how do you feel now?
34. M1ita:	**boh, boh, i feel more relaxed (..) what have you written of what I have said?**
35. ((F1ita and M2ita, laughing, beckon "so-so"))	

36. LMita: don't worry
37. M1ita: **o: how "don't worry"? Are you writing what I didn't say.**
38. LMita: they didn't have -?

In S12, M1ita's perspective is negatively assessed by the leader as a result of mis-understanding, which cannot be accepted as it prevents education from positively changing the child's mind.

8.5   Ambivalent coordination and mediation

The activities proposed and the forms in which they are managed offer few op-portunities of active participation to children and adolescents, and conflicts are considered incompatible with activities. Nevertheless, there are cases in which adults' dialogic actions open up to children's and adolescents' participation. In this section, we present two examples: S13 concerns adults' partial and ambiva-lent coordination of a conflict between children, and S14 concerns mediation of adolescents' positions in a summer camp.

In S13, similarly to previous examples, we observe a debriefing session re-suming a conflict which emerged during the activity *Peace-war-peace*. Communi-cation is focused on the meanings of war and peace. As usual (Chapter 6), the sequence starts with an adult's question (turn 1) supported by a clarifying refor-mulation (turn 3) aimed at encouraging the participation of the hesitant child (turn 2), who reacts in turn 4 with a controversial opinion ('to make war is fun'). LFnzl firstly echoes M2nzl's opinion (turn 5) and then tries to involve the whole group stressing its meaning (turn 7). The opinion is not assessed although it is not in line with the CISV narrative. LFnzl's action promotes participation and development of the conflict in a creative way for the purposes of the activity. While LFnzl actively listens to M2nzl's perspective, she also motivates him to clarify its meaning, involving the other participants. This provokes a conflict between M2nzl's and F1nzl's contrasting opinions. While adults support F1nzl's perspective (turns 11, 12, 14), projecting her display of satisfaction (turn 15), they do not negatively assess F1usa's opinion in favour of the war (turns 17, 20). While adults appreciate 'positive' contributions, they do not, however, assess 'negative' ones. The result is that the interaction is not concluded with children's complete alignment to the mainstream perspective, but with the repetition and partial enrichment of the two controversial opinions.

(S13)

1. SFusa: **R., what about you? Are you (?)?**
2. M2nzl: **ahm:**
3. LFnzl: **how did you feel about making war?**
4. M2nzl: **it was fun.**
5. LFnzl: **it was fun.**
6. *((laughing))*
7. LFnzl: **ok.** *((she smiles)).* **What do you mean-** [**What he means**
8. F1nzl: [Can I say something?
9. SFusa: yes of course.
10. F1nzl: I think that you feel better about making peace, but it's harder to do it, and it's easier to do war but you feel bad about it.
11. *((SFusa nods)).*
12. LFnzl: **you got the point.**
13. F1nzl: does that make sense?
14. LFnzl: **yea.**
15. F1nzl: **ok** *((laughs)).*
16. SFusa: what about you Miss S.? (.) Was it easy to create war?
17. F2usa: **mm: yes, it was fun.**
18. *((Laughing))*
19. F1nzl: it was fun (more).
20. F1usa: **I (was) like walking and everyone else do it more though.**
21. *((F1usa starts narrating amusing episodes of destruction, while the other children are laughing))*

In this interaction, children can express their personal meanings and adults accept all their contributions, coordinating the interaction. Adults' actions confirm and support children's contributions, check their perceptions, actively listen to their self-expression, ask for their understanding, appreciate their actions and experiences. Distribution and promotion of participation allow them to avoid the polarization of different perspectives, and to coordinate those perspectives. The interaction creates a quiet and welcoming confrontation without anxiety and tensions. However, adults support one position, while accepting the expression of the other.

  S14 is probably the most significant example of mediation in summer camps, although it also shows some controversial aspects. It displays the kind of conversational work that adults may do in order to mediate conflicts, and considering the unpredictability of communication processes. In turns 2–5, we observe a contradiction between Mdut and the rest of the group during the activity called *Peace War Peace*. This conflict concerns how to stick together recycled materials that adolescents are using to build 'the ideal city'.

Mdut has decided to use glue, whereas his group-mates would have preferred sellotape. In this case, LFdut does not avoid or block the conflict, rather she displays her intention to face the contradiction and to acknowledge different positions, acting as third party. In turns 6, 8 and 10, she asks an explorative question ('*what are you doing?*') partially repeated ('*what what are you*') and an interrogative formulation ('*so that it stays up?*'), in order to check her understanding of her delegate's position. These actions succeed in promoting group's participation: adolescents self-select their turns, explaining what is happening (turns 7, 9) and expressing different positions (turn 11), thus making the adult realise the reasons for the conflict. In the subsequent turns (12, 14), LFdut combines two feedback token showing understanding and a formulation (turn 12) with a practical suggestion and a check on perception: these dialogic actions show the leader's acknowledgement of different opinions, and elicit further developments of the conflict (turns 15–22). In turn 23, while showing affection towards her delegate, the leader evokes a practical reason to convince Mdut that the solution chosen by the rest of the group is probably better than his own ('*so maybe the tape is quite practical*'). Thus, after many dialogic efforts to develop and mediate the conflict, the adult seems to turn to persuasive actions to settle the dispute.

(S14a)

1. LFdut: [*reaching the group*] oh, look at that! Fantastic! I love it, that is
             [so -
2. Mdut.   [and they say it doesn't work!!
3. Mcos: it's not going to work
4. Mdut: I'm confident it will work
5. Mcos: you've been hold here like 15 minutes
6. LFdut: **what are you doing?**
7. Mdut: I'm holding now for 1 minute and 15 seconds
8. LFdut: **what what are you – ?**
9. Feng: to stick up
10. LFdut: **so that it stays up?**
11. Mcos: with glue, no
12. LFdut: ok, ok. **Well, you've got tape down**
13. Mcos: I know, but he doesn't want to use
14. LFdut: ah ok. **Is there a problem with tape or – ?**
15. Mdut: we can, we can
16. Feng: H., it just needs to be stable
17. Mdut: why don't we try!
18. Feng: H., trust me. It needs to be stable
19. Mdut: it is stable! The tape isn't stable

20. LFdut: (??)
21. Mdut: why don't we just wait before we try, then we can discuss about whether is
            stable or not
22. Feng: (??)
23. LFdut: **it might be difficult, H.** ((*her delegate*)). We don't have an amazing
            amount of time, **so maybe the tape is quite practical** ((*putting a hand
            on his shoulder; in the meanwhile Mcos uses the tape to stick the bottles
            together*))

In the second part of the sequence, however, Mdut (turns 26, 28, 33, 35) and
Feng (turns 27, 32, 41), ignoring LFnor's suggestion in turn 25, both reinforce and
keep on opposing one another. While LFdut formulates his delegate's perspective
to make it more understandable to the rest of the group in turn 29, at the same
time she seeks to convince him to use the tape (turns 34, 36, 39). LFdut once
again turns from dialogic mediation to a mitigated hierarchical resolution, based
on persuasion: exploiting her role and the affective closeness to her delegate, she
tends to distribute "the right" and "the wrong", although without any impositions,
and this strategy shift seems to project the conflicting parties' withdrawal from
the interaction (turns 38 and 41). Nevertheless, the renewal of the conflict (turns
42–44) stimulates a new change in the leader's action: she promotes the understanding and coordination of the two perspectives through a sequential set of
formulations, addressing the conflicting parties separately (turns 45, 47). These
dialogic attempts promote new participation, as in turn 48, where Mcos self-selects and formulates Feng's viewpoint, addressing Mdut and promoting mutual
understanding and a new contradiction in the group (turns 49–52). In the subsequent turns, LFdut (a) uses a formulation to check her understanding of Mdut's
position (turn 53), (b) acknowledges the value of Feng's perspective (turn 57),
and (c) suggests the possibility to cooperate to the conflicting parties, in order to
increase the aesthetical quality of their work, beyond its necessary stability (turns
55, 59, 61). However, instead of promoting the conflicting parties' empowerment,
i.e. their decisions on how to manage the different perspectives and continue their
work, LFdut suggests her own solution. Although LFdut's actions fail in promoting Mdut's and Feng's participation, they activate the participation of other interlocutors (turns 66, 67, 69, 71), who make proposals in order to allow the work to
go on. In the interaction with Mdut, LFdut uses the other-disclaiming 'but' in a
number of turns (47, 53, 55, 57, 63): in this way, the leader tries to enhance mediation, contrasting her delegate's deliberate self-positioning.

(S14b)

24. Fola: ok
25. LFnor: **you can have the project like in your own room**
26. Mdut: the tape is ugly
27. Feng: it doesn't matter
28. Mdut: it matters! I want (??)
29. LFdut: **he wants it to be pretty**
30. Mcos: it's not very (??)
31. LFdut: (??)
32. Feng: (this is not fair)
33. Mdut: it is cool!
34. LFdut: *((touching the shoulder of her delegates))* **you can, you can use the tape (.) listen**
35. Mdut: it won't
36. LFdut: *[caressing his head]* **you can use the tape**
37. *((Feng shows them that their handmade work is unstable))*
38. Mdut: ok, do what you want!
39. LFdut: **ok**
40. Mdut: do what-
41. Feng: I'm just saying (??) *((moving a little bit out of the group and looking irritated))*
42. Mdut: you're saying that (??)
43. Feng: (??) (you can see if it's stable or not)
44. Mdut: (??)
45. LFdut: **ok. So you think it's not working?** *((turning to Feng))*
46. Feng: I've just put all together
47. LFdut: **but you are not (sure) that it will work** *((turning to Mdut))*
48. Mcos: she's just saying that it's not stable
49. Mdut: it's stable, you can put it
50. Mcos: no, no
51. Mdut: if we do more tape we can also can do this
52. Mcos: we can do –
53. LFdut: **(??) but maybe you can work on (.) on make it (..) I think you don't like it because you don't like the tape, right? You don't like [the tape**
54. Mdut: [it's just ugly
55. LFdut: **but maybe you can help –**
56. Mdut: she is just saying, the only thing she's saying is that it has to be stable
57. LFdut: **but it is important that**
58. Feng: ok, it doesn't matter if it is stable or not
59. LFdut: **I do think, well you can still make it pretty, that doesn't mean that –**
60. Feng: yea yea

61. LFdut: **so maybe you can concentrate on that, even if you don't like the tape, you can try and try to make a nice building**
62. Mdut: we only have few minutes
63. LFdut: **but it's plenty of time**
64. Mdut: (??)
65. LFdut: **well few people can (??) and few can make the building pretty**
66. Mcos: (??)
67. LFnor: and then we can have a swimming pool, right?
68. LFdut: oh (..) I like the swimming pool!
69. Mcos: do you know how to draw it?
70. LFdut: ok so maybe
71. Mcos: then the roof

The last part of the sequence opens with LFdut's moving away from the group and with a renewal of the conflict, in which Mdut keep on rejecting Feng's viewpoint and repeating his position (turns 73 and 75). Interestingly, however, Mdut's monologues now project Feng's dialogic action (turn 77): she no longer expresses either refusal or opposition, rather she displays openness to Mdut's interests and, consequently, the intention to cooperate to improve the aesthetical quality of the handmade city. This expression of respect and inclusion projects the alignment of Mdut, who in his turn starts to collaborate introducing his ideas (turns 78 and 80), supported by adults. From this point on, the atmosphere appears more relaxed, the level of cooperation seems higher, and the contradictions have more playful tones. However, LFnor concludes the sequence reframing conflict management with educational meanings. In turn 84, she assumes the role of expert and expresses cognitive expectations, leading adolescents' reflection towards the (positive) values of group cohesion and team work, implicitly distinguishing them from the (negative) value of conflict, using an other-disclaiming 'but'. This emphasis on cooperation reinforces the transcultural form of the CISV narrative, based on the idea that conflict can menace the harmony of the community.

(S14c)

72. *((LFdut stands up and goes away, while LFchi translates for her delegate))*
73. Mdut: **but if you do more tape, it's so ugly. If you don't more tape it won't**
74. LFnor: you can also correct that one
75. Mdut: **you can do like this and you can put more tape, but it isn't stable**
76. LFchi: (??)
77. Feng: **look, we have this** *((passing him some paper))*
78. Mdut: **ah, we can make the the, yes, the garden!**
79. LFnor: and also you can make the (??), yeah?

80. Mdut: **look, the garden**
81. *((The Norwegian leader cuts a piece of paper and puts it on the handmade city))*
82. Mdut: but we don't see anything!
83. *((They laugh, then the boys work together though Mdut continues to lead a bit, while*
      Feng remains a little bit apart but she laughs))
84. LFnor: **but can you see how it works better to work as a team? Can you see that**
      now?
85. Mdut: mmm
86. LFnor: yea!
87. *((The boys are working together; Mdut asks Feng her opinion about their work and*
      little by little she reaches the group and collaborates; the atmosphere is more
      relaxed, the leaders are joking and supporting the adolescents))

Dialogic conflict management does not guarantee that conflicts are concluded with shared agreements. However, it is important to guarantee the involvement and responsibility of all participants. This means to pass from 'operative consensus' to operative coordination and mediation, whose outcomes are not predictable. While CNR require that decision-making is based on those elements which share or adapt to guiding cultural presuppositions, coordination and mediation enhance multiple contributions which spread responsibility of choices, thus empowering participation in decision-making.

8.6   Conclusions

During activities with children and adolescents, conflicts are often prevented or avoided, and when they arise, conflict normative resolution and requests of understanding are their main treatment. Conflicts are managed primarily through prevention and avoidance strategies, and secondarily through hierarchical forms. There is a predominant reference to we-identities, indicating the necessity to 'act as one'. As we-identities are predominant, adults do not generally need to change footing from 'I' to 'we' to assert their authoritativeness. These results clearly indicate the consequences of the CISV transcultural narrative and CISV cultural presuppositions in terms of educational guiding values, role hierarchies and prevailing cognitive and normative expectations.

The main guiding values concern cooperation and sharing. Role hierarchies appear to be primarily relevant in the few cases of conflict, where normative expectations and impositions of adults' perspective are prominent. In summer camps, interactions seem to be more ambivalently structured than in villages, in which, however, ambivalent coordination may be observed (see also Chapter 6). On the one hand, the promotion of adolescents' participation may prevail over hierarchical relationships. This means that awareness of differences between villages and summer camps (Chapter 3) is translated into actions by adults. Dialogic actions and effective empowering dialogues may be observed more often in summer camps, in the two forms of coordination and mediation.

On the other hand, this promotion of different perspectives does not seem to enhance many conflicts, and We-identity prevails in interactions involving adolescents. In summer camps, as in villages, dialogic actions and promotion of participation are almost abandoned in cases of conflict. This confirms that a weak aspect of the CISV experience is conflict management, especially mediation as a dialogic form of conflict management, which is based on coordination of different perspectives and mutual satisfaction of the parties.

Activities 4

Adolescents' coordination

Claudio Baraldi and Alessandra Braglia

Chapter 9 highlights adolescents' participation in the activities held during summer camps. Adolescents are more actively engaged in interactions than children, they are more encouraged to be active by adults and seem to be particularly competent in coordinating activities. In particular, they are competent in equally distributing participation among their mates and in presenting personal proposals dialogically, although ambivalences and disempowering monologues are not absent from their interactions. Like adults, adolescents tend to avoid conflicts in their interactions rather than adopting forms of mediation; ballots, withdrawal from conflict, and elusion through forms of diversion prevail in their interactions. Overall, interactions among adolescents show interesting forms of empowering dialogue.

9.1 Adolescents in the interaction

This chapter analyses communication processes among adolescents during summer camps, in particular in two settings:

1. Planning groups (PGs) in which adolescents may work together without external influences, where a small number of participants plan the activities that will be proposed to other participants.
2. Activity time (AT), i.e. discussions and assessments on specific activities.

Similarly to what we have seen in Chapters 6 and 8, the analysis focuses on the cultural forms of the interaction which may or may not promote adolescents' participation. In particular, we will see if and when empowering dialogue can promote adolescents' active participation in interactions in these settings, allowing adolescent participants to self-express and act as responsible persons.

According to developmental theories, adults are supposed to be more competent than adolescents in communication, whereas participatory theories claim that adolescents may be competent in their own way, if they are given the opportunity to act autonomously and if they are supported in their right to be social agents. According to its cultural presuppositions, and in compliance with developmental theories, CISV gives adolescents the opportunity to exercise their right to participation in a much more evident way than it does with children. However, this is only partially true as it is evident that the physical and interactional presence of adults in summer camps influences the social processes involving adolescents (see Chapters 6 and 8). Nevertheless, the observation of interactions involving only adolescents in summer camps is an interesting opportunity to understand if and in which ways competing theories about adolescents' competence are useful to interpret naturally-occurring interactions involving them.

9.2   Coordination as distribution of participation

In PGs and AT, adolescents may act as coordinators of the interaction; they may coordinate contributions of their peers, according to the role which has been assigned to them in the organisation of the interaction. The main form of this coordination is a form of action which does not include the coordinator's personal contributions. Renouncing her/his personal expressions, the adolescent coordinator can show the primary importance assigned to her/his interlocutors' participation.

S1 concerns an instance of AT. The interaction is coordinated by Fbra and is part of the Brazilian Cultural Activity. In turns 1, 3, 5, Fbra tries to promote a social space in which adolescents are allowed to self-express, with the help of Mita (turn 2). In turns 3 and 5, Fbra introduces normative expectations about the organisation of the meeting. In turn 7, Fgre aligns with her expectations and projects Ffra's alignment (turn 8). In turns 9 and 11, Fbra starts explaining the meaning of the activity and at the end of turn 11 she tries to promote the interlocutors' participation according to her cognitive expectations ('*How is in your country?*'). This question projects Marg's contribution in turn 12. In turns 13, 15, 17, 19 and 21, Fbra supports Marg's participation, asking questions, and showing her interest and active listening. In turns 23, Fbra tries to extend participation to other adolescents. However, Farg (turn 24) is ready to reciprocate Fbra's attention, which is immediately and easily attracted (turn 25). In turn 27, Mnor takes the turn and Fbra immediately supports his contribution with a question (turn 28). The whole interaction features a recurrent display of We-identity: this is a typical framework in meetings between adolescents, in which participants tend to position themselves as 'members' of national delegations.

(S1)

1. Fbra: how are you?
2. Mita: I think we have to sit by group
3. Fbra: ah: ok. You sit all together, **you don't have to separate by groups**
4. (22)   *((The participants sit around the table))*
5. Fbra: ah: (02) **I'll talk about how:** *((noise for 02 seconds))* J.! (04) D.! D.! **Come here!** (??) **So we are altogether!** (Next to each other)
6. (11)
7. Fgre: **she's talking!**
8. Ffra: sorry! (04)
9. Fbra: ah: I'll talk a little bit ah:: the nature in Brazil (02)
10. M(??):   (it's very:)
11. Fbra: nature. Ah: I'm sorry. *((the group near Fbra's group complains about the high tone of her voice))* Like we have a lot of biodiversity (.) biodiversity (.) in Brazil, like a lot of animals and ecosystems a:nd lots of (things) in Brazil a:nd wheat else (..) people that cut down trees ah because some people pay them to get like this wood a:nd for they: like (this wood) cut down trees because like ah: they have to have money to get food for ah: the children and I'd like to know how is in your country (.) how is like ah: the biodiversity (.) ah: do you have projects to help ah:m the environment? (03) **How is in your country?**
12. Marg: environment is ok. All the diversity of the world, so. We have all the diversities
13. Fbra: **all the diversities?**
14. Marg: all.
15. Fbra: **like how?**
16. Marg: deserts, mountains (.) tropical, non tropical (.) (all the things we have)
17. Fbra: **you have deserts?**
18. Marg: what?
19. **Fbra:**   **you have deserts? (.)   [deserts?**
20. Marg: [yeah (..) in the [Patagonia
21. Fbra: [where? (..) Like in the South?**
22. Marg: south. South Patagonia (02)
23. Fbra: **and in Indonesia?**
24. Farg: (you) have biodiversity of animals and plants and we have biodiversity of environments.
25. Fbra: **yeah: (.) animals, plants (.)   [whatever**
26. Farg: [everything (03)
27. Mnor: we have protected areas.
28. **Fbra:**   **you have protected areas?**
29. Mnor: yeah (??)

In S1, after her presentation at the beginning of the interaction and the display of her expectations, Fbra renounces expressing her personal perspective when she is not explicitly asked. In general, she uses questions to empower her interlocutors' self-expression, starting from cognitive expectations about the meaning of the activity. In this way, the presentation of the Brazilian Cultural Activity enhances dialogic coordination of communication about natural features of different countries. The potential ethnocentric approach to the National Activity is transformed into transcultural interaction.

S2 concerns another instance of AT, namely the *Fantasy Island* activity. A small group of adolescents must decide how the country, which is supposed to include the group itself, can be shaped for the future. The perspective is obviously one of sharing values and symbols, for instance, adolescents must decide the shape and colours of the flag, the national anthem and the people who can live in the country. Fcan has the task to coordinate the discussion. In turn 1, she starts her coordination inviting discussion. She decides what to do and when to go on with the next topic, showing her cognitive expectations concerning interlocutors' performances. In turn 2, Mdut and Fnor propose together what they would like to work on and, in turn 3, Fcan supports this proposal through an echo (repeating what Mdut and Fnor have said). This echo allows Mdut to express his opinion (turn 4), thus empowering his participation. In turn 5, Fnor supports Mdut's proposal and in turn 6 Fcan continues to empower participation through a question enhancing further elaboration. Fcan coordinates this activity setting up a dialogic space within which the other participants are allowed to self-express. In turns 7, 8 and 9, the other participants suggest answers to her question while she continues to coordinate the interaction by inviting them to clarify their assertions (turns 11, 13, 16, 20). In particular, Fcan's turns may be observed as repairs of Mdut's, Fnor and Ffin's assertions in turns 9, 12, 15, 19: Fcan allows her interlocutors to reflect upon their assertions, without correcting them; rather, with her questions she initiates and supports a chain of self-repairs of their assertions in turns 11–21. In this way, Fcan promotes the interlocutors' perspectives on what they can decide. Her action leads the participants to a better understanding of their reciprocal perspectives, through self-repair, which finally leads to a shared decision (turn 21).

(S2)
1. Fcan: **ok, next thing.**
2. Mdut-Fnor: *((together))* **who lives there**
3. Fcan: **who lives there**
4. Mdut: **people and (??) rich**
5. Fnor: **oh yeah**
6. Fcan: **how many people live there?**

7. Mdut: **six million**
8. Fnor: **no! four billion**
9. Mdut: **yes, no ten billion. Ten billion of rich**
10. Fnor: **what?**
11. Fcan: ten billion?
12. Ffin: **no!**
13. Fcan: **less?**
14. Ffin: less
15. Fnor: **four**
16. Fcan: **four billion?**
17. Fnor: four
18. Ffin: less *((drowning out of voices))*
19. Mdut: **what about one million?**
20. Fcan: **one million?**
21. Fnor-Ffin: **yes**

The use of questions is the main linguistic form signalling dialogic coordination in adolescents' AT. Questions work as verbal cues for both active listening, inviting the interlocutor to continue with further details or suggestions, and cognitive expectations about the reaching of positive results and the fulfilment of assigned task. Active listening and cognitive expectations do not lead to corrections of perspectives, but invite enrichment of reciprocal knowledge and, occasionally, self-repair. The conjunction of dialogic actions and cognitive expectations is the main feature of coordination among adolescents.

9.3   Coordination as active proposal

Coordination may present another feature. In some interactions, adolescents coordinate the different perspectives, supporting and encouraging the interlocutors' self-expression, and in the meanwhile expressing their own perspectives.

S3 concerns a discussion on the Danish Cultural Activity called *Homeless people*. Coordination is managed by the Danish delegation, above all by M1dan, M2dan and F1dan, while F2dan is less involved. In turn 1, M1dan starts organising the turns of speech, obtaining F1arg's alignment (turn 2), and in turn 3 M2dan supports F1arg's participation asking for a feedback. As we have seen in S1 and S2, this kind of promotional question shows the interest for the interlocutor's contribution and creates a space for other contributions. F2arg adds her contribution to the discussion in turn 4. In the following turns, M1dan and M2dan, and later F1dan, actively and intensively participate in the conversation expressing their opinions without imposing their perspective (turns 5, 9, 10, 11, 12, 13, 14). Their active participation is not an obstacle for other contributions, rather it supports them. In turn 7, F2arg shows interest for what has been said by M2dan, asking for repetition. In turns 16, 21 and 24, F1arg and F1ind actively participate asking information: F1arg shows her interest for M1ind's previous explanation (turn 16), and F1ind shows her interest for the Danish situation, which seems different from that of her country (turns 21, 24).

(S3)

1. M1dan: C. ((F1arg))
2. F1arg: we have the homeless.
3. M2dan: you have homeless? (??)
4. F2arg: after crisis I suppose.
5. M2dan: (??) in Denmark, if you are a homeless, you usually have chosen by yourself.
6. (??):   wow
7. F2arg: you could have what?
8. F(??):   chosen by yourself.
9. M2dan: (we have) a very high social support (..) so you can actually live from it. You can have an apart-, a sole apartment and enough for food, but some choose to ahm, some choose to ehm (??) they choose
10. M1dan: yeah, and also ehm those that are
11. M2dan: mentally ((whispering))
12. M1dan: mentally ill, so they can't stay by themselves.
13. F1dan: (??) when they get an apartment from the government or social service, they can't live there, because they are used to live everywhere (??) ((noises; in the other room the KS are cleaning with the radio on))
14. M1ind: in our country also we have homeless, but ah:m the government (is also poor) so: (??), but usually they (?) because they usually get illegal houses, like maybe (?) that they don't have. One day the government kicked them off. (??) (03")
15. M1dan: C.
16. F1arg: (??) homeless is in all the country or just in the capital?
17. M1dan: it's all over.
18. F1dan: yeah, all over, but mostly in the capital.
19. M2dan: yes. Way more in the capital. (there are better places to sleep there) (??)
20. F1dan: N. ((F1ind))
21. F1ind: I just wanted to ask about the hippies. We don't have them in Indonesia, is there, (are there) many of the hippies in Denmark?
22. M2dan: we have some (.) Five hundred? (We don't know many hippies) but they are not hippy, they are Christianiased, they live in Christiania, Christania. Soren will tell (.) please tell the story about Christinia.

23. M1dan: ahm Christiania first was a military base *((M1dan passes a photo of Christiania))* it was first a military base, but then the military went out and then was (??) (for years), and then the hippies ah:m some socialists (entered the fence) and then they came in and then (got into the building)
24. F1ind: **ah it's legal to (get into buildings)?**
25. M2dan: no it's (not)
26. M1dan: no

It is evident that all adolescents feel supported and free to self-express. They show their competence in both coordinating and actively expressing their perspective, without preventing the interlocutors' participation; on the contrary, the coordinators' active participation and self-expression enhance further participation and therefore a balanced distribution of participants' contributions.

S4 concerns an instance of AT called *The ideal city*, which is similar to *Fantasy Island*. Adolescents work in small groups and each group has to build its own country and decide its government, its capital city, its traditional dances, and so on. In turn 1, Fbra tries to promote the interlocutors' participation through a promotional question and in turn 2, Fleb aligns proposing her idea. In turn 3, the other participants echo Fleb's action in order to ask for more information. In turn 4, Fleb explains her idea; apparently she perceives the interlocutors' laughter (turn 5) as support because she keeps explaining the idea in turn 6. In turn 7 her suggestion is supported by Fbra through a continuer. In turn 8 Fleb, feeling supported, tries to include her interlocutors in her proposal. This chance of participation is taken by Mecu, who aligns, asking for advice in turn 9. In turns 10–15, the adolescents actively discuss the idea. The interaction takes the form of a question-answer pair which has the function of creating a shared project of "ideal city", where the communicated contradictions (turns 11–12, turns 16–22) improve the interaction. In particular, in turns 16–22, (1) Fleb suggests that religion can be chosen in the ideal city, (2) Fbra shows her perplexity, (3) Fleb aligns with her perplexity, (4) Fbra confirms her perplexity, (5) Fspa denies the importance of religion, (6) Fleb aligns with this denial, (7) Fbra asserts her adversity to religious matters. Finally, the adolescents confirm Fbra's position (turn 23). In this process, Fleb's position is abandoned through a negotiation process in which Mspa's denial is a turning point which projects Fbra's dissent and therefore the beginning of an alternative story which is confirmed in turn 23.

(S4)
1. Fbra: ok, guys **do you have an idea?**
2. Fleb: **ice(h)-cream(h)**
3. Different voices: **ice cream?**
4. Fleb: we can do like Ice-cream, we scream, all screams for ice-cream

5. *((laughter))*
6. Fleb: **and capital could be chocolate**
7. Fbra: **yeah**
8. Fleb: **who wants to write?**
9. Mecu: *((takes the markers))* **and what name I have to write?**
10. Fleb: ice-cream
11. Mecu: **not ice-cream land?**
12. Fleb: **I don't think so** (..) cause when you say 'Brazil' you don't say 'Brazil land'
13. Fbra: yeah
14. Fleb: and capital city? Chocolate? (..) I don't know. (..) Strawberry?
15. Fger: and what we have to choose too?
16. Fleb: **religion**, weather. (.) Weather is cool (05) and also we to find a history
17. Fbra: **what religion?**
18. Fleb: **religion?**
19. Fbra.   **yeah**
20. Mspa: **no religion**
21. Fleb: **yeah, no religion**
22. Fbra: **for me the perfect society don't have religion**
23. Different voices: **yeah, yeah**

In S4, the effects of active participation on positioning, narratives, and collective decisions are clear. Fbra starts as coordinator but she can actively contribute to the decision-making process only thanks to Mspa's support. Fleb starts as 'project manager', coordinating the actual project but she is ready to abandon her ideas (e.g. about religion). Mspa's solitary comment can enhance a change in decision-making, as it supports Fbra's doubts. This mix of coordination and expression of personal opinions creates the conditions for equal distribution of participation and is a key-factor for enhancing decision-making.

9.4   Ambivalence and monologues

Coordination fails when the focus on the coordinator's perspective prevails, as the interlocutors are not sufficiently supported in their self- expression (or attempts at self-expression).

In S5, adolescents are working in a small group. They must cooperate to build a sort of parachute for an egg. In turn 1, Mcan expresses his worries and doubts about the final result of the activity, introducing it with an other-disclaiming 'but' referring to the previous work. These doubts are indirectly supported by Fcos with a promotional question (turn 2). In turn 3, Mcan confirms Fcos's reframing and explains his concern. In turn 4, Mbos aligns with this concern, however he cannot continue because of his poor English. In turn 5 and 7, Mcan tries to support Mbos's self-expression through continuers. In turn 6, Mbos tries to explain himself through gesture, but in turn 8 he gives up his contribution. In turn 9 Mcan encourages him again, coupling his vocal encouragement with gesture. However, this support is weak and in turn 10 Mbos refuses to continue and Mcan (turn 11) aligns with this refusal. Despite Mcan's attempts to empower his action, Mbos does not feel supported enough to self-express.

(S5)
1. Mcan: **but I see a problem, maybe it doesn't work -**
2. Fcos: **over there?**
3. Mcan: **yes. This doesn't have anything like open to catch air, so it can go slowly**
4. Mbos: **yeah –**
5. Mcan: *((Mcan turns towards Mbos))* **mhmm**
6. Mbos: *((He tries to explain with gesture))*
7. Mcan: **mhmm**
8. Mbos: *((He shows with gesture that it doesn't matter))*
9. Mcan: **no, no** *((Mcan uses gesture to invite Mbos to try again))*
10. Mbos: *((He says no with a shake of his head))*
11. Mcan: **ok**

S5 demonstrates that a weak support may fail in promoting the interlocutors' participation. The simple use of continuers or mild encouragements (*no, no*) is not sufficient to overcome linguistic or cultural obstacles. Promotion of active participation requires more active coordination of the interaction.

S6 concerns a discussion about the Italian Cultural Activity called *House of feelings*, which aims to make participants aware of the treatment and feelings of migrants when they arrive in Italy. Fita asks some questions about the other participants' feelings and understanding during the activity. In turn 1, Fita tries to promote adolescents' self-expression with a promotional question. In turns 2–8, adolescents express their opinions, but they show they are not taking the conversation seriously (see the non verbal cues in turns 2, 6, 8). Fita pays little attention to her interlocutors' contributions (she only utters a continuer in turn 5). In turn 9, she gives the turn of speech to Mcan who expresses his opinion, which she weakly supports in turn 11 with another continuer. In turn 13, Fita tries to involve other adolescents in the discussion, addressing them with a rather educational question about the activity. In turn 14, Mcan tries to give his contribution, but in turn 15, Fita ignores him and starts explaining the activity, imposing her educational perspective. Starting from this turn, she gives up promoting the interlocutors' participation, simply imposing her perspective about the activity. In turn 15, she does not give space for the translation time until one of the Italian delegates points out to her that someone needs the translation (turn 16). After translation time, Fita continues her monologue (not shown).

(S6)

1. Fita:	please **what was the best moment and the worst moment?**
2. Fcos:	the best leaking Nutella ((*laughter*))
3. Feng:	they've got chocolate, we didn't!
4. Mita:	nutella
5. Fita:	**yeah**
6. Feng:	I didn't get chocolate! ((*laughter*))
7. Mdut:	I get a cookie!
8. Mcos:	I get chocolate ((*they keep joking on this topic*))
9. Fita:	C. ((*he gives the turn of speech to Mcan*))
10. Mcan:	I think the best part of it was with the chocolate (??) and the worst was the (??) ((*someone agrees*))
11. Fita:	**yeah**
12. Feng:	(??)
13. Fita:	and (.) **do you have any idea of what we wanted to represent?** So, with this activity –
14. Mcan:	**I need (??)**
15. Fita:	**nobody? So, I will explain you.** The first part was, it's a story about immigrants because in Italy we have erm like erm a little (.) a problem about immigrants. People come in our country and (..) has to live with us. And yeah. In the first part they were still at home, in their country, but they were not happy, so they walked on stones, so they were not so (.) comfortable (.) and they've got also –
16.	((*Someone asks for the Translation Time, but she wants to go on; then, the Italian male delegate makes her notice that someone is asking for the Translation Time, so she stops*))

In S6, Fita switches from an initial attempt to promote participation (turns 1, 9, 13) to a monologue, which leaves no space for the other participants. She appears more interested in educating her interlocutors than in promoting their participation.

The weakness of a coordination based on dialogic actions strongly reduces collective participation, and the communication system gets stuck in the perspective of the coordinator. In this way, coordination is substituted by direction and hierarchical structures become unexpectedly relevant in the interaction.

9.5   Conflict management

Conflicts do not appear very frequently during the interactions among adolescents in summer camps. In particular, we have observed role/task conflicts and interpersonal conflicts.

Role conflicts focus on role performances during activities in which the achievement of a goal is involved. Competition concerning role performances is the most important starting point for conflicts. In these cases, coordination is substituted by competition, which blocks the activity, at least until somebody is able to impose her/his perspective. Apart from S4, in which conflict management is fruitful, because included in active coordination, we have observed three main ways in which adolescents manage these conflicts: ballot, withdrawal and diversion.

9.5.1 Ballot

In S7, during the *Fantasy Island* activity, adolescents work in a small group and must decide how to make the flag which will represent their country. In the first part of the sequence (turns 1–5), Mdut is trying to mediate between Fnor's and Fcan's proposals. In turn 5, Mdut announces the 'best solution' for the group, but in the meanwhile he introduces a new proposal (*'and we can put this here'*) which opens a conflict with Fnor (turn 6). In turn 7, Mdut defends his proposal, but Fnor insists in her conflicting position with a firm and unusual *'no'* (turn 8). Facing this refusal, Mdut introduces a new idea (turn 9), but Fcan suddenly blocks the negotiation proposing a democratic ballot (turn 10). This proposal closes the conflict: in turn 11, Mdut accepts this solution, aligning with Fcan's proposal, and starts managing the ballot (*'Who's only for lucky money and who's for lucky and happy money?'*). After voting, in turns 13 and 15, Mdut checks Fnor's acceptance of the decision, and Fnor aligns with his position (turns 14 and 16). Finally, Mdut confirms the shared decision (turn 16).

(S7)
1. Fnor: why don't we do like erm like that?
2. Fcan: the trees?
3. Fnor: yeah
4. Mdut: this is two doors! (…)
5. Mdut: **yes, everybody is happy too and put it we can put this here**
6. Fnor: **no here!**
7. Mdut: **it's the way -**
8. Fnor: **no!**

9. Mdut: **lucky and happy money**
10. Fcan: **why don't we vote?**
11. Mdut: **yes. Who's only for lucky money and who's for lucky and happy money?**
           Lucky and happy money?
12. *((Almost everybody raises their hand))*
13. Mdut: **yes, we are four. Lucky**
14. Fnor: **yes**
15. Mdut: **and happy**
16. Fnor: **just**
17. Mdut: **ok**

Ballot seems to be a quick and useful way of solving conflicts in adolescents' per-spective. It is easily accepted because it is a 'democratic procedure', and therefore avoids prolonged disputes. However, it also avoids negotiations and their possible coordination.

9.5.2 Withdrawal

In S8, adolescents are involved in a planning group where they have to decide and prepare some activities for the whole camp. They are talking about warm-up ac-tivities. In turn 1, F1arg tries to include the interlocutors in the conversation with a promotional question ('*what do we do?*'), at the same time making her proposal in a doubtful tone ('*The one of the personal belongings?*'). In turn 2, F1nor does not align with F1arg, suggesting a different solution. In turn 3, following the con-flict, F2arg opens a space for alternative proposals. The laughter which follows her opening (turn 4) might be a way to relieve the tension created by the conflict. In turn 5, F1dan aligns with F1arg and implicitly contradicts F1nor's proposal, as she does not seem interested in doing any other kind of warm up. Her change of foot-ing from 'I' to 'we' shows a claim for authoritativeness which is rather unusual in the interactions between adolescents. In turn 6, F1nor replies with her proposal, showing little attention for the consequences of her action: she expresses her idea without listening to other proposals, she neither supports nor encourages people to take part in the interaction. In turns 7-9, the conflict becomes explicit between F2dan, who supports F1dan's solution with a different argument (turns 7 and 9), and F1nor, who keeps supporting her idea of doing the "shark song" (turn 8). In turn 10, F1ind suddenly aligns with F1nor's proposal, through a candidate answer within her question (see Chapter 6). After this alignment, F1dan withdraws from the interaction (turn 12).

(S8)
1. F1arg: as a warm up, **what do we do? The one of the personal belongings?**
2. F1nor: **shark song!**
3. F2arg: **or we should do something else?**
4. *((Laughter))*
5. F1dan: **I think we should just do personal belongings**
6. F1nor: **and the shark song**
7. F2dan: **it's not very long**
8. F1nor: it's very funny!
9. F2dan: **it's a short warm up**
10. F1ind: **what are we going to do? Shark song?**
11. F1nor: shark?
12. F1dan: *((She nods))*

Withdrawal seems to demonstrate that in absence of coordination, proposals are rather volatile. Although she has repeatedly supported F1arg's and her proposal, and she has found some further support, F1dan easily gives up, and the opposite view prevails. F1ind's use of a candidate answer demonstrates that this use of language is not successful only in conditions of role hierarchy; they can also be successful as support to proposals. The consequence, however, is the same: making the decision-making process unbalanced and provoking the withdrawal of a conflicting party.

9.5.3 Diversion

Diversion is the most frequent form of conflict management among the adolescents. In S9, during a planning group, M1ita introduces the theme of the activity, while some participants are not listening, and others are eating. M2ita is building a kind of arena for horse races, and the members of the group pay attention to what he is doing. In turns 1 and 2, M1bra and M1ita seem interested in what M2ita is doing, and ask for explanations. In turn 3, M2ita tries to answer, but he is immediately stopped by M1ita who disqualifies his action (turn 4). His assertion projects laughter (turn 5) which amplifies disqualification and derision of M2ita's action. M1ita's action and the other participants' reaction (the laughter) make the interpersonal conflict explode. In turn 5, M2ita starts with a defensive self-disclaiming 'but' (*'I know but I try'*), and continues offending the other participants (turns 6, 8), who keep laughing at him (turns 7, 9), projecting M2ita's anger. In turn 10, M2bra reacts with a derisory joke which projects new laughter (turn 11). In turn 12, M2fra interrupts this conflict diverting the attention of the participants, but M2ita gets offended and withdraws from the interaction.

(S9)
1. M1bra: **what are you doing?**
2. M1ita: **what are you doing?**
3. M2ita: **no: it's -**
4. M1ita: **that is tomorrow night!** ((*he addresses M2ita*))
5. ((*They start laughing at M2ita*))
6. M2ita: **I know, but I try. I try stupid guys, I try!**
7. ((*Laughter*))
8. M2ita: **stupid boys!**
9. ((*Laughter for 06 seconds*))
10. M2bra: **boyfriend of mine!**
11. ((*Laughter*))
12. M2fra: **A.? A.? So how many activity, how many games do we have?**
13. M1arg: two pokers, one black jack (.) horse and maybe   [we have like
14. M2fra: [slot machine
15. M1arg: what?
16. M2fra: do you know: ahm
17. M1arg: ah, the machine as well

In S10, during the *Fantasy Island* activity, a small group of adolescents must decide how to make the flag which will represent their country. In turn 1, Mdut positions himself, self-assessing his abilities. In turn 2, his action is supported by Fcan with a continuer (*ok*), anticipating her expectations which enhance a recommendation ('*make them beautiful*'). In turn 4, Fcos introduces a proposal, consequently a conflict arises between Fcos and Mdut about the marker to be used, as Mdut has proposed to draw. In turns 7–9, Mdut and Fcos engage in a role/task conflict: their conflict concerns their role performances and the goal they want to achieve. In turn 8, Mdut underlines that he is able to draw something beautiful, while in turn 9, Fcos underlines that she is able to draw something bigger. Both Mdut and Fcos announce their role competences as well as the different objectives they will be able to reach. The use of the modal verb *can* associated with an assertive construction of the sentence, shows that they want to impose their perspective. Fnor interrupts this conflict in turn 10, diverting her mates' attention.

(S10)
1. Mdut: **I can draw people**
2. Fcan: **ok, then, make them beautiful**
3. ((*Mdut starts drawing and the girls in the group are amused*))
4. Fcos: **why don't we do like (..) ?** ((*she takes the marker and starts drawing something*))
5. Fnor: ((*Addressing Fcan*)) C. ! *don't laugh at her!*

6. Fcan: no, at this
7. ((Mdut and Fcos are fighting for the marker))
8. Mdut: **I can make it beautiful**
9. Fcos: **I can make it bigger!**
10. Fnor: **why don't we do like erm like that?**
11. Fcan: the trees?
12. Fnor: yeah

In S11, during a debriefing session, adolescents play a soccer match with an invisible ball. In turn 1, Mdan tries to promote the interlocutors' participation asking for assessment of the activity. In turn 2, almost all adolescents express their negative opinion and, due to the noises caused by the participants, in turn 3 Mdan tries to restore some kind of order. In this way, he is able to offer the turn of speech to Marg and Fcan (turns 4 and 6). Fcan's turn (6) opens an interpersonal conflict with Mcan (turns 7–10). In turn 12, Mdan invites Fnor to speak, ignoring the conflict between Fcan and Mcan, and diverting the participants' attention.

(S11)
1. Mdan: **did you guys like the activity?**
2. All together: <u>**no!**</u> ((noise and overlapping))
3. Mdan: **please! Please! Please! One, one at the time!** C. ((Marg))
4. Marg: I liked, but I didn't like the football because it had no sense. It's not our fault, because you said to us. It's very difficult. ((he probably refers to the match with the invisible ball))
5. Mdan: ok ((he points towards Fcan))
6. Fcan: I (would be) the goalie, right? And my team got closer to the net and the other team (would) come and then shoot in mine and
7. Mcan: (??)   [**you didn't save it!**
8. Fcan: [**no::! I caught it like ten times!**
9. Mcan: **no**
10. Fcan: <u>**yes!**</u>
11. ((Overlapping and screams due to the conflict between Fcan and Mcan; 10))
12. Mdan: **ok, Molly.**
13. Fnor: (I didn't like football), because (??) the other one made a goal that wasn't a goal, but I liked the Frank's running up and down.

Adolescents tend to avoid conflicts or to solve them in the simplest possible way. Avoidance and quick conclusion of conflicts are directly correlated with preference for peaceful coordination which, however, implies the abandonment of coordination. When avoidance does not work, participants show their lack of concern for their interlocutors.

S12 concerns the activity *Peace War Peace*. The group is building part of a city with cardboard, paper, cans and other materials. In turn 1, Mdut criticises Mchi, disqualifying his participation. Mdut tries to use the glue but his action is in turn disqualified by Feng (turn 2). This opens a conflict based on role performances: in turns 4–6 and 8–9, Feng contradicts Mdut, who reacts with a protest (turn 6), followed by the interlocutors' laughter. In turn 9, Feng concludes the conflict imposing her perspective ('*it doesn't matter*') and disqualifying Mdut.

(S12)
((MChi is trying to put something under the roof))
1. Mdut: **no, no don't put. You broke it** *((then he tries to use the glue))*
2. Feng: **no, no, no it smells, it smells**
3. *((laughter))*
4. Mdut: **we can put it here**
5. Feng: **no, wait. We put in the middle. Yeah, just take this off a bit**
6. Mdut: **oohh!**
7. *((laughter))*
8. Mcos: that doesn't look like a part of a building
9. Feng: **it doesn't matter.** It's in the future

Turn 9 shows Feng's lack of concern for Mdut's actions as well as for the consequences of her action.

9.6   Conclusions

Adolescents show their competence in coordinating the interaction and managing participation, and they are able to promote their interlocutors' participation without hierarchical structures. They are able to create reciprocal empowerment in the interaction, supporting each other, through two forms of coordination: coordination as distribution of equal participation, and coordination through personal proposals.

In general, adolescents' coordination is mainly expressed through recurrent promotional questions, which are based on cognitive expectations about the results of the interaction, but which can also work as encouragements in participation, which is not assessed. The effective management of the interaction combines coordination through promotional questions with active contributions through the expression of personal perspectives, which can improve participation both qualitatively and quantitatively. Active contributions seem to be particularly effective for decision-making. Disclaimers and competitions are much less frequent than during adult's organisational meetings; adolescents try to impose their perspective less frequently than adults when participation is scarce and conversations are limited. Furthermore, these interactions recurrently display non competing we-identities, while changes of footing asserting speaker's authoritativeness are infrequent.

Adolescents who coordinate activities are able to develop a dialogic space in which their interlocutors feel supported and confirmed in their expressions, while only occasionally do failures in promoting participation provoke ambivalences and hierarchies. Adolescents' actions seem particularly effective because they express their perspective, without imposing their positions in the interaction. Active contribution shows coordinators' personal involvement in the interaction; this form of action testifies the opportunity to speak and the meaning of coordinated actions in decision-making.

The mixture of questions (promoting equal distribution of participation) and assertions (promoting new proposals) in coordination gives new impulse to a fruitful and satisfying interaction. As we have seen in Chapter 3, the adolescents' narrative is that shared decisions are ineffective without a fruitful dialogue, as people adhere only contingently to collective decisions and stick to their previous opinion.

Comparison with organisational meetings involving adults and in some cases adolescents shows a common framework: in both conditions decision-making is the main task and dialogic coordination is the cultural form which allows its achievement. Therefore, dialogic coordination is a secondary structure of the interaction: its achievement is not the main task for it. These conditions of coordination clearly differentiate these situations from those in which coordination is educationally promoted (see Chapters 6, 7, 8).

However, it is not unusual to observe important differences between organisational meetings with adults and activities involving only adolescents. Firstly, the prominent hierarchical structure of organisational meetings is different from the symmetrical form of activities involving adolescents. This difference explains more frequent coordination in adolescents' activities, and easiness in equal distribution of participation. Secondly, adolescents do not seem to give particular value to role performances in their interactions; their interactions are much more frequently person-centred, because their actions tend to distribute participation rather than to demonstrate competence. Paradoxically, this lack of displayed competence in role performance highlights competence in dialogic action, i.e. in exercising agency. While interactions between adults frequently demonstrate competence through performances, interactions between adolescents give frequently voice to participants' ideas.

This kind of management of the interaction fails in case of conflicts. Conflicts are not very frequent and concern role performances and interpersonal disputes.

In both cases, avoidance and simple solutions are preferred, with few exceptions. Conflicts are mainly managed in ways which seem simple and apparently reduce the risks of escalation. In particular, ballot, withdrawal and diversion seem to avoid escalation of conflicts. However, these forms of management prevent development of participation and expression of different perspectives, and this is also an obstacle to coordination.

The analysis of conflicts shows the problems caused by actions which do not pay attention to their communicative consequences, i.e. mainly the imposition of personal perspectives. It is evident that conflicts are treated as risky and their appearance creates the conditions for an easy solution. Therefore, while participation is promoted in situations in which there is shared coordination, it is impeded in situations in which coordination is not shared and adolescents must face difficulties and contradictions in continuing communication.

Activities 5

Interpreting as mediation?

Claudio Baraldi and Rosanna Blasi

Chapter 10 deals with translations during educational activities. Translations are important because children display a strongly differentiated competence in understanding and speaking English as a lingua franca. In villages, adults' translations are frequently instrumental to the achievement of assigned tasks while promotion of children's active participation is scarce. During their translation activity, adults tend to strategically reduce renditions of translated turns and to avoid possible conflicts. Nevertheless, during the translation activity, dyadic interactions in the first language may be useful in promoting children's active participation, and adults may also highlight the possibility to change decisions and reopen discussions. Dialogic mediation seems to be more likely in adolescents' occasional translations for their mates in summer camps.

10.1 The importance of translation

The CISV narrative considers non-verbal communication important for effective interpersonal relationships in multilingual contexts. However, the increasing value assigned to English as a lingua franca in many countries has produced two consequences for CISV activities. Firstly, the power of English-speaking children and adolescents has been enhanced, both in understanding activities and, above all, in communicating during activities. Secondly and consequently, 'translation time' has become a very important activity. These phenomena might disappear when all children and adolescents are able to speak English very well, however, at present, translation is an essential component of CISV activities. In villages, most children need systematic linguistic support, because their linguistic knowledge is limited, or very limited. Even in summer camps, however, where adolescents are in general much more competent in English, translation is often a necessary tool for promoting participation. Therefore, translation has a fundamental function in the interaction.

This chapter deals with translation and the need for clarification in the interactions between adults and delegates and among delegates, where participants are not very competent speakers of English. The analysis highlights the practices of interlinguistic and intercultural mediation which should promote children's and adolescents' understanding and participation in the activities. These practices primarily involve leaders, and occasionally staff members and JCs. The analysis aims to discover the effects of interlinguistic and intercultural mediation in multilingual villages and summer camps. For linguistic and practical reasons, the analysed translations concern Italian and Spanish delegations.

10.2   Translations as monologues: Selection of information

In the last ten years, the literature on dialogue interpreting or community interpreting (e.g. Angelelli 2004; Brunette, Bastin, Hemlin & Clarke 2003; Hale 2007; Mason 1999, 2001; Wadensjö, Englund-Dimitrova & Nilsson 2007), has been widely influenced by the idea that interpreting is achieved in the interaction (Wadensjö 1998), and that interpreters are active participants with important functions in the interaction (Davidson 2000). A number of studies highlight the relevance of interpreter-mediated interactions in terms of interpreters' coordination of the conversation during translation. Research demonstrates that it is not infrequent for translation to be performed by ad hoc interpreters, or cultural mediators, who lack specific professional training in interpreting. In CISV initiatives, interpreting is 'ad hoc' as it is performed by leaders, JCs and staff members without specific professional skills, who are primarily intended as coordinators and mediators.

According to Baraldi & Gavioli (2007), in this kind of situations, and particularly in healthcare institutions, interpreting presents two main structures: (1) after-turn translation, which are rare, and (2) combination of dyadic monolingual interactions and summarized or expanded translations, which are much more frequent. Similarly, during CISV activities, after-turn translations are not frequent and are never merely after-turn, as exemplified in S1 and S2.

In S1, the chef of the village is explaining to the children how to make bread and biscuits. She speaks Italian and the camp director translates her explanations into English for the children. The distribution of turns is unequal, as the children participate only with non-verbal forms. DMita's turn-by-turn translation is strictly informative. At the end of turn 15, however, DMita adds new information; this expanded translation might establish contact with the children, underlining their possible perception of vinegar through a shift in register ('It smells') but it has no effect. In turn 18, DMita strengthens the normative connotation of the chef's original utterance (turn 16), turning his informative utterance to explicit instructions, and forbidding the children to touch the table after they have cleaned it. Finally, in turns 26, 27, and 28, DMita and SFita repeat a concept that has already been translated in turn 25: these turns are non renditions which highlight the normative expectations introduced in turn 18.

(S1)

1. CHEF: perfetto. Oggi facciamo il pane e i biscotti
          perfect. Today we are going to make bread and biscuits.

2. DMita: ok, today we're gonna do bread and biscuits

3. Children: wow! yes!

4. CHEF: per iniziare a fare questo, ognuno avrà una postazione davanti al proprio tavolo
          to begin, each of you will have a place at the table

5. DMita: to do this, to start doing this, each of you has a place, his place, in front of the table

6. CHEF: questo tavolo ora lo dobbiamo rendere pulito per mangiare
          we have to clean this table to eat

7. DMita: we start with cleaning it

[…]

12. CHEF: usiamo l'aceto
          we're going to use vinegar

13. DMita: [we use

14. CHEF: [perché non è un detersivo
          [because it is not a detergent

15. DMita: we use vinegar because it's not a soap, it's natural. **It smells, but it's natural**

16. CHEF: quindi, da ora in poi questo tavolo non dobbiamo più sporcarlo
          from now on we must not dirty this table

17. (02)

18. DMita: **ok. so, once you clean it, once you clean it don't touch it anymore**

[…]

22. CHEF: e: chi ha finito
          erm: who has finished

23. DMita: ok, and now, listen! who's finished go to the [shower and –

24. CHEF: [va a lavarsi le mani
                                                       [must go to wash their hands

25. DMita: wash - wash your hands

26. SFita: **it's very important that you wash your hands**   [**so please**

27. DMita: [**wash your hands**

28. SFita: **use soap! ok? (??) water is not enough!**

In S2, LFita translates Meng's utterances in Italian, in order to promote Fita's understanding. This is a turn-by-turn translation involving two participants. Fita intervenes only in turns 8, 10, and 14, giving feedback to LFita or implicitly inviting translation. In turn 16, LFita abandons the role of interpreter and assumes the role of leader, inviting Fita to express her preference. LFita's translation allows Fita to make a choice in turn 17. Nevertheless, LFita does not translate Fita's contribution: consequently the leader does not promote mutual understanding. Her translation has an informational value only for Fita. In particular, she gives instructions to Fita about what to do and how to participate in the activity.

(S2)

1. LFita:	can you say it?	
2. Meng:	women's rights	
3. LFita:	erm i diritti delle donne	
	erm Women's rights	
4. Meng:	free speech	
5. LFita:	diritto di parola	
	the right to speak	
6. Meng:	democracy	
7. LFita:	democrazia	
	democracy	
8. Fita:	**sì, democrazia**	
	yes, democracy	
9. Meng:	health care	
10. Fita:	**che cosa sono –**	
	what are they -	
11. LFita:	servizi sanitari	
	healthcare services	
12. Meng:	education	
13. LFita:	e l'istruzione	
	and education	
14. Fita:	**mmm**	
15. Meng:	health care and education	
16. LFita:	**ok, adesso li dovete mettere in ordine di importanza (..) secondo te, qual è il più importante?**	
	ok, now you have to rank them (..) which is the most important in your opinion?	
17. Fita:	**questo**	
	this one	

Similarly to what happens in healthcare settings, during CISV activities, a frequent form of translation is the combination of dyadic monolingual interactions and summarized or expanded translations (Baraldi & Gavioli 2007). After a sequence in English, leaders translate in a summarized or expanded way and their delegations can interact with them to obtain further information or make comments.

In many of these cases, as we have seen in S1 and S2, adults' translations are followed by children's nodding as a sign of understanding, short answers which often follow yes/no questions (see also Chapter 6), and non-verbal communication in general. This structure of translation successfully promotes activities, but it is not effective in promoting delegates' self-expression.

In S3, during the activity *Life boat*, seven children are acting as characters defined by their job and social status. Only six of them will be able to remain on the boat, while the seventh will be abandoned, as the least useful to society. The aim of the game is to deal critically with the problems of prejudices and stereotypes in society. During the activity, LFita translates LFcan's turns, but does not translate the children's contributions (for instance, she does not translate turns 3 and 4). This selection of information influences F1ita's understanding of the communicative process, as she can only understand LFcan's contributions. Moreover, LFita's translation reduces F1ita's active participation: in particular, in turns 8 and 11, LFita's translations guide F1ita's actions through yes/no questions which prevent the Italian child from a critical participation in the interaction; F1ita cannot actively participate in the interaction because she is solicited to make quick choices. LFita's translation is therefore a one-sided translation: from LFcan, who directs the activity, to the child, whose actions are oriented to the leader's expectations. This action does not seem very effective and, in turn 22, the child is obliged to ask for the translation to follow the activity, thus confirming the informational value of translation.

(S3)

1. LFcan: the alcoholic captain of the ship
2. LFita: il capitano alcolizzato della barca *((to F1ita))*
          the alcoholic captain of the boat
3. F1arg: (??) **drive us**
4. M1spa: **he's going to kill all the people on the boat**
5. LFcan: not necessarily because (??) people are alcoholics and drink a lot, you
          can't tell   [(??) and we don't know (??)
6. LFita: [però L. *((LFcan))* dice che comunque non è
          detto che sia – ti dice che è alcolizzato, per cui solitamente beve molto,
          però non ti dice se effettivamente è ubriaco mentre guida la barca
                             [however, L. says that he may not actually – she
          says he is alcoholic, so he normally gets drunk, but she is not saying that he
          is drunk while he pilots the boat
7. LFcan: the mayor of Madrid, mayor of Madrid, mayor of Madrid, yes? Do you
          understand? If you want him on the boat put your hands up

8. LFita: *((to Flita))* **lo vuoi sulla barca il sindaco, oppure no?**
            do you want the mayor on the boat or not?
9. LFcan: one, two, three, four, ok, so it's (down) between the single pregnant woman who is sixteen years old or the eighty years old scientist
10. F1arg: this one, out *((she indicates the paper))*
11. LFita: **(??) incinta e (??) lo scienziato**
            (??) pregnant and (??) the scientist
12. LFcan: do you all agree that the eighty years old scientist should be the person off?
13. *((Some children say "yes"))*
14. LFita: sta dicendo che lo scienziato ottantenne dovrebbe - on the boat? *((to LFcan))*? on the boat?
            she is saying that the eighty-year- old scientist should -
15. LFcan: the one (??) him off
16. LFita: ok, fuori dalla barca, in mare, ok?
            ok, outside the boat, in the sea, ok?
[…]
20. LFcan: yeah, (??) he knows (??) so, yeah, (??) who was the single pregnant woman, C.
21. F1ita: **cosa dice?**
            what is she saying?
22. LFita: chi era la mamma single incinta
            who was the single pregnant mother

In S1, S2 and S3, the informational value of translation is evident, but translation is not effective in promoting the children's participation. Although children can understand what they have to do, they do not participate actively in the interaction: they follow the adults' instructions (S1) or stand aloof from the interaction (S2 and S3).

These results confirm that this type of translation does not easily promote active participation (Baraldi & Gavioli 2008). In particular, when translating, adults select information, to convey to their delegates only the questions the latter are supposed to answer; consequently, non-English-speaking children understand the communicative processes differently from children with better competences in English. According to Davidson (2000), the selection of information is the main feature of interpreting as *gatekeeping*: interpreters protect institutional roles from risky situations created by their interlocutors. This consideration may well apply to CISV educators: their gatekeeping concerns both the achievement of activities and the cultural presuppositions of CISV education. However, there are two oversimplifications in this interpretation. Firstly, gatekeeping is much more crucial for its effect in reducing children's participation than for its protection of the institution. Secondly, the selection of information does no satisfactorily explain gatekeeping.

10.3   Translations as formulations: Gatekeeping and conflict management

Gatekeeping is based on the tendency on the part of adults to change the meanings of original utterances during translation, influencing their interlocutors' understanding of communicative processes. This happens for two reasons. Firstly, these changes can *adapt* children's understanding to the organisation of activities and their guiding values. Secondly, they can enhance *cognitive forms* of children's contributions. Therefore, these changes establish normative and cognitive expectations. Formulation is the most relevant form in which these expectations are established and these changes produced.

In S4, turn 1, LMbra announces his intention to highlight the importance of respect among children; in particular, he remarks that when somebody raises her/his hand to talk, the other participants should keep silent and listen to her/him. In other words, LMbra promotes a cooperative atmosphere based on the cultural presupposition of active listening, and avoidance of power relationships. In turn 2, LFita translates LMbra's turn, emphasizing the normative expectations presented. She highlights the gap between adults and children, and does so by saying that adults must be listened to by children.

(S4)

1. LMbra: ok everybody? Just to remind you that (.) **when (.) an adult or any of you participants raise your arm (we know you have) to say something (.) so (.) other people will respect you (..) and when you also raise an arm and remain in silence and everyone can listen to what you-** […] all right? I'll tell you one more time. A raising hand, a high five means: "ehi people, I want to speak. Please, can you hear me? (..) It is not necessary for us to <u>shout</u>, so we can also be respectful. (..) For the next activities we're gonna have some running games inside the gym (.) because outside *((indicating outside the gym))* it's too hot (03) so we will stay here <u>inside</u>. (..) we don't go outside *((indicating again outside the gym))*, because outside (.) it's too hot *((pretending to dry off his forehead))* The most important for us now is to remain (.) here, inside the gym. Translations.

2. LFita: ok *((standing up and talking to her delegation))*, allora, **prima di tutto ricordatevi che quando un leader alza la mano dobbiamo stare in silenzio, perché significa che vuole dire qualcosa, quindi innanzitutto come segno di rispetto**, ok? Adesso facciamo invece un'attività, un gioco

in cui bisognerà correre, stiamo in palestra, non andiamo fuori perché è
troppo caldo. Ok? *((sitting down again))*
*ok, so. First of all remember that we have to keep silent when a leader
raises his hand, because this means that he wants to say something, so,
above all in sign of respect, ok? Now we are going to do an activity, a
running game. We are going to stay in the gym. We won't go outside
because it's too hot. Ok?*

This formulation can easily produce a reduction of children's active participation,
as a consequence of their lesser right to be listened to.

In S5, during the first part of the interaction within the Italian delegation,
SF3ita promotes the children's reflection about the ways in which the activity
can be performed (turns 61, 67, 75, 79). In turn 93, she translates their contributions by formulating the children's utterances, presenting them in a better cognitive form. In this way, SF3ita's translation adds her perspective to the
children's. SF3ita makes her delegates aware of the meaning of her translation
(turn 95), but she presents her formulation as if it was the children's original
utterance. Moreover, she avoids translating LMusa' turn (94), which underlines
the importance of participation.

(S5)
61. SF3ita: **ehm: come siete riusciti a comunicare nella vostra squadra?**
              what are the ways you communicate in your team?
62. M2ita: [coi gesti, poi in inglese
              with gesture, then in English
63. F1ita: [in inglese!
              in English!
64. M2ita: gli facevi vedere così –
              you did like this -
65. F1ita: anke un po' in inglese!
              a little bit in English too!
66. M2ita: eh!
67. SF3ita: **lui ha detto anche in inglese-**
              he says in English too-
[...]
75. SF3ita: **ma secondo voi nel primo gioco si comunicava bene?**
              do you think that there was a good communication in the first game?
76. F2ita: ma quale, quello de:l treno(.) secondo me abbastanza
              which one? The one of the train? (.) Enough, in my opinion
77. F1ita: soprattutto in quello delle sedie
              above all in the game of the chairs.

78. M1ita: in quello della penna pure (..) quello delle sedie, se non capivi potevi
cadere per terra
*in the pen game too (..) in the chair game, if you did not understand, you
could fall down.*

79. SF3ita: **ma secondo voi, in quale gioco era più facile comunicare quello dei
treni, quello della penna nella bottiglia o quello della sedia**
*from your point of view, could you communicate easily in the train game,
the pen game, the bottle game or the chair game?*

80. M1ita: le sedie
the chairs

81. F2ita: sedia
chair

[…]

93. SF3ita: and: they are saying they communicate even in English, with signs but: **it
was: (.) easier to communicate with signs in the last game, because: it
was easier, just in the structure of the game, it was easier to communicate
with signs, like: they pass the chair and it was obvious that you have to
pay attention to the signs while you take it**

94. LMusa: **[that's very very important, the signs, talking is very important (.)
if they don't understand what you say, you have to say it in another way**

95. SF3ita: **[(*(to M2ita)*) gli ho detto quello che avete detto voi,** che
praticamente era più semplice l'ultimo gioco perché ti passavano la sedia
e tu sapevi che per forza la dovevi andare avanti e: quindi era più semplice
questo che gli altri
*[I told him what you told me, the last game was easier because they
passed the chair and you knew you had to go on and: that's why it was easier
than the other games*

Translation also establishes the opportunity to create normative expectations
about children's contributions, when these are followed by adults' comments
about children's participation.

In S6, children are invited to avoid the destruction of a nation struck by
the fall of a huge meteorite. In turn 7, LFita translates LFphi's turns (1, 3, 5)
after some continuers by the children (turns 2, 4, 6). M1ita and M2ita try to
express their preference for developing the activity in a different way from what
expected (turns 8, 10). LFita's reaction is a formulation of LFphi's instructions
(turn 11) which binds their actions to the fixed structure of the activity, rather
than promoting their self-expression. In turn 11, LFita introduces her normative expectations preventing the children from changing the way the activity is
developed.

(S6)

1. LFphi: your countries are really perfect. However, °however, there was a hu:ge
meteorite°. Everybody knows what a meteorite is?

2. Children: **yes, yes**

3. LFphi: from the (upper) space?

4. Children: **yes**

5. LFphi: ((*imitating the noise of a falling meteorite*)) niaw: pciuf! now, they gave
your country a problem, that you have to solve! ah! or else, the country
will be dead

6. Children: **yes! dead!**

(2)

7. LFita: **c'è stato un cataclisma che ha praticamente: portato un problema nel
vostro- praticamente se non volete che il vostro pianeta praticamente
scompaia**
*there was a catastrophe which created a problem in your- if you don't
want your planet to practically disappear*

8. M1ita: **no ma se   [lo vogliamo?**
but if   [we want

9. LFita: **[il vostro, la vostra terra, dovete risolvere il problema**
                [your, your planet, you must solve the problem

10. M2ita: **se vogliamo (??)**
if we want (??)

11. LFita: **no, non c'è possibilità, dovete assolutamente risolvere il problema che
vi è stato dato, ok? dovete parlare, discutere, poi risolvete il vostro
problema qua, dite come lo avete risolto.**
*no, there is no other possibility. You must absolutely solve the problem we
gave you, ok? You must talk, discuss, then solve your problem, tell us how
you solved it.*

In S7, in a summer camp F1bra and LMpor are coordinating the interaction. In
turn 177, LMspa translates LMpor's turn in 175. In the first part of turn 177, he
conveys the meaning of the original utterance then he proposes a formulation
which tries to guide his delegates' selection towards his own preferred choice,
aligning with LMpor's suggestion, which is presented as more convenient. In
turn 178, M1spa tries to express his position, but LMspa interrupts him (turn
179) saying emphatically that he is not responsible for what he is translating. In
fact, M1spa's very short turn 178 might be interpreted as disagreement, but
it does not imply LMspa's responsibility for what he has translated; nevertheless, LMspa tries to legitimise his own position. In the following turns, LMspa
continues to strengthen his preference (turn 183), avoiding answering M2spa's
question in turn 182. LMspa uses his linguistic competence to influence his

delegates' perspective, rather than to promote their self-expression and their mutual understanding.

(S7)

175. LMpor: one hour and a half. (.) ya. If you want to do some bigger activity, something like a cultural activity or anything (..) and all the activities will be small, you really think to need an extra half an hour of delegation time? I really like the delegation time, but I think it would be good for you guys to place one activity bigger, but it's only – just think about that.

176. Fbra1: ya, ok. So let's vote. Who wants to take time from the activity- oh sorry translation.

177. Lmspa: para él está bién, porque le gusta mucho el delegation time pero que: si queréis hacer alguna actividad larga, o cultural o algo así, os conviene tener una actividad de dos horas. A lo mejor una actividad de dos horas no se hace, pero si un planning group planea una actividad de una hora, bien. **Pero si va a planear una actividad de una hora y media, y si sobra tiempo hay free time. Tu te das cuenta que a lo mejor que el planning no rellena a las dos horas.**

he agrees with you, because he likes delegation time, but if you want to do longer activities, cultural ones or something like that, it is advisable to have a two-hour-long activity. Maybe we won't have an activity of two hours, if a planning group plans an activity of one hour, ok. Otherwise, if it plans an activity of one hour and a half and there will be some time left, you will have free time. You realise that the planning does not fill up two hours.

178. Mspa1: **bueno –**
ok, but -

179. Lmspa: **¡haced como creéis! ¡Estoy contando lo que dicen!**
do as you like! I'm reporting what they're saying!

180. Mspa2: y las soluciones que han propuesto ahora, ¿qué son?
and which solution do they propose now?

181. Lmspa: las soluciones que han propuesto ahora son si quieres quitar media hora de la actividad o si quieres que la actividad sea de dos horas.
now they propose to remove half an hour from the activity or to have a two-hour-long activity.

182. Mspa2: **no sé (..) De verdad no sé que: (..) ¿Me puedo abstener?**
I don't know (..) I really don't know. Can I abstain ?

183. Lmspa: **yo: erm: Yo: voy a votar que:: hagan las dos horas de actividad (..)**
I: erm: I'm going to vote for the two-hour-long activity.
ya, we finished the translation.

The establishment of normative and cognitive expectations is very frequent in interlinguistic mediation during the activities. These expectations guide the selection of information in order to achieve expected results, the meanings of formulations which reinforce educational values, and the management of possible interactions with the children in their first language. However, they also prevent children from expressing their perspectives.

10.4   Dyadic management of conflicts

As we have seen, when children express either their need for clarifications or their perspectives in their first language, adults often establish cognitive and normative expectations. While leaders promote children's understanding by clarifying their doubts and answering their questions, their main aim is to guarantee a 'correct' development of the activities. Adults highlight explanations of rules and objectives, while other aspects are not considered relevant, and are frequently not translated. This enhances normative conflict resolutions in dyadic monolingual interactions.

S8 concerns an activity planned by some adolescents and LMpor. From turn 1 to turn 17, LMpor coordinates the planners' contributions explaining the activity to the adolescents and interacting with some of them (not reported). In turn 18, LMpor invites the leaders to translate for those who did not understand. In turn 19, LMspa's summarized rendition formulates the utterances of previous turns for his delegation. He openly appreciates the activity, and then summarizes the main aspects of the preceding explanation. In turn 20, M2spa asks for clarifications. In turn 21, LMspa answers to his delegate, but in turn 23 he seems to be bothered by his interruption (turn 22), and his answer blocks M2spa's opportunity to participate ('*Espera, joder*'), maintaining a hierarchical positioning. Ignoring LMspa's turn, the Spanish adolescents continue to ask (turns 24, 26), without receiving proper answers. In turn 27, LMspa asks about M2spa's need for clarifications (turn 26) without translating his question (turn 26) and M2bra answers the Spanish leader (turn 28).

(S8)

18. LMpor: before dividing into groups you want the translation
19. Lmspa: **a ver. Ésta es una actividad guapísima.** A mí me la explicaron desde el principio. Vais a ir en grupos de cinco grupos, cada grupo tiene una fábrica que produce determinados objetos, puedes ser roba, puede ser comida. En los grupos de cinco hay dos financieros, uno del sindicato, uno del ambiente y el presidente. A cada uno de vosotros van a dar un rol de esto, tenéis que ateneros a vuestro rol, vale? El objetivo es comprar la mayor cantidad de objetos en la fábrica, vale, comprar la mayor cantidad, y: contaminar lo menos posible

so. This is a very nice activity. They explained it to me from the beginning. You will be in groups of five people, each group has a factory to produce certain objects like clothes, food. Each group has two financiers, a trade unionist, one environmentalist and the president. Each of you will play one of these roles and you have to keep it, ok? The aim is to buy the largest quantity of objects for the factory, ok? To buy as much as you can by polluting as less as you can.

20. M2spa: **¿y si nos dan poco dinero? ¿Si nos dan cien? ¿Si nos sacan los cien?**
and what happens if they give us less money, if they give us one hundred, if they take out one hundred?

21. Lmspa: para sacar los cien van a ir los lideres con propuestas de financiación, los del planning con propuestas de financiación. Vale? Y lo que decia vosotros decidís si os conviene o no. Entonces están, como os había dicho, los dos financieros, el ecologista y el sindicato y el presidente. Y solo van a votar estos cuatro, vale? Los financieros, el ecologista y el del sindicato, vale?
to take out one hundred, the leaders and the planners come to you with financial proposals, ok? What I told you is to decide if you agree or not. So there will be, as I told you, the financiers, the ecologist, the trade unionist and the president. Only the financiers, the ecologist and the trade unionist are going to vote, right?

22. M2spa: **y el presidente?**
and the president?

23. Lmspa: **espera, joder!** Si los dos financieros que seguramente si van a hacer su rol bien, van a ser un conjunto y quieren producir más y no les importa de la contaminación, y luego si el ecologista y el del sindicato se unen serán dos contra dos y luego será el presidente que tomara la decisión.
wait! Damn! If the financiers, who normally are going to act well, agree, want to produce more and don't care to reduce the pollution, and the ecologist and the unionist join their forces, they will be two against two. So the president will take the decision.

24. M1spa: **y el sindicato que sindicato es?**
and the trade union, what kind of trade union is that?

25. Lmspa: **es de los trabajadores,** y a lo mejor sabes, le interesa producir más, para que suba el sueldo o a lo mejor le interesa conservar el medio ambiente, y está de acuerdo con el ecologista. Bueno si estos dos se unen, la decisión es del presidente, y bueno si uno de estos dos vota con el financiero, pues el presidente no vota. Entonces el objetivo del juego es comprar la mayor cantidad de objetos y que produzcan poca contaminación. Lo que hay que encontrar es el balance, (.) o a lo mejor los financieros lo que le pasa es comprar los más baratos y les da igual que contaminar y el ecologista el contrario. Y el presidente es que ya realmente le toca decidir cuando se empatan estos dos, le toca realmente decidir

the workers' union. Maybe they are interested to produce more in order to earn more or maybe they want to protect the environment and agree with the ecologist. In this case the decision is in the president's hands; otherwise, if the ecologist or the unionist vote with the financiers, the president won't vote. Indeed, the aim of the game is to buy the largest quantity of objects at a low contamination level. The president is going to decide whenever two members unite, he has to decide.

26. M2spa: **y el presidente les puede pedir –**
can the president ask them –

27. Lmspa: **no ha dicho nada sobre el presidente**
he didn't say anything about the president
((to Mbra2 who approaches them)) the leaders do not play?

28. M2bra: no, if they just wanna stay there and helping kids.

In S9, in turns 6, 8, 10, 13, and 15, M1ita and M2ita express their doubts and disappointment regarding the meanings of the activity, while F2ita seems to adapt to its rules, although not agreeing with them (turn 12). LMita reacts creating a "double bind" (Watzlavick, Beavin & Jackson 1967): in turns 17 and 19, he urges the children to participate, however his tone and words discourage the children's participation rather than promoting it. This is confirmed by the fact that LMita highlights only the 'right' way to perform the activity (turns 14, 22, 24). He pays more attention to the prefixed framework than to the delegates' points of view. As a consequence, the children hesitate to express their perspectives, staying silent for a long time (turns 16, 21). In particular, F1ita seems to feel uncomfortable in participating (turns 18, 20). In turn 23, M2ita seems to give up his scepticism, and adapts to his leader's perspective.

(S9)

6. M1ita: <u>**è insensato –**</u>
<u>*it's senseless –*</u>

7. *LMita:*   <u>*cosa?*</u>
<u>*what?*</u>

8. M1ita: **eh, che la peste venga uccisa dalla morte –**
that death killed the plague –

9. LMita: perché?
why?

10. M1ita: **eh, perché: vabbè-**
yes, because:, ok-

11. F1ita: perché la peste è una malattia
because the plague is a disease

12. F2ita: **vabbé: è un gioco**
ok, but it's a game

13. M2ita: **un gioco che finisce così:**
            a game which is concluded like that:
14. LMita: <u>**la morte uccide 'sta malattia, no?**</u>
            <u>*death kills this illness, right?*</u>
15. M1ita: **vabbé, sì –**
            ok, yes –
16. ((06))
17. LMita: <u>**no, dì, (.) parlate, o;h, madonna!**</u>
            <u>*no, tell me (..) Speak! O:h my gosh!*</u>
18. F1ita: **no, perché-**
            erm: because-
19. LMita: **dì**
            speak
20. F1ita: **e:h-**
            erm-
21. ((08))
22. LMita: *((annoyed))* **praticamente se tu sei un coniglio e ti prende un cacciatore
            e tu gli devi dare due bigliettini, ma ne hai solo uno, tu sei morto, e devi
            entrare qua dentro in questa stanza**
            *if you are a rabbit and a hunter catches you, you will have to give him two
            little cards. If you have got only one card, you are dead and you must go into
            this room.*
23. M2ita: **e quindi chi rimane vince (.) chi rimane vince –**
            *indeed, the winner is the one who remains alive (.) the one who remains
            is the winner –*
24. LMita: **eh (.) e praticamente dice che: tra i conigli, tra volpi, vi potete: aiutare, che
            ne so, vedete che c'è uno che sta vicino a zero, e gliene potete dare un po'
            (.) capito? Capito? Vi ricordate queste cose?**
            *he says that rabbits and foxes could help each other, for example, when you
            see who is on the point of having zero card, you could give him a few, right?
            Right? Do you remember this?*

It is clear that children's opportunities to participate in interactions in their first
language do not guarantee their self-expression. Frequently, adults use first languages in a normative framework: they direct delegates' actions towards the accomplishment of activities and the acceptance of values, without listening to their
perspectives and normatively managing the arising conflicts. Children's opportunities to speak in their first language are bound to their role performances.

10.5   Dyadic and triadic mediation

In some cases, interactions in the first language promote children's reflection and favour the decision-making process. In S12, LFecu promotes her delegates' opinions
about the national problems of their country by coordinating their turns in Spanish.
She promotes their reflection on the causes of the Ecuadorian migration (turn 1),
using promotional questions (turns 7 and 9), without trying to influence their answers. She expresses her point of view without imposing it (turns 11 and 13). After
turn 13, LFecu listens to the children's perspectives; consequently the children freely
express their ideas and their emotional affiliation. Their common cultural identity
facilitates mutual understanding, without judgement, while affective communication with their leaders facilitates their self-expression. In this situation, the use of a
first language is a tool for promoting reflection and active participation.

(S12)

1. Lfecu: **cuidamos que cada uno tenga un punto y no nos interrompamos. O
            sea, cada idea que fluya, explican.** Ya hemos hablado de los puntos que
            creemos que son las causas de la migración y que (..) >me van a explicar
            eso< por qué la gente sale, y además las sugerencias, lo que podemos
            cambiar, o sea, ahorita como es el gobierno.
            *we take care to explain your point of view and do not interrupt . Let's say,
            give voice to your stream of ideas. We already talked about what we think
            are the causes of migration and (..) >explain it to me< Why people go away
            and then your suggestions, the things we can change, let's say, what kind of
            government we have now.*

2. Mecu2:   en un corto plazo
            in a short term

3. Lfecu: o sea si se puede cambiar
            if a change is possible

[…]

7. Lfecu: **¿pero de qué depende?**
            what does it depend on?

8. Mecu1:   de qué haya una nueva opción de qué: una buena opción de cambio
            on a good opportunity to change

9. Lfecu: **¿pero qué es esa opción?**
            what kind of opportunity is it?

10. Mecu2: no hay todavía
            there isn't one yet.

11. Lfecu: **no pensamos tener. Pero es que nosotros siempre nos vamos diciendo
            en todas las conversaciones siempre lo mismo, es que depende de que la
            gente se una.**

we don't think we have it. We always say the same thing, but it depends on
the union of the people

12. Fecu1: depende de nosotros también
it depends on us too.

13. Lfecu: **también! Muchos van buscando la gente jóven.**
too! Lots of them are looking at the young generation.

14. Fecu2: es que siempre son los mismos *((she refers to politicians))*
they are always the same

15. Mecu2: pero es que todos, todos lo que queremos es tener una vida normal, mis papas también dicen eso.
the fact is that all we want is to have a normal life, my parents say it too.

16. Fecu2: o sea hay gente que no se quiere meter en la política
let's say, many people don't want to be involved in politics

17. Mecu1: pero eso es verdad, porque tu dices eso, 'yo sí vivo', si quiero llegar a la política e influenciar, si tu dices 'yo voy a tener una vida normal', claro que no va a haber cambio. O sea como dices '¡no! Usted ahorita decimos que vamos a cambiar, pero yo voy a tener una vida normal' dices '¡no! Yo me gradúo y voy a la Salme de Concejal hacer diputado para llegar a ser alguien' o sea si tu quieres cambiar lo haces. Si no quieres, vives una vida normal y el país sigue yendo donde se está yendo.
this is true, 'cause you say 'I live', if I want to have political career and influence, if you say 'I want an ordinary life', there will be no possibility to change. Let's say, you say 'No! Now we are saying we're gonna change, but I want an ordinary life'. You say: 'I graduate and go to the Salme de Concejal to be a deputy, to be somebody'. Let's say, if you want to change, let's do it. Otherwise, you can live an ordinary life and our country goes on in the same direction it's going right now.

In S13, a dyadic interaction between LMspa and his delegates follows a decision about the time of silence taken in a plenary session. In turns 116 and 117, the Spanish delegates express their disagreement with this decision. As the decision has already been taken, LMspa suggests that they talk with the other delegates at the end of the camp meeting (turn 118). His proposal promotes the Spanish delegates' initiative. In turn 120, LMspa underlines the possibility for delegates to ask for a new camp meeting, in order to change the decision – a possibility which is appreciated by M2spa (turn 121). LMspa's suggestion is part of the regular development of camp meetings, which have the function of promoting delegates' perspectives and initiatives.

(S13)

116. Fspa1: **no, no. Podemos otra vez –**
     no, no. Can we again -
117. Mspa1:   **puedo hablar con ellos en pla:n (hhh)**
     can I talk with them in a way: (hhh)
118. Lmspa: **habladlo luego, con la gente en vuestra habitación.**
     let's talk after, with people in your room.
119. Fspa1: se puede hacer otro camp meeting, ¿no?
     can we have another camp meeting?
120. Lmspa: **claro, claro. Va a haber más camp meeting. Se puede hacer todos los camp meeting que quereis.**
     yes, yes. We will have other camp meetings. It's possible to have all the camp meetings you want.
121. Mspa2: también podemos si pedimos que mañana haya otro camp meeting y lo hacemos? *((LMspa nods))* Bueno, ¡Camp Meeting todos los días *((laughter))*!
     can we have another camp meeting tomorrow if we wanna do it? Ok, Camp meetings every day

Acting as responders, adults may facilitate their delegates' expressions, promoting their participation. In the dyadic promotional interactions shown, however, there is no promotion of mutual understanding, because adults do not translate children's utterances into a lingua franca and consequently they do not involve the other delegations participating in the activity. Translation is significant in that it is complementary to dyadic support of reflection in promoting participation. Translation transforms dyadic mediation into triadic mediation.

In S14, during the final phase of an evaluation activity, SF3ita translates only the question which has to be answered (turns 98, 100), leaving out part of LMusa's turn ('*these games all you had to collaborate with your time*'). Nevertheless, SF3ita's feedback to her delegates' turns shows her understanding of their points (turn 106) and opens new spaces for their reflection (turn 107). The use of a first language is fundamental for promoting reflection and children's perspectives. However, another decisive aspect is that SF3ita translates the Italian delegates' perspectives (turn 113), thus also promoting the other participants' understanding. By acting as recapitulator (Wadensjö 1998), she passes the Italian children's contributions; she recapitulates their contributions by formulating them; she expands M1ita's turn ('*because when someone has difficulties in the family you cooperate to solve this problem*'), leaving out part of F1ita's turn (105) '*anche: presentando delle piccole cose*' (when you have to show little things), and changing the meaning of Mita2's turn (107), formulating the expression '*ognuno fa: un lavoro simile*' (everyone does a similar job) as '*everyone has his tasks*'.

(S14)

97. LMusa: last question ehm: **these games all you had to collaborate with your time**
so: was there some other places in your life (.) where collaboration is very
important? When you had to collaborate, two minutes to talk, and then
we discuss

98. SF3ita: **allora: la cooperazione-**
so: cooperation-

99. Fita1: eh?

100. SF3ita: **dice: in quali altre situazioni della vostra vita è importante cooperare,
tra di voi o altri?**
*he's asking what are other situations in your life where cooperation among
you or among people is important.*

101. F1ita: in progetti!
in projects!

102. M1ita: e: ma secondo me in tutte quante, perché: te la dicono sempre questa
cosa, tipo: metti caso che: una persona è in difficoltà nella famiglia così
no:i   [collaboriamo
*but I think it's always important, because everyone always says this. For ex-
ample, if a person has family problems, so we [collaborate*

103. F1ita: [in un progetto, quindi
                                                                    [*let's say in a project therefore*

104. M1ita: oppure noi collaboriamo eh: ehm: beh secondo me in tutta quanta la
nostra vita è importante cooperare
or we collaborate erm: I think cooperation is always important in our life

105. F1ita: per me nei progetti, cioè quando **anche: presentando delle cose piccole**,
comunque devi stare con qualcuno che:
*I think in projects, let's say, **when you have to show little things**, you must
be with someone who:*

106. SF3ita: **quindi quando devi lavorare con qualcuno ad un progetto, devi
collaborare con lui**
*let's say, whenever you have to work with someone to a project, you have
to collaborate with him*

107. M2ita: **secondo me anche qua al CISV devi cooperare con altri, quando ci sono
le pulizie, ognuno fa: un lavoro simile**
*I think you have to cooperate here, at CISV too, when we have the cleaning
groups, everyone does a similar job*

[…]

113. SF3ita: L. ((M1ita)) was saying that almost in everything, in everyday life you have
to collaborate, he made an example in the family, **because when someone
has difficulties in the family you cooperate to solve this problem** and:
L. ((F1ita)) was saying that when you are working with someone else at a

project, a common project you have to cooperate, and M. ((M2ita)) was saying that even in CISV, like in the cleaning group you have to cooperate because everyone has his tasks.

This idea of translation as transformative formulation seems to be particularly important. In S15, during a debriefing session, SF2ita asks the Italian delegates to explain the strategies they adopted during the previous activity (turn 2), and then she promotes their understanding, translating the Italian utterances into English. She translates (turn 7) conveying M1ita's explanation (turn 6), and informing the other participants of the reasons for the latter's action.

(S15)

2. SF2ita: lo scopo del gioco era (fare più punti) per tutti, quindi se dicevate per esempio "dai giallo" e poi alla fine davate blu, perdevate tutti e non è che alcuni vincevano, cioè perché facevate questo? (03) o comunque magari nelle negoziazioni dicevate una cosa e poi facevate tutt'altro
the aim of the game was (to score more points) for everybody. For example, when you said "give yellow" and at the end you gave blue, each of you lost and it's not as if someone won, so why did you do like this? (03) Also in negotiations you said something and acted in the opposite way

3. M1ita: uhm uhm.

4. SF2ita: come mai?
why?

5. (02)

6. M1ita: perchè se ti capitava il giallo hai più probabilità di perdere o comunque guadagnare meno punti, invece tu devi spe- stavi sperando che: (.) l'altra squadra cascasse, insomma metteva il giallo, e tu intanto mettevi il blu e guadagnavi più punti e loro li perdevano.
because if you had yellow, you have more probabilities to lose or anyway earn fewer points. Otherwise, you hoped that the other team believed you were putting yellow, while you put blue and they lost points while you gained them.

7. SF2ita: **ok. He said if you put yellow was a risk and so - if you put- you hope that the other ones will put yellow and (..) you will put blue so that you will gain (..) more points.**

In sequences S14 and S15, SF3ita and SF2ita shift from their role as staff members (asking the delegates to explain their strategies during the activity) to the role of interpreters (promoting understanding). This is particularly useful to create co-ordination in the groups. During CISV activities, the two-phase translation, i.e. the dyadic interaction in a first language and the transfer of information to other interlocutors through formulations, is particularly important in promoting both understanding and participation among children.

10.6 Triadic mediation among adolescents

As we have seen, adults' linguistic facilitation of children's understanding have the frequent effect of reducing their self-expression, because of its orientation to pre-fixed normative and cognitive expectations. On the contrary, the infrequent, but interesting adolescents' attempts at interlinguistic mediation promote their mates' understanding and, consequently, their active participation.

In S16, during a planning session, F2bra, who speaks English fluently and a little bit of Italian, tries to involve F2ita, who stands aloof from the interaction because of her limited linguistic competence. By asking her point of view and pronouncing her name (turn 46), F2bra promotes F2ita's inclusion in the communication process. Here we can see again that "calling the name" is a way of involving the participants, but in an opposite way as compared to debriefing sessions in villages (see Chapter 6). LMspa takes care of F2ita's participation too, promoting her expression in her first language (turn 47) and echoing F2bra's translation (turn 51). The empathic atmosphere created by F2bra and LMspa enables F2ita to express her opinion in her first language (turns 49, 54 and 59). F2bra promotes a triadic interaction by translating from Italian into English (turns 50, 56) and from English into Italian (turn 58), in order to promote communication between LMspa and F2ita. Even if the translation is imprecise, because of F2bra's scarce knowledge of Italian, and the communication presents some difficulties, the aim of promoting F2ita's participation is reached, as demonstrated by turns 60 and 61.

(S16)
45. LMspa: **can you put an example of this topic?**
46. F2bra: **(..) I don't know (..) S.?**
47. LMspa: **S.? (12) You can say it in Italian**
48. (03)
49. F2ita: °dobbiamo rappresentare gli oggetti°
             °*we have to represent the objects*°
50. F2bra: **we have to represent the objects**
51. LMspa: represent the objects like doing a representation-
52. F2bra: <With all the objects or only by taking one object for the representation?>
             ((F2ita nods))
53. LMspa: ok. *((to F2ita))* Do you understand anything when I talk in English (..)
             or more or less?
54. F2ita: io ho capito erm: che: (..) per ogni base ci deve essere un oggetto da
             rappresentare
             I understood erm: tha:t (..) there must be an object to represent for each
             base
55. LMspa: what did she say?

56. F2bra: **she said that it has to be an object in a group (.) in base (.) I think it's base** ((*looking at F2ita for confirmation; F2ita nods*))
57. LMspa: sorry (..) have to be an object for all the bases and they have to use the objects
58. F2bra: **it could be (.) (rappresentare queste cose (.) con oggetti?)**
59. F2ita: anche
             also
60. F2por: **we can represent the fear with the objects**
61. LMspa: (..) yes (..) There are good ideas.

The continuation of this sequence highlights the importance of interlinguistic mediation based on affective expectations, promoting not just the delegates' self-expression in their first language, but also their efforts to express in the lingua franca. F2bra keeps on supporting F2ita's self-expression by proposing that she speaks in English and offering her help with Italian (turn 112). The Brazilian delegate's support and reassuring verbal and non-verbal contributions allow F2ita to express her point of view in English (turn 114). LMspa supports this effort in turn 115.

(S17, continuation of S16)
112. F2bra: ((*to F2ita*)) **try to say what do you think in English and I can help you with the Italian**
113. (02)
114. F2ita: I think erm: (..) that the nineteen persons can represent the problem and every group find (..) the solution
115. LMspa: **good (..) good idea.** (.) How many problems? Because this is an activity for an hour and a half. Do you think that they will be – How many time they take for: the problems?

In S16 and S17, even if mutual understanding seems to be jeopardized, affective expectations and dialogic actions promote not just F2ita's active participation, but also her potential to speak English. In general, in the few cases of interlinguistic mediation among adolescents that we have observed, the interaction is never oriented to normative and cognitive expectations: the promotion of both understanding and participation is the only observable feature of adolescents' translations.

10.7   Conclusions

The lack of both a shared linguistic code and linguistic competence in the lingua franca can create difficulties in communication in villages and summer camps. In these conditions translation is very important to promote children's understanding and participation. However, frequently, adults' linguistic competence and their translations are used to control communicative processes and systematically direct them towards pre-fixed normative and cognitive expectations.

In villages, adults translate explanations of the activities during translation time and answer children's questions in first languages. They do so by alternately engaging in dyadic interactions and translations. Nevertheless, children who lack linguistic competence often participate in a marginal way. Translation is effective in promoting children's understanding of activities, but its primary cultural presupposition (being a tool for the achievement of activities) determines significant limitations for children's active participation. Translations have an informational value and are frequently followed by non verbal forms signalling understanding, and short answers. Often, translations are selections of information which promote the pre-arranged structure of activities, rather than children's self-expression. Reflection in dyadic interactions in the first language is promoted in the context of normative and cognitive expectations: diversions from these expectations are negatively assessed. Children's doubts and perspectives are not always translated; their contributions are not translated if they are not considered relevant for pre-arranged activities. Frequently, adults' formulations of original utterances guide children's understanding towards fixed normative and cognitive expectations.

To sum up, translation reduces children's active participation when adult interpreters:

1. Negatively assess children's actions when they are not aligned to pre-arranged expectations.
2. Reduce information about children's perspectives and/or formulate them in better cognitive forms.
3. Reduce other adults' appreciation of children's actions, by translating only the information which is useful for the activities.

Since the adult interpreters belong to the organisation, they tend to align to its normative and cognitive expectations: the use of both the first language and the lingua franca is instrumental to this purpose, rather than to the promotion of children's self-expression. The approach whereby adults dedicate translation time mainly to the explanation of activities reduces children's self-expression and highlights power hierarchies: adults control the interaction by translating. Indeed, the function of translation in promoting coordination among personal and cultural diversities, expressed in different linguistic codes, does not seem to be sufficiently taken into account.

Nevertheless, dyadic interactions in the first language seem to be particularly useful for establishing affective expectations between adults and children. Adults may promote children's active participation by coordinating their actions and listening actively to their contributions. Adults may highlight the possibility to change decisions and reopen discussions. It seems clear that children's reflection is promoted by the use of first languages. Translation has to be coupled with promotional dyadic interactions in order to obtain dialogic interlinguistic mediation, which can open the doors to personal and cultural diversities.

Dialogic mediation seems to be more likely in interactions among adolescents in summer camps. Adolescents' occasional translations promote both understanding and active participation in the activities, without displaying normative and cognitive expectations. Adolescents promote inclusion of their mates in communicative processes by creating an atmosphere of affective affiliation through reassurances, active listening and linguistic support. This means that adolescents are able to achieve effective coordination also through translation.

Conclusions

Claudio Baraldi

Conclusions highlight the ways in which the use of language in interactions provides important cues for analyzing the cultural presuppositions of CISV activities, through both empowering dialogues and disempowering monologues. The analysis of interactions and participants' narratives shows both (1) dyadic hierarchical interactions associated with conflict avoidance, normative conflict resolution and instrumental translation, and (2) dialogic empowering relationships based on specific dialogic actions supporting and confirming active participation, such as promotional questions, continuers, echoes, systematic appreciations, transformative formulations, and suggestive narratives. In the activities analysed, promotion of agency and personal expressions, through coordination and dialogic mediation, seems to be more important than insistence on intercultural relationships, and improvements in this promotion seems to be crucial for education to peace in intercultural settings.

1. A short summary

The huge, complex and difficult work of CISV consists in a large number of activities and obtains important positive results. Each year, CISV organises hundreds of international villages, camps and exchanges, involving thousands of children and hundreds of trained volunteers. This huge involvement of people in very complex activities from the relational point of view (see Chapters 4–10), without any external generalised institutional support, contributes to enhance the participants' perception of high-quality initiatives in education to peace and intercultural/interpersonal relationships. In Chapter 3, we have seen children's and adolescents' generalised interest and appreciation for CISV activities.

However these activities do not seem to create similarly generalised changes in children's and adolescents' interest in intercultural knowledge and relationships (Chapter 3). Children's and adolescents' assessments of the experience demonstrate that at the end of the day, a significant number remained indifferent to the cultural and personal differences observed in villages and summer camps. Moreover, all participants (adults and children) declared an ambivalent attitude to dialogic actions.

Interactions in villages and camps show divergences from CISV cultural presuppositions (see Chapter 2). In the following five points, we will try to focus on these divergences, as they emerged from the research presented in the previous chapters.

1. During organisational meetings we observed: (1) frequent hierarchical relationships between staff members (particularly camp directors) and leaders or adolescents presenting planned activities and proposals; (2) frequent forms of conflict avoidance which favoured the quick conclusion of meetings but did not let problems and voices come out; (3) frequent normative resolutions for conflicts which could not be avoided. Overall, disempowering monologues, and in particular staff members' monologues were frequent. While these monologues seem to be functional to the organisation of meetings, coordination and dialogic mediation seem to give better results in promoting active participation and creative ideas.

2. During the most complex educational games and their debriefing sessions within villages, we observed: (1) frequent hierarchical relationships between adults (leaders, staff members, sometimes JCs) and children, based on a pattern of difference in competences (expert and competent adults vs. inexpert and incompetent children); (2) frequent worries for the achievement of tasks. Adults' educational monologues frequently prevailed and children were frequently guided by adults in their participation and reflections about participation.

3. During educational and organisational activities in summer camps, interactions between adults and adolescents were more frequently based on coordination and dialogic mediation. The different age of young participants and the different way of looking at them enhanced adults' more frequent promotion of participation. However, dialogic actions were limited in cases of conflicts, which were mainly managed through strategies of avoidance and normative resolution. Consequently, monologues tended to prevail when problems of communication arose.

4. Interactions among adolescents in summer camps were much more reciprocal. Adolescents were able to position themselves in coordination and dialogic mediation, both promoting and actively formulating new proposals. Overall, peer-to-peer interactions seemed to work in enhancing active participation and proposals, showing the effectiveness of summer camps in promoting autonomy and responsibilities among adolescents. This result demonstrates the effectiveness of promoting adolescents' autonomy in working together. How-

ever, in this case too, conflicts were frequently avoided rather than managed through dialogic mediation.

5.   During translation time, adults' translations were prevalently instrumental. Adults' translations, as well as monolingual side sequences in which adults explained the meanings of activities, were mainly used to improve the organisation of activities and the achievement of tasks, rarely encouraging children's active participation. An interesting exception to this instrumental use of translation was evident in the interactions among adolescents, where they occasionally assumed the role of "ad hoc interpreters". In these situations, they were able to promote participation through translation more effectively than adults.

The participants' observation of the CISV experience mainly confirmed that an important pattern of interaction was monologue. In particular, adults observed frequent difficulties in empowering dialogue with other adults, most children preserved their prevailing attitudes for non-dialogic actions after the experience, adolescents were critical towards their relationships with adults. Therefore, participants' narratives confirmed the presence of disempowering monologues in villages and camps.

2.   The relevance of language in interactions

These divergences from CISV abstract cultural presuppositions may be easily explained. These presuppositions, written in official texts, are transformed during empirical experiences in two different ways. Firstly, they are applied through a specific use of language in the interaction. Secondly, they are transformed into the participants' narratives, i.e. into the participants' expectations and observations about values, contributions and results. There is a circular relationship among CISV cultural presuppositions, participants' narratives of their meanings, and linguistic cues in interactions. Interactions are the social processes which embody and possibly change abstract cultural presuppositions and enhance participants' narratives. Participants' narratives transpose abstract cultural presuppositions into social representations (see Chapter 2), influencing the course of interactions. Abstract cultural presuppositions are the starting point of participants' narratives and interactions, but they are subject to change throughout the very same narratives and interactions.

Our primary interest in interactions is based on their importance in reproducing and changing cultural presuppositions and narratives. For this reason, this book has mainly focused on the value of adults' and children's actions in projecting further interlocutors' actions, rather than on participants' representations or on topical orientations of interactions. The interaction is a communication system, and its analysis concerns a complex chain of actions guided by cultural presuppositions as revealed in the use of language.

We have highlighted that the same lexical and grammatical forms may indicate different cultural presuppositions in different communication systems. This means that language is meaningful because it is (1) produced in particular communication systems, and therefore (2) contextualized through the cultural presupposition of these systems. Some examples can be extracted from our research.

The first example concerns questions. Questions are very frequent in most communication processes, but different cultural presuppositions give them different meanings. Within educational systems, the meaning of questions is related to their main function in assessing role performances. In Chapter 7, we have observed the meaning of questions within the QAA (question-answer-assessment) structure, during reflections on activities. We have also observed an alternative, promotional meaning of questions, included in dialogic mediation. Promotional questions can be interpreted on the basis of different cultural presuppositions and are consequently included in different interactional structures, such as 'asking for support' and 'inviting clarifications' during organisational meetings (see Chapter 4), or the QAAp (question-answer-appreciation) structure during reflection about activities (see Chapter 7). Promotional questions are particularly frequent in interactions among adolescents (see Chapter 9), probably for two reasons: their insufficient knowledge of English, which leads to more simple structures of conversation, and their genuine interest in knowing each other, which is encouraged by the CISV narrative.

The second example concerns changes of footing, in particular between 'I' as self-positioning pronoun and 'we' as other-positioning pronoun. These changes can have two different interactional meanings, derived from two different cultural presuppositions: they can both (1) assert speakers' authoritativeness, when the interaction is hierarchically structured, and (2) demonstrate speakers' personal responsibilities for their positions as agents promoting the interaction, when the interaction is dialogically structured. These changes of footing are particularly frequent in organisational meetings, where hierarchies and needs to assert responsibilities are frequent, while they are infrequent in interactions between adults and children/adolescents, where the success of we-identities in conversations is frequent, and cues for authoritativeness are generally not requested.

The third example concerns the use of 'but'. In linguistics, 'but' is generally observed in its function as a connective. Robin Lakoff (1971) distinguishes between the function of 'but' in "semantic oppositions", marking a contrast between elements of a text, and the function of 'but' as "denial of expectations"

(G. Lakoff 1971). This distinction is a generalised blueprint for the discussion. For example, according to Schiffrin (1987) 'but' introduces a statement in support of an argument, signalling a contrast with the information currently in focus, and marking this contrast with a new position; according to Segal & Duchan (1997), 'but' guides interpreters in the construction of meanings for texts, providing "cues for how events and objects in the story relate to one another" (p. 99); according to Blakemore (2000, 2002), 'but' contradicts and eliminates assumptions in texts. In all these interpretations, the function of 'but' is observed *within* texts, in which 'but' connects two different clauses. Although some of these approaches include a reference to readers (or interpreters) and imply a pragmatic use of 'but' (Dascal 2003), they do not consider the function of 'but' within communication systems, particularly within sequences of turns. In this specific function, 'but' is not a connective, i.e. it does not have the function of connecting different parts of the same text; rather it has a "disclaiming" function (van Dijk 2000), i.e. it is a cue for denying, or introducing doubts on participants' positioning in communication. More precisely, 'but' may be interpreted as a cue for (1) the promotion of personal expressions or (2) the assessment of roles, depending on the cultural presuppositions of the interaction in which it emerges.

First, 'but' is a cue for self-disclaiming, i.e. for disclaiming the position of the speaker. The self-disclaiming 'but' can mitigate possible negative expectations on speakers' positions, enhancing and strengthening their positive *roles* (e.g. Chapter 4, S8, Chapter 5, S12) or *proposals* (e.g. Chapter 5, S14). The self-disclaiming 'but' can also promote interlocutors' personal contributions, through a mitigation of speakers' positive positions (e.g. Chapter 4, S3). In all these cases, 'but' is a cue for the promotion of interlocutors' participation and the reduction of speakers' authoritativeness. This reduction may be doubtful and ambivalent (e.g. Chapter 5, S8); more infrequently, it softens normative expectations, opening up opportunities for participation (e.g. Chapter 6, S14).

Second, and more frequently in our data, 'but' is a cue for other-disclaiming, i.e. for denying or creating doubts about the interlocutors' positive positions. The other-disclaiming 'but' can open a direct contradiction with interlocutors' assertions (e.g. Chapter 4, S14, S9). These contradictions are more frequent in interactions between adults and children than in organisational meetings, where they are generally more subtle and indirect (e.g. Chapter 5, S10, S12). This also depends on the fact that among children and adolescents 'but' results from an uncertain and simplified use of English as a lingua franca, as it is a simple and direct cue for any form of dissent. Among adults, the other-disclaiming 'but' is more frequently combined with a confirmation ('yes'); the combination 'yes but' is a cue for mitigated other-disclaiming. The mitigated other-disclaiming 'but' is mainly a hierarchical disclaiming of the interlocutors' positions (e.g. Chapter 4,

S14), however it can also be a defence (e.g. Chapter 4, S4) or a mitigation (e.g. Chapter 5, S5) of subordinated positions. In all these cases, 'but' is a cue for power distribution among participants. The other-disclaiming 'but' can also be mitigated through other doubtful expressions (e.g. Chapter 5, S9).

In our data, 'but' does not occur only as a disclaimer. Among children, for example, it is frequently used in "semantic oppositions", within stories which do not address interactions and participants' positions. Our point is not that 'but' is always a cue for cultural presuppositions of interactions, rather that it *can* have a function of disclaiming in interactions, which means that it can be a cue for self-positioning and other-positioning. In our analysis, its connective value within the text is less relevant than its effects on positioning within the interaction.

Finally, the fourth example concerns formulations. The analysis of formulations is particularly complex because it concerns the ways in which a turn (1) takes the previous positions of interlocutors and makes them explicit, glosses, or comments on them, and (2) projects the next turn. Formulations can (1) demonstrate attention and sensitivity for the interlocutor's expressions, and (2) project a direction for subsequent actions, promoting active participation. In this case, we call them *affective* formulations, because they take into account participants' self-expressions. In our data, formulations make previous utterances explicit (Chapter 4, S7, S11, Chapter 5, S11, Chapter 6, S9, S11, S12, S13, Chapter 7, S9, Chapter 8, S4, S14) and develop them (Chapter 5, S11, S12, Chapter 6, S11) using suggestions (suggestive narratives). Both these kinds of formulation are effective in promoting interlocutors' active participation. We have called the latter *transformative* formulations as they create the conditions for change in participants' positions, above all in cases of conflicts, and therefore they are particularly useful in dialogic conflict management. However, formulations can also have other functions, such as checking the understanding of interlocutors' utterances (Chapter 4, S13, Chapter 5, S7, Chapter 8, S14), and, as we have seen in Chapter 10, projecting adults' normative and cognitive expectations about children's actions. These different functions depend on the different cultural presuppositions of the interactions in which formulations are included.

All these linguistic forms have a meaning and a function only in specific communicative systems; they are cues for cultural presuppositions of these systems. The main features of these communicative systems are summarised in the following few sections. In particular we will try to answer the main research issues introduced at the beginning of this book (Chapter 2), namely:

1. The difference between dyadic interactions and dialogic mediation.
2. The relationship between education and promotion of children's participation.

3. The ways in which empowering dialogue can enhance education and children's participation.
4. The relationship between empowering dialogue and intercultural communication.

The answers to these issues are based on the generalised overview of linguistic cues emerged in differently structured interactions.

3.   Linguistic cues: A summary

3.1   Disempowering monologue

The linguistic cues for the cultural presuppositions of disempowering monologues consisted of: (1) long or repeated turns in which detailed explanations and normative expectations were redundantly narrated; (2) speaker-centred turns, in which the speakers presented themselves in the interactions as experts, teachers or judges. Redundancy, insistence and self-presentation were the main components of a normative hierarchical structure.

In organisational meetings, this normative structure was sometimes supported through alliances among some participants, which were forms of coordination in constructing hierarchies. These alliances were expressed both as explicit co-construction of normative expectations and as continuers indicating agreement with normative expectations. In adult-children interactions, the projections of normative expectations were frequent both at the beginning and at the end of stretches of interactions concerning tasks and planning in lingua franca, monolingual explanations, and translations. These projections constitute normative narratives which give meanings to the interaction, guiding it towards some basic value. These meanings were supported through the recurrent construction of We-identities in the interaction, and through cognitive expectations projecting the importance of achieving specific tasks.

Assessments were frequent, either in the form of direct negative assessments, prevalently in adult-children interactions, or as mitigated other-disclaimers which were used to contradict the interlocutor without starting a direct conflict, prevalently in organisational meetings. In adult-children interactions, assessments were frequently expressed in the third position after a question/answer pair, i.e. in Question-Answer-Assessment triplets (QAA). Consequently, questions projecting correct answers and assessments of these answers were the basic elements of the hierarchical structure. Questions were often used to suggest answers, through the inclusion of candidate answers, the use of interrogative negative forms, and the projection of 'yes/no' answers – all forms which legitimise the adult as primary meaning giver, and facilitate positive assessments enhancing the sharing of meanings.

Hierarchical monologues, associated with adults' socio-epistemic claims, were particularly frequent in adult-children interactions. Since these monologue were 'adapted' to children's and adolescents' supposed cultural and linguistic competence, cognitive expectations were much more frequent in villages, where the educational value of tasks was considered particularly important, while normative expectations were distributed in all activities, as adolescents and children are both considered in need of control. Therefore, normative structures were generalised in villages and summer camps, they inhibited children's and adolescents' dissent, and encouraged their alignment with the interlocutors. In particular, the projection of normative expectations was frequently followed by a two-phase alignment: (1) children aligned with adults' actions which might be either self-selected as second turns (assessments or normative requests) or actively projected as first turns (questions, often calling the child's name); (2) children referred to adults as experts or leaders who had in this way asserted their expertise or leadership. Through this two-phase process, adults can set up values and tasks which project their own leading role.

Translation time enhanced both cognitive narratives creating information for the children's and adolescents' achievement of tasks, and normative narratives reinforcing value orientations. These functions were accomplished in different ways, such as through the selection of information, unilateral translations (from adults to children), normative formulations which emphasized some selected aspect of the translated turns, cognitive formulations which improved children's performances through translation. Translations were mainly instrumental in two ways: for the accomplishment of cognitive tasks and for the understanding and acceptance of normative expectations. Adults assumed the double role of translators and educators in the same turns.

Normative expectations and assessments did not always work properly. On the contrary, they projected frequent difficulties in the interaction, such as silent alignments, uncertain positioning, embarrassed self-repairs, and defensive reactions (e.g. through mitigated other-disclaimers). Sometimes, they projected open contradictions, provoking the rise of conflicts.

In fact, conflicts were infrequent in adult-children interactions, as they were mainly prevented through normative structures which effectively projected children's and adolescents' alignment. In general, children accepted adults' leadership, and sometimes cooperated in its interactional construction, e.g. downgrading their competences and cooperating in the management of rights and responsibilities. It is evident that CISV educational cultural presuppositions were frequently accepted because they are contextualized through educational meanings of adult-children interactions generalised in society. Sometimes, children and adolescents resisted adults' claims without opening conflicts, i.e. through non type-conforming answers which displaced adults' questions.

When conflicts arose, during both organisational meetings and educational activities, normative resolution was not surprisingly a frequent form of their management. In organisational meetings, conflict normative resolution affirmed the staff's and directors' leadership. It was enhanced through negative assessments, mainly through mitigated other-disclaimers, imperatives and normative summaries of problematic interlocutor turns. These normative actions frequently projected the interlocutors' alignment, enhancing winning alliances based on superior power in decision-making, minimising disclaimers, withdrawals, or attempts to divert attention. However, the conflicting party's insistence could mitigate this hierarchy. Mitigated other-disclaimers were frequently used both to contradict and to respond to contradictions. In adult-children interactions, conflict normative resolution implied direct negative assessments and normative closures which readdressed the interactions, reducing children's opportunities for participation. Within monolingual sequences coupled with translations, conflict normative resolution was sometimes explicitly based on the expression of adults' disappointment at and irritation about children's objections.

Normative resolution increased the intensity of conflicts rather than reduce it, when they were not mitigated. These normative-resolution-related problems demonstrated the fragility of hierarchical structures as bases for conflict management. Consequently, forms of conflict avoidance were frequently and successfully adopted.

In organisational meetings, conflict avoidance was mainly based on (1) minimisations of conflicts, through disclaimers which de-escalate the conflict, and subsequent minimising explanations of its motives, and (2) diversions which drop contradictions, announced by prefatory 'false' confirmations ('yes', 'yeah', 'ok'), which open or project a diverting turn. The difference between minimisation and diversion is indicated through the difference between disclaimers and false confirmations: while disclaimers state the existence of conflicts, although they minimise them, false confirmations state that conflicts do not exist. In organisational meetings, a third, more complex form of conflict avoidance was based on mitigation, as self-reversal of the normative resolution, that is as hierarchical self-repair. Mitigations were projected by the superior role position, following lack of opposition, that is withdrawals and lack of insistence: contradictions were mitigated because they did not find the expected opposition. In adult-children interactions, conflict avoidance was mainly based on normative narrative, which projected normative expectations, avoiding further contradictions, and reconstructed shared representations. Normative expectations were projected in the same way in cases of alignment and in cases of contradiction. Educational cultural presuppositions were so clearly established that children's and adolescents' contradictions were often eluded through the simple projection of normative expectations. Moreover, during translation time, conflict avoidance was achieved through non renditions of children's translatable turns.

3.2   Empowering dialogue

Adults' dialogic actions are particularly meaningful for analysing the promotion of participation.

The first and most basic cues for empowering dialogue were promotional questions. In particular, in organisational meetings, these questions were positioned at the end of turns in which proposals were presented. They consisted of (1) invitations to ask for clarifications, which allow speakers to complete their narratives or reflect about the narrative which they have presented, (2) questions through which speakers ask for their interlocutors' support in constructing their narratives. These questions promoted the interlocutors participation and active co-construction of proposals.

Promotional questions made coordination and mediation likely. The cues for coordination and mediation were continuers, echoes, open invitations to participate, feedback of clarification, appreciations expressed through acknowledgement tokens ('good', 'fine', 'ahhh!!!', 'that's cool', etc.), formulations projecting active participation (transformative formulations), additional promotional questions in which calling names invited participation in reciprocal interactions, and narratives projecting suggestions (suggestive narratives).

In particular, continuers ('mhm', 'yeah', 'yes', 'ok', etc.) and echoes (repetition of previous turns or parts of turns) seem to be frequent cues for coordination and mediation. Continuers and echoes are considered fundamental in a famous theory of counselling based on a person-centred approach, which assigns them an important function in "reflecting" (Mearns & Thorne 1999) or "active listening" (Gordon 2002), and sees them as actions which should mirror interlocutor's attempts at self-disclosure. Continuers allow interlocutors to feel that their actions are effective in the interaction and this encourages them to continue in their expressions. Echoes reinforce encouragement in reflecting interlocutors' perspectives; this is considered the most important form of encouragement as it avoids risks of misinterpretation of interlocutors' utterances, allowing them to deepen their alternative stories.

During reflections in villages, the main form of empowering dialogue was the simplified QAAp (Question-Answer-Appreciation) sequence, which is formally analogous to QAA sequences, but it introduces a systematic appreciation of children's actions and expressions, avoiding differentiated assessments, and therefore displaying an "unconditional positive regard" (Mearns & Thorne 1999) for their active participation. During translation time empowering dialogue was displayed in monolingual side interactions, through promotional questions and suggestive narratives. The use of the first language seemed to improve the opportunities for empowering dialogue.

Coordination and mediation were also able to manage conflicts which arose in the interaction, mainly through a combination of formulations (particularly transformative formulations) and suggestive narratives. This combination was supported by promotional questions, further supportive formulations and collaborative narratives. This chain articulated decision-making as *mediated coordination*. Only in few cases did the combination of transformative formulations and suggestive narratives efficiently work as conflict management during educational activities. During activities with children and adolescents, the difficulties of empowering dialogue were demonstrated by the rarity of (1) dialogic conflict management and (2) translation through transformative formulation. Although infrequent, empowering dialogue did promote children's autonomous construction of meanings and, more significantly, adolescents' autonomous coordinated decision-making.

Empowering dialogue was more frequent, although less varied, in interactions among adolescents. These interactions presented two interesting form of coordination. The simplest form was based on distribution of participation, through promotional questions (also as other-initiated repairs), continuers and echoes. A more complex form of coordination was based on active proposals, through suggestive narratives, which displayed the importance of active participation, and consequently projected further contributions with the same features. A third interesting, although infrequent, form of coordination among adolescents was observed in cases of translation support of mates' understanding and participation. In these cases, imprecision in translation was not an obstacle, as interpreting was clearly understood as mere support for participation. However, once again conflict management was not dialogic among adolescents: they preferred quick or simple forms of conflict avoidance (above all diversion) or resolution (above all ballot), while they did not consider coordination and mediation as forms of conflict management.

4.   The meanings of dyadic hierarchical interactions

4.1   Dyadic education, expectations and participatory processes

The observed contextualization cues demonstrate the importance of *dyadic education* in the interaction, both during activities with children/adolescents and during organisational meetings. Dyadic education is achieved through monologues, i.e. through a role hierarchy between a leading position and a subordinated position, and implies the intention to give up third voices. The reduction of complex group interactions to dyads is the most important feature of disempowering monologues: disempowering monologues are based on a dyadic interactional structure, even when the number of participants is higher, or much higher, than two.

Dyadic education is associated to cognitive expectations concerning the achievement of tasks, and normative expectations concerning the consolidation of values. Dyadic education may be successful because these expectations are expected by both adults and children/adolescents.

In the participants' narratives of values, intentions and activities (Chapter 3), expectations of children's and adolescents' participation regard 'development'. Consequently, children's and adolescents' participation is considered important if it is subordinated to adults' educational guidance of their development. This perspective indicates an insufficient integration between values and practices, above all for the coupling of education and participation. This insufficient integration is confirmed by the analysis of interactions between adults and children/adolescents.

Role hierarchies in the interaction are based on these forms of expectations. The generalised cultural presupposition in society is that both organisational meetings and educational activities should be based on leading roles and normative/cognitive expectations. It is not by chance that the CISV narrative includes the meaningful expressions 'camp director' and 'leader', as well as 'counsellor', to indicate the main positions in the organisation of activities.

Dyadic education implies the importance of individual role performances in accomplishing the requested tasks. Our analysis demonstrates the great importance in CISV villages and camps of confrontations concerning role performances, both in organisational meetings and educational activities, especially with children. Role performances give an important contribution to children's positioning and socialisation.

In these cultural and structural conditions, it is not strange that active participation and promotion of agency are less frequent than should be expected considering CISV cultural presuppositions. There is an evident difference between *abstract* cultural presuppositions, presented in official narratives, and *empirical* cultural presuppositions, observable in the interaction.

4.2   Conflict prevention, avoidance and normative resolution

On these premises, conflicts are prevented through role hierarchies and normative/cognitive expectations. The contradictions which arise are avoided or normatively resolved through these very same structures. These forms of conflict management largely impede the insurgence of contradictions. Contradictions are considered avoidable obstacles for 'good' relationships, and conflicts are observed as problems in communication. Children and adolescents are not considered interlocutors who can contradict adults' actions, and in organisational meetings only staff members (especially camp directors) are openly encouraged to contradict their interlocutors and propose resolutions of problems. The common result of conflict prevention, avoidance and normative resolution is a substantial reduction of active participation and self-expression as possible sources of productive conflicts.

Conflict prevention and avoidance show that CISV cultural presuppositions make normative conflict resolution and, at the end of the day, the imposition of hierarchical structures difficult. The CISV narrative promotes sharing and peaceful coordination, leading the participants to make efforts to reduce at least conflicts, if not hierarchies. Hierarchical structures seem to be useful for decision-making, value orientation and task achievements, but they clash with the narrative of agency, active participation and coordination.

4.3   Instrumental translation

Translation is an increasingly significant phenomenon, especially in CISV villages. The increasing attention for 'good' communication makes the use of English as a lingua franca increasingly important, far beyond the traditional significance of non-verbal communication in the CISV narrative. Side conversations in the first language during translation time are equally important for those delegations in which children are less competent in English. Recent trends in translation studies and community interpreting underline the importance of interpreters' active participation in the interpreter-mediated interaction. Our research has confirmed that adult 'interpreters' are active, but their active participation has mainly non participatory effects.

Adult are 'ad hoc' interpreters, as they are not professionals. However, their interpreting function is scheduled in CISV programs and they are officially in charge of this task. Their condition is hybrid: they are not professionals, yet they are given the task of interpreting as well as of educating. Their double task (interpreting and educating) causes the overlapping of two functions and roles, promoting a form of instrumental translation. Adult interpreters perform both education and translation in the same interaction and specific turns: this prevents them from a 'neutral' stance. Neutrality here does not mean passive participation, rather it implies competence in empowering both parties in the interaction. The problem is that translations and side monolingual sequences do not make children's empowerment relevant in the interaction, because adult interpreters display greater attention for the successful accomplishment of tasks and for normative orientations. Consequently, adult interpreters are mainly gatekeepers for the educational institution.

The final result is that translation and side monolingual interactions promote children's understanding of CISV activities, but they do not guarantee their active participation. While interpreting is functional to accomplish these activities, it is not functional to promote children's active participation. For this reason, linguistically incompetent children are not sufficiently involved in interactions and decision-making. The different competence in English as a lingua franca creates inequalities in children's opportunities for active participation.

5.   The meanings of dialogic relationships

5.1   The importance of empowering dialogue

Our research demonstrates that it is difficult to achieve empowering dialogue and children's active participation when cultural presuppositions encourage convergence and conjunction of educational values and active participation.

We do not think that this problem is restricted to the CISV experience. The plan to involve children as social agents cannot be easily applied in the interaction, when in society they are only trained to follow values or to accomplish tasks. The same is true for organisational meetings, in which the institutional task of decision-making can contradict the active involvement of participants. Task achievement, value orientation, and decision-making are not easily transformed into opportunities for empowering dialogue and active participation, as they are much more easily promoted through role hierarchies and their socio-epistemic claims, based on normative or cognitive expectations, i.e. disempowering monologues.

These presuppositions may also favour ambivalences in the interaction, as a result of the attempts to maintain orientations to both hierarchical roles and active participation. These ambivalences create uncertainties, especially in adult-children interactions, as in the same interaction participants, particularly children observe hierarchical structures and dialogic actions. However, the low frequency of such ambivalences demonstrates that interactions strongly encourage the choice of some orientation, and that this choice is prevalently for monologues. In institutional settings, role hierarchies, although based on participatory principles, are frequently the primary structures of the interaction.

Nevertheless, empowering dialogue is an important form of communication. Its achievement demonstrates that it is possible to improve decision-making and education, while changing their interactional meanings, i.e. promoting participatory forms of communication. Although this is not an easy task in interlinguistic groups of people who do not know each other at all, communications in English as a lingua franca, translations, and first-language interactions present opportunities for dialogic action and consequently for empowering dialogue. Empowering dialogue allows both the opening of actively participated sessions of decision-making and the management of emerging conflicts, without recurring to hierarchical structures and positioning. Last but not least, the achievement of empowering dialogue demonstrates adolescents' specific competence in improving good practices of interpersonal and intercultural relationships.

Empowering dialogue can work in improving both decision-making and educational activities in complex group interactions, as it promotes interactions which are impeded by hierarchical structures and positioning. In particular, dialogic actions promote active participation and deliberate self-positioning in three different phases. Firstly, they promote active participation and self-positioning at the beginning of the interaction, through promotional questions. Secondly, dialogic actions promote group reflection about particular topics, leading to decision-making during organisational meetings and enhancing assessments of activities in children's and adolescents' groups. Thirdly, dialogic actions promote coordination and mediation of second-order positioning and conflicts. In these three phases of the communication process, dialogic actions are useful for educational and organisational purposes, and can validly substitute hierarchies and expertise as incentives for accomplishing tasks, first and foremost because they do not focus on such accomplishment, but on the relevant communicative aspects that the accomplishment highlights and helps facing. This also means that empowering dialogue is more coherent with CISV cultural presuppositions than hierarchical structures are.

5.2   Prevailing dialogic actions

Our research has made it possible to observe a scale of 'intensity' regarding successful dialogic actions. The first level includes promotional questions, which enhance interlocutors' participation, starting empowering dialogue. The second level includes continuers and acknowledgement tokens, which are useful for supporting interlocutors' active participation, showing speakers' attention in listening. The third level includes echoes, which confirm interlocutors' narratives, encouraging their expansion. The fourth level includes systematic appreciations, which confirm interlocutors' actions, showing an unconditional positive regard for them. To avoid assessments, appreciation must be systematic and generalised during the interaction. The fifth level includes transformative formulations, which reproduce the gist of the previous narrative and project interlocutors' active contributions, thus allowing a "depth reflection" (Mearns & Thorne 1999) in the interaction, by facilitating interlocutors' understanding and promoting their further participation. The sixth level includes suggestive narratives, which display speakers' personalised contributions, without imposing them, thus encouraging further contributions. The combination of transformative formulations and suggestive narratives seems to be particularly effective in promoting, coordinating and mediating active participation.

These dialogic actions can avoid stereotypes and prejudices in the interaction, as they are centred on interlocutors' personal expressions instead of speakers' monologues. This does not mean that speakers are inactive. On the contrary, in particular appreciations, formulations and narratives are the most active forms of participation which may be successful in institutional interactions: their specific dialogic value resides in their attention and respect for personal participation, connected with affective expectations and personal disclosure. Therefore, we may well refer to unconditional appreciation, affective formulations (see Chapter 4) and suggestive narratives (see Chapter 5).

Dialogic actions are particularly infrequent in adult-children interactions, and opportunities for acting dialogically are frequently missed. Narratives have often a non-dialogic form, both in organisational meetings, where they describe activities or display superior expertise, and during educational activities, where they project normative or cognitive expectations. Active listening is mostly based on continuers and echoes as 'reflecting' actions, as suggested by a person-centred approach: while continuers and echoes are effective in projecting next turns, these simple reflecting actions determine the partial missing of potential opportunities for promoting participation. Affective formulations are potentially the starting point of another form of feedback, i.e. perception checking. However, this kind of dialogic action seems to be particularly difficult to perform. In our data, feedback only concerns understanding and only refers to the speaker's previous actions; therefore, participants' feelings are rarely checked, and participants may be less confident in being supported during the interaction.

The limits in continuity, quantity and typology of dialogic actions might be considered an intrinsic limitation of empowering dialogue. Alternatively, they might be considered the consequence of the prevailing form of dyadic hierarchical education. The latter explanation seems to be more likely, although not certain, as the adults' narrative displays hierarchical attitudes and scepticism towards dialogue (Chapter 3). These considerations seem to suggest that there are opportunities to improve dialogic actions.

5.3   Coordination and mediation

Coordination and mediation are the two fundamental forms of empowering dialogue emerging in the interaction. Coordination is a chain of participants' actions, based on symmetrical interactive and reflexive positioning, which leads to some decision. In the specific case of conflict, it is a form of management which promotes changes of opinions in sequences of co-constructed decisions, avoiding the distinction between winners and losers. Coordination emerges through the alignment, intended as co-production of different actions. While this alignment is cognitively oriented, it is based on affective expectations concerning mutual support and confirmation; therefore, this form of alignment is also a form of affiliation. According to Pearce (1989), coordination is like a "dance": in CISV organisational meetings and educational activities, it is a choral dance; it is performed as a group interaction in which participants are affiliating in producing decision-making, achieving tasks and managing conflicts.

In mediation, a single participant promotes empowering dialogue through her/his dialogic actions. The mediator coordinates her/his interlocutors who are trying to make a decision, achieve a task or disputing some topic. Mediation promotes the interlocutors' self-management of the interaction, enhancing their symmetrical reflexive and interactive positioning and satisfying their expectations. Mediation does not necessarily imply conflict management, as it firstly promotes the interlocutors' active participation and reciprocal sensitivity. Mediators' dialogic actions enhance these two features of the interaction, while only occasionally do they face open conflicts when active participation creates contradictions. Therefore, dialogic mediation concerns more reflection and decision-making than conflict resolution.

Coordinators and mediators can (1) equally distribute opportunities of participation among the interlocutors, and (2) enhance mutual sensitivity among the interlocutors. Affective formulations, suggestive narratives and unconditional appreciations are important for this function as forms of coordinator's and mediator's deliberate self-positioning, i.e. self-disclosure. Moreover, coordination and mediation may also be enhanced through simpler supporting actions, such as promotional questions, continuers, and echoes showing the mediator's and coordinator's reflecting attitude.

Coordination and mediation are forms of empowering dialogue, improving decision-making, task achievement, group reflection and possibly conflict management. These forms of empowering dialogue interrupt dyadic interactions. Dyadic interactions are frequently based on hierarchical structures, as hierarchies are encouraged in the mainstream narrative contextualizing decision-making and educational activities. The re-contextualization of hierarchical structures may be achieved through coordination and mediation, as they imply the reversal of dyadic structures. The contradiction between dyadic education and coordination/mediation seems evident. This is also demonstrated by the fact that coordination and mediation are more frequent in interactions among peers (adults or adolescents) than in interactions in which the hierarchical difference of age is considered important, reflecting the generalised idea that adults should be expert educators for children and adolescents.

In other settings (Baraldi & Gavioli 2007, 2008), dialogic mediation faces difficulties, as the 'third' position is less efficient than dyadic interaction in achieving affiliation and fulfilling affective expectations. Consequently, institutional mediation often supports hierarchies and disempowering monologues rather than discourage them. Research has demonstrated, however, that this is true only in some circumstances, probably where the 'mediator' is conceived as in charge of a double, potentially contradictory task (e.g. educator *and* translator). Otherwise, mediation can break and substitute hierarchical dyadic structures with important results, ultimately making a person-centred approach relevant.

6.   Transcultural communication and cosmopolitanism

As expected, during CISV organisational meetings and educational activities, cultural diversities are systematically transformed. However, this transformation is rather surprising: cultural diversity seems to be largely neglected. Following Helen FitzGerald's suggestion, we should assume that "situational context must always be taken into consideration when discussing intercultural communication: the findings from one type of situational context cannot be extrapolated to other dissimilar ones" (2003, p. 206).

Studies about intercultural communication are generally based on the comparison among different cultural (often national) styles in the interaction, which permit us to understand different cultural cues (e.g. Kiesling & Bratt Paulson 2005). In the analysed interactions, however, we did not find meaningful cues which could be related to either national styles or gender.

In one of the few direct linguistic analyses of intercultural communication, Gumperz (1982) suggests looking at conversational asynchronies in the interaction to identify the verbal and non-verbal cues of misunderstandings which are correlated to cultural styles in the use of language. In our analysis, we have neither found significant asynchronies and 'misunderstandings' nor indications of different cultural styles of conversation.

Differently from Gumperz, who does not reduce contextualization cues to communicated contents, FitzGerald (2003) proposes analysing the contents of the interactions to observe culturally variable cues. For example, in her data she shows that culturally different participants in group interactions display their individualistic rather than collectivist attitudes, and culturally different expressions of disagreement. We have not found such culturally formed differences in the analysed interactions. We have observed few conflicts concerning cultural habits, but they have been managed by avoiding the prominence of 'cultural' aspects and shifting to role performances and personal needs. On the other hand, FitzGerald concludes that in the interaction "individuals are not cultural automatons who passively act out cultural values and expectations" (2003, p. 207).

The only conditions in which in interactions during CISV activities, 'cultural differences' seem important concern the differentiated competence in speaking English. Gumperz (1982) demonstrates that differences in cultural interpretation cannot be reduced to problems of linguistic competence and literacy. However, it is evident that great differences in linguistic competence play an important role in the interaction and in particular in positioning participants, and undoubtedly these are cultural differences. In our case, these differences create inequalities in the positioning of children, regarding the opportunities for their active participation in the interaction. In particular, they create a privileged access to information and decision-making for English native speakers and the most competent non-native speakers either coming from countries where learning English is normal and linguistically straightforward (e.g. Scandinavian countries and The Netherlands) or belonging to the upper social class in countries where this implies a privileged access to learning English (e.g. some South American and Asian countries). The paradox is that the universalising use of narratives in English as a lingua franca promotes the emergence of cultural inequalities, which are badly faced during translation time, as we have seen. There seems to be a mitigated but observable intolerance for those children who do not display an adequate knowledge of English.

To sum up, if we exclude the important problem of English as a lingua franca, in CISV initiatives cultural diversity is confined to National Nights in villages and National Cultural Activities in summer camps. In this way, cultural diversities are explicitly institutionalised in the public presentation of national events, and their reappearance is discouraged in other kinds of interactions. This also means that cultural diversity is confined within the We-identity of national delegations, while it is discouraged in interpersonal and role relationships. However, as we have seen, these We-identities emerge in the interactions which involve children and adolescents, and collective positioning is frequent during the activities. Consequently, within communication and narratives, there may be ambivalences between orientations to the CISV We-community and orientations to differentiated National We-identities (Chapter 3).

In the CISV abstract narrative, intercultural diversity should be transformed through interpersonal friendship. This should correspond to the planning of transcultural education: friendship should be the form of communication whereby cultural diversity is accepted in its personalised expressions. Consequently, effective interpersonal communication is considered the best expression of successful transcultural communication.

This may be true in the informal part of the CISV experience, although only for some selected relationships. We did not investigate this important part of the CISV experience. However, during the activities, cultural diversity is often transformed into confrontation of role performances and intercultural communication is often transformed into educational hierarchical communication, rather than in interpersonal communication. The impact of experiential learning (Biesta 1994; Dewey 1955; Kangaslathi & Kangaslathi 2003; Kolb 1984; Rogers 1969) on intercultural relationships is as high as expected, but in the sense that positioning in role performances creates opportunities to reduce cultural diversity and achieve shared forms of relationship. Interactions transform cultural identities above all through role performances.

The effort to improve transcultural communication through interpersonal relationships might be appreciated when empowering dialogue promotes personalisation in the interaction. As the literature suggests (Chapter 1), dialogic actions promote person-centred communication. Consequently, dialogic actions confirm the CISV general narrative concerning the importance of interpersonal communication for intercultural purposes: the treatment of participants as persons encourages their self-positioning and self-disclosure, which can also be positioning and disclosure of cultural identities.

However, our data do not confirm the equivalence between personal and cultural positioning. On the contrary, it seems that cultural differences are more evident in the framework of hierarchical structures than in cases of interpersonal communication. The observation of problems in intercultural relationships is linked to these structures: hierarchical structures promote ethnocentric communication which highlights differences between We-identities, while interpersonal communication encourages participants to express their own *personal* views. Paradoxically, the best way of promoting intercultural communication does not effectively promote the display of cultural identities and diversities. It seems that the idea of effective transcultural communication is not coherent with empower-ing dialogue, as there cannot be 'trans' without 'cultural'.

Empowering dialogue seems to be a cosmopolitan form of communication. In its traditional version, cosmopolitanism is applied to individuals and means openness, flexibility, universalism, togetherness with absence of cultural roots (Beck 2004; Hannerz 1996; Tomlinson 1999). These presumed features of cosmo-politan people are less interesting than the consequences of cosmopolitanism for communication. According to Tomlinson, cosmopolitans can "be able to enter into an intelligent relationship of dialogue with others who start from different assumptions" (1999, p. 195). Although cosmopolitanism is often associated with the treatment of cultural diversity, its intrinsic features concern communication, particularly empowering dialogue. While transcultural forms are focused on the paradoxical maintenance and dissolution of boundaries between cultures, cosmo-politanism concerns the process of empowering dialogue itself, i.e. coordination of different voices (Pearce 1989). Cosmopolitanism takes the incommensurability between cultural forms for granted, avoiding cultural confrontations, despite be-ing achieved through social processes of coordination and mediation.

Cosmopolitanism implies dialogic communication. Participants are not posi-tioned in-between, they are positioned in-dialogue. Is this a plausible alternative global form with respect to role performances? Is affectivity a functional equiva-lent of cognitive and normative expectations in globalising the world? We leave these questions to further investigations to conclude with some final consider-ations about the CISV experience, and more generally about experiential learning in complex intercultural and interlinguistic communities.

7.   Empowering dialogue, personal expressions and successful socialisation

Our research indicates that the generalised success of the CISV experience is mainly connected with the We-identity created as an effect of normative and cognitive expectations in the daily living together. The particular organisation of CISV creates the normative and cognitive meanings of a strong We-identity, which is confirmed through an intense community life, while national activities maintain We-identities smaller avoiding their sudden risky deflagration.

The CISV experience is particularly surprising and displacing for children for two reasons. First, they are not accustomed to such an intense community life as they live either in private houses and close relationships, or in relatively imper-sonal educational settings. Second, they are exposed to a setting in which they need to make unusual linguistic and relational efforts. When the trauma of this surprising total condition is overcome, the global We-identity can be achieved, in spite of a number of obstacles, including linguistic difficulties in communication, compelling and challenging close relationships with different perspectives, unusual and tiring lifestyles. CISV activities mainly aim to overcome the trauma and create the global We-identity.

In this complex and fascinating task, an important part is played by the importance assigned to role performances, learning and cognitive expectations, and normative expectations about the correct planning and execution of performances. These global cultural presuppositions help children (and adolescents) to establish connections with the organisational and educational life which is usual for them, therefore finding some kind of helpful familiarity in a very unfamiliar place. This creates a fascinating differentiated and at the same time homogeneous "global multiculture" (Nederveen Pieterse 2007) within the community, which makes the experience a fabulous hybrid of familiar and unfamiliar. As the difficulties of Chinese delegations demonstrate (Chapter 3), complete unfamiliarity creates many problems.

Our research has shown the extent to which this unusual global multiculture is implemented in the interactions which make up the CISV experience. This complex organisation requires solidity of expectations, clear orientation to tasks, and competence in quick decision-making. The consequence is that the promotion of personal expression may be limited, open conflicts may be discouraged and, when contradictions arise, they are frequently avoided or treated in a normative way.

In CISV villages and summer camps, interactions create many opportunities to support and confirm the meanings and value of positive relationships and peace. Moreover, the informal part of the CISV experience may be important in balancing the weight of role performances and cognitive/normative expectations, both for children/adolescents and adults. However, it seems evident that formal institutional activities are not always effective in socialising with differences of perspectives and personal expressions. The construction of positive and peaceful interpersonal/intercultural relationships is based on interactions which partially contradict the meanings that formal institutional activities would like to carry.

Despite being a very important achievement, the participants' generalised satisfaction for the experience is not a sufficient indicator of success: it needs to be coupled with socialisation to agency during institutional activities, and correspondingly to the experiential meanings of dialogic interactional dynamics. Empowering dialogue can significantly support the success of the CISV experience, promoting agency as self-expression, and enhancing a cosmopolitan community. Empowering dialogue can give a coherent communicative *form* to the *contents* of institutional activities. The conjunction between the successful construction of the CISV We-identity, and the effective promotion of adults' and children's personal expression and social agency in institutional interactions is the foundation of the CISV experience.

This conclusion can be extended to all situations in which adults and children are involved in intercultural and interpersonal experiences oriented towards peaceful education and socialisation. A generalised outcome of this research is that the best improved We-identities and the most sophisticated educational activities are not sufficient to achieve successful peaceful interpersonal and intercultural forms of communication. Their achievement requires particular attention to the forms of communication which make up the activities and which are therefore essential to reach expected outcomes.

In childhood studies, it is no longer a taboo or a nonsense to sustain that effective socialisation requires children' active participation and that consequently personal expression and social agency should be carefully promoted (Baraldi 2008). However, frequently these requirements appear to be abstract values rather than empirical practices, as they are overwhelmed by traditional narratives of education, decision-making, meaning of conflict and conflict resolution. In a communicative and interactional perspective, based on empirical analyses, we can say that empowering dialogue is an effective form of communication for these requirements.

We may conclude that the awareness of the importance of promoting personal expressions and social agency, through coordination and dialogic mediation, might be very useful for adults aiming to facilitate experiential learning, and their training should include these aspects in a systematic way.

References

Alred, Geof, Michael Byram & Mike Fleming (Eds.) (2003). Intercultural experience and education. Clevedon: Multilingual Matters Ltd.

Angelelli, Claudia (2004). Revisiting the interpreter's role: a study of conference, court and medical interpreting in Canada, Mexico and the United States. Amsterdam: John Benjamins.

Arminen, Ilkka (2005). Institutional interaction: studies of talk at work. Aldershot: Ashgate Publishing.

Ayoko, Oluremi, Charmine Härtel, & Victor Callan (2002). Resolving the puzzle of productive and destructive conflict in culturally heterogeneous workgroups: A communication accomodation theory approach. International Journal of Conflict Management, 13 (2), 165–195.

Baker, Mona (2006a). Translation and conflict. A narrative account. London: Routledge.

Baker, Mona (2006b). Contextualization in translator- and interpreter-mediated events. Journal of Pragmatics, 38, 321–337.

Banks, Joseph (1998). Ethics, cross-cultural exchange and risk management. Interspectives, 16, 27–29.

Baraldi, Claudio (1993). Structural coupling: Simultaneity and difference between communication and thought. Communication Theory, 3, 112–129.

Baraldi, Claudio (2003). Planning childhood: Children's social participation in the town of adults. In Pia Christensen & Margaret O'Brien (Eds.), Children in the city. Home, neighbourhood and community (pp. 184–205). London: Falmer Press.

Baraldi, Claudio (2005). Forms of communication in multicultural classrooms: A way of exploring dialogue. In Wolfgang Herrlitz & Robert Maier (Eds.), Dialogues in and around multicultural schools (pp. 13–24). Tübingen: Niemeyer.

Baraldi, Claudio (Ed.) (2006a). Education and intercultural narratives in multicultural classrooms. Roma: Officina.

Baraldi, Claudio (2006b). New forms of intercultural communication in a globalised world. International Communication Gazzette, 68 (1), 53–69.

Baraldi, Claudio (2006c). Diversity and adaptation in intercultural mediation. In Dominic Busch (Ed.), Interkulturelle mediation in grenzregion (pp. 225–250). Frankfurt/Main: Peter Lang.

Baraldi, Claudio (2008). Promoting self-expression in classrooms interactions. Childhood, 15 (2), 239–257.

Baraldi, Claudio & Laura Gavioli (2007). Dialogue interpreting as intercultural mediation. An analysis in healthcare multicultural settings. In Marion Grein & Edda Weigand (Eds.), Dialogue and culture (pp. 155–175). Amsterdam & Philadelphia: John Benjamins.

Baraldi, Claudio & Laura Gavioli (2008). Cultural presuppositions and re-contextualization of medical systems in interpreter-mediated interactions. Curare, 31 (2–3), 193–203.

Beck, Ulrich (1997). Was ist globalisierung. Frankfurt a.M.: Surhkamp.

Beck, Ulrich (2004). Der kosmopolitische blick oder: Krieg ist frieden. Frankfurt a.M.: Suhr-kamp.

Bennett, Milton (Ed.) (1998). Basic concepts of intercultural communication: A reader. Yarmouth/MA: Intercultural Press.

Biesta, Gert (1994). Education as practical intersubjectivity: Towards a critical-pragmatic understanding of education. Educational Theory, 44, 299–317.

Blanchet-Cohen, Natasha & Brian Rainbow (2006). Partnership between children and adults? The experience of the international children's conference on the environment. Childhood, 13 (1), 113–126.

Bohm, David (1996). On dialogue. London: Routledge.

Bowling, Daniel & David Hoffman (2000). Bringing peace into the room: the personal qualities of the mediator and their impact on the mediation. Negotiation Journal, 16 (1), 5–28.

Brunette, Louise, George Bastin, Isabelle Hemlin & Heather Clarke (Eds.) (2003). The critical link 3. Interpreters in the community. Amsterdam & Philadelphia: John Benjamins.

Bush, Robert Baruch & Joseph Folger (1994). The Promise of mediation: Responding to conflict through empowerment and recognition. San Francisco: Jossey-Bass Publishers.

Carbaugh, Donal (Ed.) (1990). Cultural communication and intercultural contact. Hillsdale (N.J.): Lawrence Erlbaum.

Carbaugh, Donal (1999). Positioning as display of cultural identity. In Rom Harré & Luk van Langenhove (Eds.), Positioning theory (pp. 160–177). Oxford: Blackwell.

Carbaugh, Donal (2005). Cultures in conversation. New York & London: Lawrence Erlbaum.

Carnevale, Peter & Dean Pruitt (1992). Negotiation and mediation. Annual Review of Psychology, 43, 531–582.

Casmir, Fred (1999). Foundations for the study of intercultural communication based on a third-culture building model. International Journal of Intercultural Relations, 23, 91–116.

Chen, Guon-Ming & William Starosta (1998). Foundations of intercultural communication. Needham Heights/Ma: Allyn & Bacon.

CISV (2004). Cisv guide, Cisv resources: Document Center.

CISV (2008). Building global friendship, Cisv site, http://www.cisv.org.

Coleman Peter T., Anthony G. Hacking, Mark A. Stover, Beth Fisher-Yoshida, Andrzej Nowak (2008). Reconstructing ripeness I: A study of constructive engagement in protracted social conflicts. Conflict Resolution Quarterly, 26 (1), 3–42.

Cotmore, Richard (2004). Organisational competence: The study of a school council in action. Children & Society, 18, 53–65.

Craig, Gary (2003). Children's participation through community development. In Christine Hallett & Alan Prout (Eds.), Hearing the voices of children, social policy for a new century (pp. 39–56). London: RoutledgeFalmer.

Davidson, Brad (2000). The interpreter as institutional gatekeeper: The social-linguistic role of interpreters in Spanish-English medical discourse. Journal of Sociolinguistics, 4 (3), 379–405.

Davies, Brown & Rom Harré (1999). Positioning and personhood. In Rom Harré & Luk van Langenhove (Eds.), Positioning theory (pp. 32–52). Oxford: Blackwell.

DeChurch, Leslie & Michelle Marks (2001). Maximizing the benefits of task conflict: the role of conflict management. International Journal of Conflict Management, 12 (1), 4–22.

Deutsch, Morton (2002). Social psychology's contributions to the study of conflict resolution. Negotiation Journal, 18 (4), 307–320.

Dewey, John (1955). Democracy and education. An introduction to the philosophy of education. New York: The Macmillan Company.

Dreossi, Alberto (2006). Intercultural narratives in Italian classrooms, in Claudio Baraldi (Ed.). Education and intercultural narratives in multicultural classrooms (pp. 147–164). Rome: Officina Edizioni.

Dueñas, Guillermo (1994). Toward a theory of intercultural learning in organizations. Teoria Sociologica, 2 (3), 193–215.

Ewick, Patricia & Susan S. Silbey (1995). Subversive stories and hegemonic tales: Toward a sociology of narrative. Law & Society Review, 29 (2), 197–226.

Fisher, Roger & Daniel Shapiro (2005). Beyond reason: Using emotions as you negotiate. New York: Viking.

FitzGerald, Helen (2003). How different are We? Spoken discourse in intercultural communication. Clevedon: Multilingual Matters.

Foerster, Heinz von (1984). Observing systems. Seaside (Ca): Intersystems Publications.

Foucault, Michel (1971). L'ordre du discours. Paris: Gallimard.

Gergen, Kenneth (1991). The satured self. New York: Basic Books.

Gergen, Kenneth, Sheila McNamee & Frank Barrett (2001). Toward transformative dialogue. International Journal of Public Administration, 24, 697–707.

Giddens, Anthony (1984). The constitution of society. Cambridge: Polity Press.

Giddens, Anthony (1990). The consequences of modernity. Cambridge: Polity Press.

Goffman, Erving (1959). The presentation of self in everyday life. New York: Doubleday Anchor Books.

Goffman, Erving (1961). Asylums. Essay on the social situation of mental patient and other inmates. New York: Anchor Books.

Goffman, Erving (1963). Behavior in public places: Notes on the social organization of gatherings. New York: The Free Press.

Goffman, Erving (1974). Frame analysis: An essay on the organisation of experience. New York, Evanston, San Francisco & London: Harper & Row.

Goodwin, Charles & John Heritage (1990). Conversation analysis. Annual Review of Anthropology, 19, 283–307.

Gordon, Thomas (1974). Teacher effectiveness training. New York: Wyden Books.

Gordon, Thomas (2002). Good relationships. What makes them, what breaks them. Solana Beach (Ca): Gordon Training International.

Gudykunst, William (1994). Bridging differences. Effective intergroup communication. Thousand Oaks & London: Sage.

Gudykunst, William (Ed.) (2005). Theorizing about intercultural communication. Thousand Oaks & London: Sage.

Gumperz, John (1982). Discourse strategies. Cambridge: Cambridge University Press.

Gumperz, John (1992). Contextualization and understanding. In Alessandro Duranti & Charles Goodwin (Eds.), Rethinking context: Language as an interactive phenomenon (pp. 229–253). Cambridge: Cambridge University Press.

Gumperz John & Celia Roberts (1991). Understanding in intercultural encounters. In Jean Blommaert & Jef Verschueren (Eds.), The pragmatics of intercultural and international communication (pp. 51–90). Amsterdam & Philadelphia: John Benjamins.

Gwartney, Patricia, Lynne Fessenden & Gayle Landt (2002). Measuring the long-term impact of a community conflict resolution process. Negotiation Journal, 18 (1), 51–74.

Hale, Sandra (2007). Community interpreting. Melbourne: Macmillan.

Hannerz, Ulf (1996). Transational connections. Culture, people, places. London: Routledge.

Harré, Rom (1984). Personal being. A theory for individual psychology. Cambridge (Ma): Harvard University Press.

Harré, Rom & Luk van Langenhove (1999). The Dynamics of Social Episodes. In Rom Harré & Luk van Langenhove (Eds.), Positioning theory (pp. 1–13). Oxford: Blackwell.

Harré, Rom & Luk van Langenhove (Eds.) (1999). Positioning theory. Oxford: Blackwell.

Heritage, John (1985). Analysing news interviews: Aspects of the production of talk for an overhearing audience. In Teun Van Dijk (Ed.), Handbook of discourse analysis, Vol. 3. Discourse and dialogue (pp. 95–117). London: Academic Press.

Heritage, John (1995). Conversation analysis: Methodological aspects. In Uta M. Quasfthoff (Ed.), Aspects of oral communication (pp. 391–416). Berlin & New York: Walter de Gruyter.

Heritage, John (2002). The limits of questioning: Negative interrogatives and hostile question content. Journal of Pragmatics, 34, 1427–1446.

Heritage, John (2005). Conversation analysis and institutional talk. In Kristine Fitch & Robert Sanders (Eds.), Handbook of language and social interaction (pp. 103–46). Mahwah (NJ): Lawrence Erlbaum.

Heritage, John (2008). Conversation analysis as social theory. In Bryan Turner (Ed.), The new Blackwell companion to social theory (pp. 300–320). Oxford: Blackwell.

Heritage, John & Geoffrey Raymond (2005). The terms of agreement: indexing epistemic authority and subordination in talk-in-interaction. Social Psychology Quarterly, 68 (1), 15–3.

Hill, Malcolm, John Davis, Alan Prout & Kay Tisdall (2004). Moving the participation agenda forward. Children & Society, 18, 77–96.

Hofstede, Geert (1980). Culture's consequence. Beverly Hills & London: Sage.

Holdsworth, Roger (2004). Taking young people seriously means giving them serious things to do. In Jan Mason & Toby Fattore (Eds.), Children taken seriously. Theory, policy and practice (pp. 139–150). London: Jessica Kingsley Publishers.

Holland, Sally & Sean O'Neill (2006). We had to be there to make sure it was what we wanted. Enabling children's participation in family decision-making through the family group conference. Childhood, 13 (1), 91–111.

James, Allison & Adrian James (2004). Constructing childhood. Theory, policy and social practice. Houndmills: Palgrave.

James, Allison, Chris Jenks & Alan Prout (1998). Theorizing childhood. Oxford: Polity Press.

James, Allison & Alan Prout (Eds.) (1997). Constructing and reconstructing childhood. London: Falmer Press.

Jans, Marc (2004). Children as citizens. Towards a contemporary notion of child participation. Childhood, 11 (1), 27–44.

Jenks, Chris (1996). Childhood. London: Routledge.

Jong, Ho-Won (2008). Understanding conflict and conflict analysis. London & Thousand Oaks: Sage.

Kangaslahti, Antti (2004). Non-profit sector macro-shift: the importance of measuring social impact. Interspectives, 20, 16–18.

Kangaslathi, Jukka & Antti Kangaslathi (2003).The facilitator: Building constructive experiences for learning. Interspective, 19, 17–19.

Katz Jameson, Jessica, Andrea Bodtker & Tricia Jones. 2006. Like talking to a brick wall: Implications of mediation metaphors for mediation practice. Negotiation Journal, 22 (2), 199–207.

Kelman, Herbert (2005). Building trust among enemies: The central challenge to peacemaking efforts. In Walter Krieg, Klaus Galler & Peter Stadelmann (Eds.) Richtiges und gutes management: vom system zur praxis (pp. 349–367). Bern: Verlag Haupt.

Kiesling, Scott F. & Christina Bratt Paulson (Eds.) (2005). Intercultural discourse and communication. The essential readings. London: Blackwell.

Kim, Young Yun (2001). Becoming intercultural. An integrative theory of communication and cross-cultural adaptation. London & Thousand Oaks: Sage.

Kolb, David A. (1984). Experiential learning: Experience as the source of learning and development. New Jersey: Prentice Hall.

LeBaron, Michelle & Nike Castarphen (1997). Negotiating intractable conflict: The common ground dialogue process and abortion. Negotiation Journal, 13 (4), 341–361.

Littlejohn, Stephen (2004). The transcendent communication project: Searching for a praxis of dialogue. Conflict Resolution Quarterly, 21 (3), 327–359.

Luhmann, Niklas (1984). Soziale systeme. Frankfurt a.M.: Suhrkamp.

Luhmann, Niklas (1990). Die wissenschaft der gesellschaft. Frankfurt a.M.: Suhrkamp.

Luhmann, Niklas (1997). Die gesellschaft der gesellschaft. Frankfurt a.M.: Suhrkamp.

Luhmann, Niklas (2002). Das erziehungssystem der gesellschaft. Frankfurt a. M.: Suhrkamp

Luhmann, Niklas & Karl Heberardt Schorr (1979). Reflexionsprobleme im erziehungssysteme. Frankfurt a.M.: Suhrkamp.

Lyotard, Francois (1979). La condition postmoderne. Paris: Minuit.

Maggioni, Guido & Claudio Baraldi (1999). Children's rights and contemporary sociological perspectives of childhood. In Francis Van Loon & Koen Van Aeken (Eds.), Sociology of Law, Social problems and Legal Policy (pp. 63–74). Leuven: Acco.

Maiese, Michelle (2006). Engaging the emotions in conflict intervention. Conflict Resolution Quarterly, 24 (2), 187–195.

Margutti, Piera (2006). Are you human beings? Order and knowledge construction through questioning in primary classroom interaction. Linguistic and Education, 17, 313–346.

Mason, Ian (Ed.) (1999). Dialogue interpreting. The Translator, 5 (2), Special Issue.

Mason, Ian (Ed.) (2001). Triadic exchanges. Studies in dialogue interpreting. Manchester: St. Jerome.

Matthews, Hugh (2003). Children and regeneration: Setting and agenda for community participation and integration". Children & Society, 17, 264–276.

Maynard, Douglas W. (1991). Interaction and asymmetry in clinical discourse. American Journal of Sociology, 97, 448–495.

Mearns, Dave & Brian Thorne (1999). Person-centred counselling in action. London & Thousand Oaks: Sage.

Mehan, Hug (1979). Learning lessons: Social organization in the classroom. Cambridge (MA): Harvard University Press.

Milhouse, Virginia, Molefi Kete Asante & Peter Nwosu (Eds.) 2001. Transcultural realities. Interdisciplinary perspectives on cross-cultural relations. London & Thousand Oaks: Sage.

Moghaddam, Fathali M. (1999). Reflexive positioning: Culture and private discourse. In Rom Harré & Luk van Langenhove (Eds.), Positioning theory (pp. 74–86). Oxford: Blackwell.

Moscovici, Serge (1976). Social influence and social change. London: Academic Press.

Moscovici, Serge (1982). The coming era of social representations. In Jean-Paul Codol & Jean-Philippe Leyens (Eds.), Cognitive approaches to social behaviour (pp. 115–150). The Hague: Nijhoff.

Moscovici, Serge (1984). The phenomenon of social representations. In Robert Farr & Serge Moscovici (Eds.), Social representations (pp. 3–70). Cambridge: Cambridge University Press.

Mulcahy, Linda (2001). The possibilities and desirability of mediator neutrality – Towards an ethic of partiality? Social & Legal Studies, 10 (4), 505–527.

Murray, Cathy & Christine Hallett (2000). Young people's participation in decisions affecting their welfare. Childhood, 7 (1), 11–25.

Nederveen Pieterse, Jan (2004). Globalization & culture. Lanham: Rowman & Littlefield.

Nederveen Pieterse, Jan (2007). Ethnicities and global multiculture. Pants for an octopus. Lanham: Rowman & Littlefield.

Onwumechili, Chuka, Peter Nwosu, Ronald Jackson & Jacqueline James-Hughes (2003). In the deep valley with mountains to climb: Exploring identity and multiple reacculturation. International Journal of Intercultural Relations, 27, 41–62.

Osler, Audrey & Hugh Starkey (2005). Changing citizenship: democracy and inclusion in education. Buckingham: Open University Press.

Parsons, Talcott (1951a). The Social System. New York: Free Press.

Parsons, Talcott (1951b). Social structure and personality. New York: The free press.

Pearce, Barnett (1989). Communication and the human condition. Carbondale: Southern Illinois University Press.

Pearce, Barnett, & Kimberley Pearce (2003). Taking a communication perspective on dialogue. In Rob Anderson, Leslie Baxter & Kenneth Cissna (Eds.), Dialogue: theorizing difference in communication studies (pp. 39–56). Thousand Oaks, CA: Sage.

Pearce Kimberley, & Barnett Pearce (2001). The Public Dialogue Consortium's school-wide dialogue process: A communicative approach to develop citizenship skills and enhance school climate. Communication Theory, 11 (1), 105–123.

Picard, Cheryl & Kenneth Melchin (2007). Insight mediation: A learning-centered mediation model. Negotiation Journal, 23 (1), 35–53.

Poitras, Jean (2005). A study of the emergence of cooperation in mediation. Negotiation Journal, 21 (2), 281–300.

Pomerantz, Anita (1988). Offering a candidate answer: An information seeking strategy. Communication Monographs, 55, 360–373.

Prout, Alan (2000). Children's participation: Control and self-realisation in British late modernity. Children & Society, 14, 304–315.

Prout, Alan (2003). Participation, policy and the changing conditions of childhood. In Christine Hallett & Alan Prout (Eds.) Hearing the voices of children, social policy for a new century (pp. 11–25). London: RoutledgeFalmer.

Ramsbotham, Oliver, Tom Woodhouse & Hugh Miall (2005). Contemporary conflict resolution. Cambridge: Polity Press.

Raymond, Geoffrey (2003). Grammar and social organization: Yes/no interrogatives and the structure of responding. American Sociological Review, 68, 939–967.

Raymond, Geoffrey & John Heritage (2006). The epistemics of social relations: Owning grandchildren. Language in Society, 35, 677–705.

Robertson, Roland (1992). Globalization. Social theory and global culture. Sage: London.

Rogers, Carl (1951). Client-centered therapy: Its current practice, implications and theory. Boston: Houghton Mifflin.

Rogers, Carl (1969). Freedom to learn. Columbus: Merrill.

Royce, Terry (2005). The negotiator and the bomber: Analysing the critical role of active listening in crisis negotiation. Negotiation Journal, 21 (1), 5–27.

Sacks, Harvey (1992). Lectures on conversation (ed. by Gail Jefferson, Introduction by Emmanuel Schegloff). Oxford: Blackwell.

Sacks, Harvey, Emmanuel Schegloff & Gail Jefferson (1974). A simplest systematics for the organization of turn taking for conversation. Language, 50, 696–735.

Samovar, Larry & Richard Porter (Eds.) (1997). Intercultural Communication. A reader. Belmont: Wadsworth.

Schegloff, Emmanuel (1991). Conversation analysis and socially shared cognition. In Lauren Resnick, John Levine & Stephanie Teasley (Eds.), Perspectives on socially shared cognition (pp. 150–171). Washington, D.C: American Psychological Association.

Schegloff, Emmanuel, Irene Koshik, Sally Jacoby & David Olsher (2002). Conversation Analysis and Applied Linguistics. Annual Review of Applied Linguistics, 22, 3–31.

Schegloff, Emmanuel & Harvey Sacks (1973). Opening Up Closings. Semiotica, 8 (4), 289–327.

Schegloff, Emmanuel, Gail Jefferson & Harvey Sacks (1977). The preference for self-correction in the organization of repair in conversation. Language, 53, 361–82.

Schoeny, Mara & Wallace Warfield (2000). Reconnecting system maintenance with social justice: A critical role for conflict resolution. Negotiation Journal, 16 (3), 253–268.

Schulz, Jennifer (2006). Confectionary and conflict resolution? What chocolate reveals about mediation. Negotiation Journal, 22 (3), 251–277.

Searle, John (1969). Speech acts. An essay in the philosophy of language. Cambridge: Cambridge University Press.

Searle, John (1992). Conversation. In John Searle et al., (On) Searle on conversation (pp. 7–29). Amsterdam & Philadelphia: John Benjamins.

Searle, John & et al. (1992). (On) Searle on conversation. Amsterdam & Philadelphia: John Benjamins.

Shah-Kazemi, Sonia Nourin (2000). Cross-cultural mediation: A critical view of the dynamics of culture in family disputes. International Journal of Law, Policy and the Family, 14, 302–325.

Shell, Richard (2001). Bargaining styles and negotiation: The Thomas-Kilmann Conflict Mode Instrument in negotiation training. Negotiation Journal, 17 (2), 155–174.

Shier, Harry (2001). Pathways to participation: Openings, opportunities and obligations. Children & Society, 15, 107–117.

Sinclair, Ruth (2004). Participation in practice: Making it meaningful, effective and sustainable. Children & Society, 18, 106–118.

Somers, Margaret R. & Gloria D. Gibson (1994). Reclaiming the epistemological 'Other': Narrative and the social construction of identity. In Craig Calhoun (Ed.), Social theory and the politics of identity (pp. 37–99). Oxford: Blackwell.

Sparrow, Lise (2000). Beyond multicultural man: complexities of identity. International Journal of Intercultural Relations, 24, 173–201.

Spitzberg, Brian (1997). A model of intercultural communication competence. In Larry Samovar & Richard Porter (Eds.), Intercultural communication. A Reader (pp. 379–391). Belmont: Wadsowrth.

Tan, Sui-Lan & Fathali M. Mogaddham (1999). Positioning in intergroup relations. In Rom Harré & Luk van Langenhove (Eds.), Positioning theory (pp. 178–194). Oxford: Blackwell.

Ting-Toomey, Stella (1999). Communication across cultures. New York: The Guilford Press.

Ting-Toomey, Stella A. & Atsuro Kurogi (1998). Facework competence in intercultural conflict: An updated face-negotiation theory. International Journal of Intercultural Relations, 22, 187–225.

Tjosvold, Dean & Haifa Sun (2002). Understanding conflict avoidance: Relationship, motivations, actions, and consequences. International Journal of Conflict Management, 13 (2), 142–164.

Todd-Mancillas, William (2000). Communication and identity across cultures. Communication Theory, 10 (4), 475–480.

Tomlinson, John (1999). Globalization and culture. Cambridge: Polity press.

Triandis, Harry (1995). Individualism and collectivism. Boulder (CO): Westview Press.

Vanderbroeck, Michel & Maria Bouverne-de Bie (2006). Children's agency and educational norms. A tensed negotiation. Childhood, 13 (1), 127–143.

Vanderstraeten, Raf & Gert Biesta (2006). How is education possible? Pragmatism, communication and the social organization of education. British Journal of Education Studies, 54 (2), 160–174.

Van Agt, Andreas (2001). In quest of global ethical standards: towards a universal declaration of human responsibilities. Interspectives, 18, 17–20.

van Langenhove, Luk & Rom Harré (1999). Introducing positioning theory. In Rom Harré & Luk van Langenhove (Eds.) Positioning theory (pp. 14–31). Oxford: Blackwell.

Verschueren, Jef (2008). Intercultural communication and the challenges of migration. Language and Intercultural Communication, 8 (1), 21–35.

Wadensjö, Cecilia (1998). Interpreting as interaction. London: Longman.

Wadensjö, Cecilia, Birgitta Englund Dimitrova & Anna-Lena Nilsson (2007). The critical link 4: Professionalisation of interpreting in the community. Amsterdam & Philadelphia: John Benjamins.

Weigand, Edda (1994). Discourse, conversation, dialogue. In Edda Weigand (Ed.), Concepts of dialogue (pp. 49–70). Tübingen: Niemeyer.

Weigand, Edda (2007). The sociobiology of language. In Marion Grein & Edda Weigand (Eds.), Dialogue and culture (pp. 27–49). Amsterdam & Philadelphia: John Benjamins.

Weizman, Elda (2008). Positioning in media dialogue. Amsterdam & Philadelphia: John Benjamins.

Welsh, Nancy & Peter Coleman (2002). Institutionalized conflict resolution: Have we come to expect too little?. Negotiation Journal, 18 (4), 345–350.

Wierbicka, Anna (2006). The concept of 'dialogue' in cross-linguistic and cross-cultural perspective. Discourse Studies, 8 (5), 675–703.

Winslade, John (2006). Mediation with a focus on discursive positioning. Conflict Resolution Quarterly, 23 (4), 501–515.

Winslade, John & Gerald Monk (2000). Narrative mediation: A new approach to conflict resolution. San Francisco: Jossey-Bass.

Winslade, John & Gerald Monk (2008). Practicing narrative mediation: Loosening the grip of conflict. San Francisco: Jossey-Bass.

Winslade, John, Gerald Monk & Alison Cotter (1998). A narrative approach to the practice of mediation. Negotiation Journal, 14 (1), 21–42.

Wyness, Michael (1999). Childhood, agency and education reform. Childhood, 6 (3), 353–368.

Yamada, Ann-Marie and Theodore Singelis (1999). Biculturalism and self-construal. International Journal of Intercultural Relations, 23, 697–709.

Zeldin, Theodore (1998). An intimate history of humanity. London: Vintage.

Index

In the series *Dialogue Studies* the following titles have been published thus far or are scheduled for publication: